50 *Hikes*

In Ohio

Day Hikes & Backpacking Trips
in the Buckeye State

Third Edition

RALPH RAMEY

The Countryman Press

Woodstock, Vermont

AN INVITATION TO THE READER

Over time trails can be rerouted and signs and landmarks altered. If you find that changes have occurred on the routes described in this book, please let us know so that corrections may be made in future editions. The author and publisher also welcome other comments and suggestions. Address all correspondence to:

Editor, 50 Hikes™ Series
The Countryman Press
P.O. Box 748
Woodstock, VT 05091

ISBN 978-0-88150-729-4

Text and cover design by Glenn Suokko
Page composition by Susan McClellan
Interior photographs by Ralph Ramey
Maps by Hedberg Maps, Dick Widhu and
Mapping Specialists Ltd., Madison, WI, © 2007
The Countryman Press

Cover photo © Jim Yokajty

Excerpt from *Idle Weeds*, copyright © 1980 by David Rains Wallace, is reprinted with permission of Sierra Club Books.

Published by The Countryman Press, P.O. Box 748, Woodstock, Vermont 05091

Distributed by W. W. Norton & Company, Inc., 500 Fifth Avenue, New York, NY 10110

Printed in the United States of America

10 9 8 7 6 5

To Carolyn Louise Ramey (1954–1997), who was unable to hike with me during her lifetime but will now be by my side on every trail, and to nieces and nephew, the author's grandchildren, who are destined to carry on the family tradition of loving the out-of-doors.

50 Hikes in Ohio at a Glance

HIKE	REGION	DISTANCE (miles)	VIEWS (Stream, Lake, Fores
1. Battelle–Darby Creek Metro Park	Central	4.5	S
2. Blues Creek Preserve	Central	2	
3. Clear Creek Metro Park	Central	4.5	F
4. Chestnut Ridge Metro Park	Central	2	F
5. Conkle's Hollow State Nature Preserve	Central	3.5	F
6. Davey Woods State Nature Preserve	Central	1.5	
7. Hocking Hills State Park	Central	6	F
8. Malabar Farm State Park	Central	5	F
9. Mohican State Park	Central	3.5	S
10. Prairie Oaks Metro Park	Central	2.5	
11. Stage's Pond State Nature Preserve	Central	3	L
12. Wolf Run Regional Park/Knox Woods State Nature Preserve	Central	2.5	F
13. Atwood Lake Park–Mingo Trail	NE	3.75	L/F
14. Brecksville Reservation Metropark–Deer Lick	NE	4	F
15. Cuyahoga Valley National Park	NE	9.5	F/S
16. Eagle Creek State Nature Preserve	NE	4.75	F
17. Fernwood State Forest	NE	4	F
18. Findley State Park	NE	3	
19. Hinckley Reservation Metropark	NE	5	F
20. Mill Creek Park	NE	6	S
21. Tappan Lake Park	NE	9	L
22. Marie J. Desonier State Nature Preserve	SE	2.5	F
23. Dysart Woods Outdoor Laboratory	SE	2	F
24. Lake Katharine State Nature Preserve	SE	4.5	L
25. Shawnee State Forest–Backpack Trail	SE	6.75–27.5	F

GOOD FOR KIDS	WATER-FALLS	CAMPING (Developed, Backpacking)	NOTES
★			Along a State and National Scenic River
★			Easy walking trails
			Forested gorge trails
			Spectacular view of Columbus from afar
★	★		Black Hand sand cliff and gorge
★			Nice woodland trail
	★	D	Old Man's Cave to Cedar Falls
			Louis Bromfield "model" farm of 1940s
	★	D	Hemlock-lined streamside trail
★			Open trails amid restored prairie
			Glacial pothole lake
			Fall trees on Illinoian moraine
		D	Full recreation area, fee in season
	★		Deep woods on deep ravines
	★		Towpath and hillside trail
★			Glacial pothole wetland complex
		D	High walls and ponds of old strip mines
★		D	From farmland to forest in 75 years
			Lakeside trail and spectacular rocks
	★		Hemlock-lined stream with grist mill
		D	Full recreation facility, fee in season
			Regrowth hill country forest
			Huge trees
	★		Sandstone cliffs and rare plants
		D/B	Backpack trail in Ohio's Little Smokies

50 Hikes in Ohio at a Glance

HIKE	REGION	DISTANCE (miles)	VIEWS (Stream, Lake, Forest)
26. Tar Hollow State Park and Forest	SE	12	F
27. Archers Fork Trail	SE	9.5	
28. Lamping Homestead Trail	SE	5	
29. Morgan Sisters Trail	SE	2, 4, or 8	
30. Symmes Creek Trail	SE	6	
31. Vesuvius Recreation Area, Lakeshore Trail	SE	8	L/F
32. Wildcat Hollow Trail	SE	5 or 15	F
33. Zaleski State Forest	SE	9.9–23.5	F
34. Caesar Creek Gorge State Nature Preserve	SW	2	S
35. Chaparral Prairie State Nature Preserve	SW	1.5	
36. Charleston Falls Preserve	SW	2	S
37. East Fork State Park	SW	14	
38. Edge of Appalachia Preserve	SW	3	F
39. Fort Hill State Memorial	SW	1.4–3.1	F
40. Germantown MetroPark	SW	6.8	F
41. Glen Helen Nature Preserve	SW	3, 5, or 10	F/S
42. Hueston Woods State Park and Nature Preserve	SW	2	F
43. Shawnee Prairie Preserve	SW	2	
44. Stillwater Prairie Preserve	SW	1.5	S
45. Goll Woods State Nature Preserve	NW	3	F
46. Kelleys Island	NW	7.5	L
47. Lockington Reserve	NW	3.5–6.5	F
48. Maumee Bay State Park	NW	2.25	L
49. Oak Openings Preserve Metropark	NW	16.6	F
50. Ottawa National Wildlife Refuge	NW	4.5	L

GOOD FOR KIDS	WATER-FALLS	CAMPING (Developed, Backpacking)	NOTES
		D/B	Steep hillsides, rugged terrain
		B	Spectacular arch and solitude
		D/B	Former homestead site with a small lake
		B	Ridgetop trail in wooded silence
		B	Peaceful trail in hill country
		D/B	Lakeside and hillside walking
		B	Good backpack training trail
		D/B	Ridgetops, ghost town, and beaver ponds
✳			Good spring wildflower area
✳			Superb July and August prairies
✳			Falls over limestone
		D/B	Easy backpack trail
			Very rugged trail but view worth the effort
	✳		Hilltop earthworks, beautiful limestone gorge
			Vast wooded preserve
✳	✳		Beautiful scenery, great wildflowers
✳		D	Mature beech/maple forest, full-service park
✳			Nature center, wetlands, and prairie
✳			State Scenic River, native prairie
✳			Best example of black swamp forest
✳		D	Great vacation spot, leave your car behind
✳			Quiet walk on wooded floodplain
✳		D	Shoreline scenery, wildlife, boardwalk
			Long trail through diverse habitat
✳			Great birding area, with nesting eagles

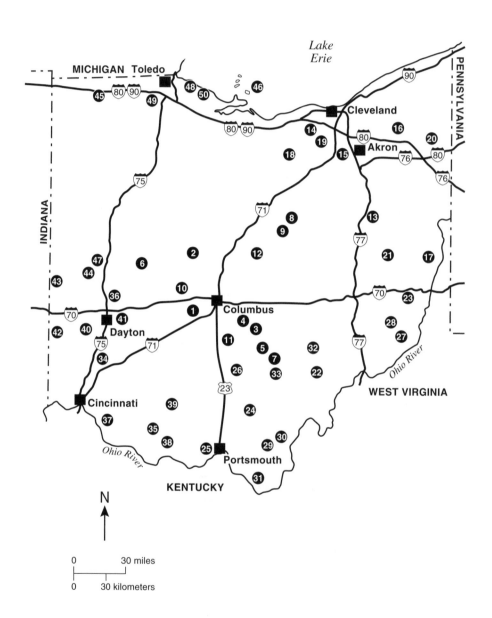

Lake
Erie

MICHIGAN Toledo

MICHIGAN

INDIANA

PENNSYLVANIA

Cleveland

Akron

Columbus

Dayton

Cincinnati

Portsmouth

WEST VIRGINIA

KENTUCKY

Ohio River

Ohio River

N

0   30 miles

0   30 kilometers

CONTENTS

Acknowledgments

My special thanks to the personnel of the Ohio Department of Natural Resources, both in the Columbus office and in the field, for sharing their knowledge and providing maps and literature. Also, thanks to the folks at the metropolitan parks, the federal facilities, the conservancy districts, the Ohio Historical Society, The Nature Conservancy, the privately owned areas, and the Buckeye Trail Association, who all readily shared their knowledge.

I will forever be indebted to the late Bill Cohn and the late Mac Henney, who as the Scoutmasters of my youth in Troop 3 in Bexley started me hiking Ohio's trails; and to the Scouts and Scouters of Troop 417 in Upper Arlington who, when I became a Scoutmaster, shared with me the joy of exploring the Ohio countryside on foot. Thanks to the staff and volunteers at Antioch University's Glen Helen Nature Preserve, where I was employed when I wrote the first edition of this book, for graciously accepting weekend program duties in my stead while I trekked Ohio's trails. Likewise, my gratitude goes to friends throughout the state who offered advice and encouragement.

I could not have done without the support of my family. My sons, John and Jim, provided hiking gear, and John got me started on the computer and bailed me out when I got in trouble. My late daughter Carolyn's cheerful, "How you doing with your hikes, Dad?" urged me on. Most important of all has been the support and encouragement of my loving wife, Jean, who kept the home fires burning while I was busy roaming the footpaths of the Buckeye State.

Lastly, I appreciated the gentle and thoughtful criticisms and suggestions given by the editors I have worked with at The Countryman Press division of W.W. Norton through three editions, especially Jennifer Thompson, a Miami University graduate, who urged me to take another look at Hueston Woods when I was about to drop it from this edition.

Introduction

When I got an e-mail from Ms. Thompson of The Countryman Press in May 2006 suggesting that it might be time for a new edition of this book, I did not hesitate to jump at the opportunity. Now that the work is behind me, it's easy to say that I wouldn't have had it any other way. But knowing what I do now, I'm not so certain. With gasoline at an all-time high, I probably will never recover my costs. On the other hand, what a wonderful summer it afforded me. I camped three or four nights a week in each of seven different parks so that I could walk nearby trails. I prepared all of my own meals, stopping at fast-food emporiums only a few times for coffee to wake me up. I completely walked more than half of the trails and explored critical parts of all of them. And all of this at the age of 77, with ankle braces on my legs and a new knee— and all alone in camp and on the trail. And I fell but five times and was not injured. I'm looking forward to being asked to do another revision in eight or ten years. It's been fun.

Hiking opportunities in Ohio are as varied as its topography. From the once mighty Ohio River on the southern border (tamed long ago by navigation locks and dams) to the "reborn" Lake Erie on the northern, the state hosts trails through deep forests or open meadows in country ranging from nearly flat to very hilly. Trail building and improvement has grown at a furious rate during the past decade. This is true of every agency, but especially the Department of Natural Resources. I tried to spur interest there over a quarter of a century ago with little success. I'm pleased to have lived long enough to see my dreams of a state with great trails come true. Trails are found in state forests, wildlife areas, parks, nature preserves, and memorials. Walking paths also crisscross national forests and recreation areas. Park district preserves and reservations offer some of the best hiking in the state, and privately owned nature centers have well-developed trail systems. In the eastern part of the state, the lands of the Muskingum Watershed Conservancy District beckon hikers, and at least one utility company has opened its landholdings to recreation. There are trails that follow lakeshores, streams, old canal towpaths, interurban and railroad rights-of-way, abandoned country roads, Native American trails, early wagon roads, game paths, and much more. Lastly, there are trails that form part of the National Trail System and paths used by the statewide Buckeye Trail system. The Buckeye Trail Association (BTA) continues to move their route from roads to fields and forests, and the North Country Trail and the American Discovery Trail have the hiking routes on the ground.

This great breadth of hiking opportunities is a result of the natural diversity of the Buckeye State. Its exposed bedrock is all sedimentary, laid down by successive warm seas, inland embayments, river deltas, and swamps. From the Cincinnati Arch, which runs from Lima to Cincinnati, the bedrock dips gently to the east and west. The edges of successive layers of bedrock are thus exposed, the oldest visible along the arch, the younger strata visible as you go east or west. In eastern Ohio the exposures are mostly sandstone, shale, and coal, the materials from which acid soils are derived. In the western part of the state, limestone and dolomites prevail—the building blocks of sweet soils. Several ice advances reshaped the northwestern part of the state, leaving boulder fields, kames, eskers, outwash plains, reversed streams, fossil beach ridges, filled valleys, and the like. The southeastern area was carved into hills by erosion, partly from glacial meltwater, forming a succession of major river systems to carry water to the ocean.

The hikes in this book visit many of the places across Ohio where the geological processes that shape the land are exceptionally well illustrated. One trail passes the world-renowned glacial grooves on Kelleys Island. At Oak Openings, you will walk on sand that was once on the bottom of an ancient lake. In Hocking Hills State Park, the trail follows the bottom of a deep gorge carved in the sandstone by meltwater; and at Glen Helen you will walk on the rim of another meltwater-carved gorge, this one of limestone and dolomite.

Before the arrival of white settlers, most of Ohio was covered by eastern hardwood forest. There were also unforested areas occupied by prairie, fen, bog, and coastal marsh. Here and there across the state are relict plant communities from times when the general climate was much different, preserved from earlier eons by microclimatic or edaphic conditions.

Bison, wolf, elk, passenger pigeon, Carolina parakeet, and other species that were common prior to settlement are now gone. When drained with ditches and tile, the extensive prairies that once supported big bluestem and baptisia became fields of corn, soybeans, and wheat. Where native herbivores once grazed in the summer on the indigenous warm-season grasses of the prairies, cool-season grasses from Eurasia were planted to support cattle and sheep. Swine were turned loose in the woods to eat whatever they could. Rivers and streams that supported dozens of species of fish and mollusks in clear, well-oxygenated water were dammed to provide for power and navigation, and polluted with chaff from mills. The industries, towns, and cities that grew along the watercourses added their waste to the streams and rivers. Virgin forests were cleared to open areas for cropland and pasture and to provide construction material and fuel. Much of southeastern Ohio's timber was cut to make charcoal for use in iron furnaces. Extractive industries mined iron, coal, sand, gravel, stone, clay, and more. Wells pumped gas and oil from below the surface. After a series of treaties, the Native Americans were driven completely from the area. In less than a century, the farmers, canallers, railroaders, road and bridge builders, and ditchdiggers had brought civilization to the rough Ohio wilderness. Yet, we now seem to be regaining some of our wildness. Bear are seen frequently enough that in some areas of southeastern Ohio I hike with "bear bells" jingling on my pack. And I continue to hear reports of badger in western Ohio. Otters are back in Ohio steams and eagles in the Ohio sky. Let us hope that the return of creatures with whom we each share this earth for our few years will continue forever.

HIKING TRAILS IN OHIO

Though Ohio ranks 36th in size among the 50 states, it is 7th in population. A major agricultural state, it is also heavily industrialized, with most of its 11 million people

Wildlife abounds in Ohio; Here beaver cuttings surround a mature tree

living in one of six urban areas. Shortly after World War I, civic leaders recognized a need for large, publicly owned natural places for outdoor recreation near the cities. Thus was born the system of local park districts, one of the nation's finest. There are now metropolitan park systems in all of Ohio's urban areas and in many rural counties as well. Most operate on a philosophy that calls for retaining 80 percent of the land in a natural state. They have many miles of trails and are great places to hike. This book includes a selection of hikes in parks with especially nice natural features from several districts.

In 1918 Ohio began to systematically acquire state forest land. Though originally established to preserve (or perhaps restore) the timber resources of the state, the 173,415-acre system now includes an area designated as wilderness where no timber-management activities occur.

The federally operated Civilian Conservation Corps (CCC) of the 1930s built many recreation facilities, including trails in the state forests, and many of these still provide great pleasure to hikers. New trails, including two backpacking trails, have been added in recent years.

In 1949 a unified Ohio Department of Natural Resources (ODNR) was created that established, for the first time, a state park system. Publicly owned lands that were being used as parks or that had the potential to be developed into parks were put under the control of the ODNR, and they became the nucleus for the present 200,884-acre state park system. Nineteenth-century canal feeder lakes, scenic areas of state forests, and lakes created for fishing, flood control, stream-flow augmentation, or water supply were among the diverse areas brought into the system. As major flood-control projects were built in the 1950s and 1960s, they joined the fledgling park system. Today, virtually all of the 72 state parks have some foot trails.

A direct descendant of the earlier Division of Conservation and Natural Resources of the Department of Agriculture, the Division of Wildlife manages areas large and small across the state that provide places for the public to hunt and fish. Though paid for with fees and taxes collected from sportsmen, state wildlife areas are now being managed for overall biological diversity as well as for fish and game production. Some offer good opportunities for hiking, and one such area has been included in this book, although hikers will want to explore these areas outside hunting season. A complete list can be obtained from the ODNR.

The newest agency within the ODNR with land holdings attractive to hikers is the Division of Natural Areas and Preserves. Since 1971 it has acquired 110 parcels totaling over 20,000 acres in all corners of the state. These areas preserve habitat for threatened and endangered plant and animal species and are examples of the wide variety of ecosystems that made up Ohio prior to settlement. Hemlock-filled sandstone ravines, fern-lined limestone gorges, fens, bogs, mature upland woods, swamp forests, and prairie are but a few of the special places now under public ownership. Hikes in a few of these areas that have good trail systems have been included here. A directory of Natural Areas and Preserves can be purchased from the division. A list of natural areas and preserves—and, often, brochures describing individual areas—is available free from the same source.

The Ohio Historical Society (OHS) has long been guardian of the state's treasury of old forts, battlefields, historic homes, and prehistoric mounds and earthworks. Explore the two state memorials included here, then seek out others on your own. Some include small, on-site museums (often with restricted months and hours of operation) and developed trail systems. The state tourism office will send you a free list of the properties operated by the OHS with information about the society.

The federal government also plays a role in providing hiking opportunities in Ohio. The United States Army Corps of Engineers (USACE), charged with the responsibility for flood control on navigable streams of the nation, has built dozens of reservoirs in all parts of the state. These are managed by a variety of agencies, including the corps itself, local park districts, and the Department of Natural Resources. In eastern Ohio, the Muskingum Watershed Conservancy District (MWCD), a local political subdivision of the state organized to control flooding, owns and manages the land behind the dams the corps built there. Hikes in two MWCD parks are included here, but there are trails in others. Information about this agency's other facilities is available from the MWCD office.

The National Park Service (NPS) operates several areas in Ohio, including the Cuyahoga Valley National Recreation Area (CVNRA), which preserves the pastoral beauty of that northeastern Ohio River corridor. The CVNRA is already a good place to hike and new facilities continue to open. The North Country National Recreational Trail is also a responsibility of the NPS, but development of the trail is up to local jurisdictions. A section of this congressionally-authorized trail uses one of the Wayne National Forest trails included in this book.

The U.S. Fish and Wildlife Service manages many acres of wildlife refuge in Ohio, principally along the southern shore of Lake Erie and around the Erie islands. A walk through the one area open to the public is included here. The U.S. Forest Service (USFS) has been present in Ohio in a quiet way for many decades. In recent years, it has consolidated land-holdings and aggressively pursued the development of recreational trails. It offers some of the best wilderness hiking in the state in its Wayne National Forest. Six trails suitable for backpacking or day hiking in the Wayne are included here.

Two university-owned nature preserves have been included, and there are many privately-owned non-profit nature centers around the state, all with good trail systems aimed at helping visitors learn more about the natural world. Self-guided, interpretive trail guides are available for many.

The American Discovery Trail, a footpath across the nation, passes through Ohio. For the most part, it uses existing trails on federal or state land or rural roads. When hiking some of the trails in this book, you may see symbols indicating that the trail is part of this system.

The Nature Conservancy (TNC) has been active in protecting natural areas in Ohio for nearly four decades. It owns and manages more than 13,000 acres of good wild land in all parts of the state, operating some in conjunction with other agencies and organizations such as the Museum of Natural History and Science of the Cincinnati Museum Center. A call to TNC's Ohio office will get you a list of its areas and information about visiting them.

With the continuing consolidation of the country's railways, many miles of rights-of-way have been abandoned. The Rails-to-Trails Conservancy (RTTC) has worked closely with many local and state organizations to convert these corridors to recreational use. To date, nearly 250 miles of such trails have been developed in Ohio. Since all of them allow bicycles and in-line skates, they are more congested than most hikers prefer. Information about such facilities in the Buckeye State is available from the Ohio office of the RTTC.

No discussion of trails in Ohio would be complete without mention of two organizations: the Buckeye Trail Association and the Boy Scouts of America (BSA). The BTA was established in 1959, originally to complete a trail from the Ohio River to Lake Erie. The trail now links the four corners of the state and is over 1,200 miles in length. It crosses public and private land and, when an off-road route cannot be found, uses lesser-traveled rural roads. Maintained almost entirely by volunteers, the Buckeye Trail takes the hiker through some of Ohio's most spectacular countryside. Though there are many loop trail opportunities along its circuitous route, it is essentially a linear path. Many of the hikes in this guide are partly or totally on the Buckeye Trail.

Over the years, a number of active Boy Scout troops around the state have established officially sanctioned Scout hiking trails. Often these are 10 miles in length, with 5-mile options to allow Scouts to complete requirements for the hiking merit badge. Unfortunately, because of their locales, many of these trails are on paved roads and city streets. Two long-established and well-maintained off-road Scout hiking trails are included.

ABOUT THIS BOOK

Most of the hikes in this book are one-day outings, but 10, all located in southern Ohio, offer overnight backpacking trips of two to nine days, as well as day walks. Nearly all of the 50 hikes are loop hikes, allowing you to finish where you started. It is always a good idea to hike with one or more companions, but many hikers prefer to travel alone, while recognizing the added risks of doing so and preparing for them. Whether you hike alone or with companions, be sure to tell someone your destination, planned route, and expected time of return. I have hiked alone for more than 50 years and, with two exceptions, I walked all of the scouting trips for the trails in this book alone. When I day-hike, I usually carry a fanny pack with some basic emergency supplies and, in recent years, a cellular phone, though I doubt if I could get reception from many of the southeastern Ohio valleys and ravines.

MAPS

The maps that accompany the trail descriptions in this book are all based on U.S. Geological Survey (USGS) 7½' quadrangles, which are available for the entire state. These "topos" have all been prepared since World War II, but changes that have occurred since they were prepared mean that they don't always exactly match man-made features. You can gain insight into the early character of an area by studying the old 15' quadrangles, most prepared around the turn of the last century. Though these can no longer be purchased from state or federal map agencies, many can be found in the federal document repositories and map rooms of libraries, colleges, and universities. They can often be copied to carry on the trail and are a great help in identifying old trolley and railroad lines, long-gone homesites, industrial complexes, cemeteries, roads, bridges, and even entire communities. Clues to early human activity are the presence of fruit trees, plantings of ornamental bulbs and shrubs, and fallen-down buildings and dumps. Other guides

for the curious hiker are the inexpensive folders sold by the OHS that show the locations of early canals, covered bridges, and iron furnaces.

Many of the managing agencies have trail maps available for their areas. These can be good supplements to the maps in this book as they sometimes reflect changes made during the current season. Nearly all can be downloaded from managing agencies' web sites. They can also usually be obtained at no charge by writing or calling the appropriate agency. In some places they are available at the trailhead, but don't depend on it. Buckeye Trail section maps can be purchased from the BTA, which will send you information and a list of available maps upon request.

HIKE STATISTICS

The *hiking times* shown for suggested routes are based on my experiences surveying the trails, and on an average of 45 minutes of hiking time per mile. Always allow ample time for road and trail travel. In both cases, expect and be prepared for the unexpected. The *vertical rise* calculation is the difference between the highest and the lowest points on the trail; there will never be a single climb of that amount. The *mileage figures* are from measurements made on the topographic maps and/or from figures provided by the managing agencies.

EQUIPMENT

There are many good books on the subject of hiking and backpacking, so there is no point in covering that material here. In my opinion, no hiker should be on the trail without at least a copy of the map as presented in this book (if not the USGS quadrangles), a compass and knowledge of how to use it, a Swiss army knife, a thunder whistle, sunscreen and insect repellent if needed, and a pocket first-aid kit. A good pair of broken-in hiking shoes and socks of a weight and material appropriate for the season are a must. Though many people hike in sneakers, I prefer an ankle-high boot of leather or nylon. A twisted ankle can ruin a hike. Dressing in layers makes the most sense for hiking, since clothing can be adjusted for the temperature during the course of the day. A day pack or fanny pack with a poncho and a water bottle of adequate size are always in order. On most of the scouting trips for this edition, I carried a hydration pack that held 2 liters of water and had room for many small items I formerly carried in my fanny pack. The weather was in the nineties on many of the days that I was on the trail, so having sufficient water was vital to my well-being. No surface water is safe to drink *anywhere* in the state.

Pocket-sized tree, flower, berry, animal track, and fern identification books, such as the "Finder" series published by the Nature Study Guild, can help you learn more about the nature of things along the trail. A pocket magnifying glass and a pair of lightweight binoculars allow a closer look at plants and animals large and small. Pentax and Eagle Optics offer close-focusing glasses that allow you to observe things like butterflies, damselflies, and dragonflies as near as the tip of your toes. Most hikers now carry digital cameras that allow them to capture incredible images under all sorts of environmental conditions. Seek advice at a camera store in choosing one for your treks. A walking staff will serve as a third leg when crossing creeks or climbing hills and as a monopod (really the third leg of a tripod when added to your two legs) to stabilize a camera in the low-light situations often found on woodland trails. I now walk most trails using a pair of trekking poles. Mine are from Leki, but there are several good brands on the market.

Some folks carry a cell phone. My experience has been that on most trails very far removed from an urban setting it is difficult to get a connection, but coverage is improving by leaps and bounds. My practice is to find a place where I can get service before arriving at the trail. It may be at the top of a nearby hill or somewhere that I can make visual contact with a cell tower. From there I call home to tell my wife where I'm about to begin walking, when I expect to be off the trail, and whom to call in the event that I don't report back by a specific time. I allow enough extra time to create the least apprehension on the home front, then I leave the phone in my car. Leaving an unoccupied car at a trailhead always makes me a bit nervous, but in a half century of doing so I've never had a problem. It goes without saying that precautions are in order. Put everything of value out of sight. If you have more than one car, use the older model. A wheel lock that is visible through the window is a good idea, and I put a sun screen in the front window to keep the inside temperature down.

ACCOMMODATIONS

Ten of the trails in this book can accommodate backpackers, and 17 hikes are located in or near public recreation areas where there are family campgrounds. Many of these areas offer boating, fishing, swimming, and interpretive programs. Most are near other suggested hikes or close to recreational or tourism resources such as amusement parks, museums, festivals, or crafts shops. Call 1-800-BUCK-EYE for information on places and events

The author at camp in the Shawnee State Forest

in the area you are planning to visit. Local convention and visitors bureaus (CVBs) can also supply useful information on area attractions. The official "Ohio Tour and Highway Map," available from the same source, lists the names, addresses, and phone numbers of all Ohio CVBs.

Much has been written about the desecration of outdoor recreation resources by careless users. The special places along the trails in this book deserve the best possible stewardship. Practice minimal-impact hiking and camping as described in many books and periodicals: Pack it in; haul it out. As I used to tell the Boy Scouts of Troop 417 in Columbus, "Let no one say unto your shame, all was beauty here until you came." Go home with good pictures and wonderful memories and leave behind only light footprints. Happy hiking!

INFORMATION RESOURCES

Acorn Naturalists
155 El Camino Real
Tustin, CA 92780-3601
1-800-422-8886
E-mail: emailacorn@aol.com
Web site: http://www.acornnaturalists.com
Catalog of resources—books, etc.—for the trail and classroom

American Discovery Trail
P.O. Box 20155
Washington, DC 20041-2155
1-800-663-2387 or 703-753-0149
E-mail: info@discoverytrail.org
Web site: http://www.discoverytrail.org

Buckeye Trail Association
P.O. Box 254
Worthington, OH 43085-0254
Web site: http://www.buckeyetrail.org
Enclose a stamped, self-addressed, business-sized envelope

Cincinnati Museum Center at Union Terminal
1301 Western Avenue
Cincinnati, OH 45203-1130
513-287-7000 or 1-800-733-2077
Web site: http://www.cincymuseum.org

Cleveland Metroparks
4101 Fulton Parkway
Cleveland, OH 44144-1923
216-635-3200
E-mail: generalinfo@cleveland-metroparks.com
Web site: http://www.clemetparks.com

Columbus Metro Parks
1069 West Main Street
Westerville, OH 43081-1181
614-891-0700

E-mail: info@metroparks.net
Web site: http://www.metroparks.net

Cuyahoga Valley National Park
15610 Vaughn Road
Brecksville, OH 44141-3018
1-800-445-9667 or 216-524-1497
Web sites: http://www.nps.gov/cuva or
http://www.dayinthevalley.com

Darke County Park District
4267 State Route 502, P.O. Box 801
Greenville, OH 45331-0801
937-548-0165
E-mail: info@darkecountyparks.org
Web site: http://darkecountyparks.org

Five Rivers Metroparks District
1375 East Siebenthaler Avenue
Dayton, OH 45414-5357
937-275-7275
E-mail: email@metroparks.org
Web site: http://www.metroparks.org

Glen Helen Ecology Institute
405 Corry Street
Yellow Springs, OH 45387-1843
937-769-1902
E-mail: annshaw@antioch-college.edu
Web site: http://www.anitoch-college
.edu/glenhelen

Kelleys Island Chamber of Commerce
P.O. Box 783F
Kelleys Island, OH 43438-0783
419-746-2360
Web site: http://www.kelleysisland
chamber.com

Knox County Park District
117 East High Street Suite 224
Mt. Vernon, OH 43050-3457
740-392-PARK
E-mail: info@knoxcountyparks.org
Web site: http://www.knoxcountyparks.org

Metropark District of the Toledo Area
5100 West Central Avenue
Toledo, OH 43615-2106
419-407-9700
Web site: http://www.metroparks
toledo.com

Miami County Park District
2645 East State Route 41
Troy, OH 45373-9692
937-335-6273
E-mail: protectingnature@miamiparks.com
Web site: http://www.miamicounty
parks.com

Mill Creek MetroParks
7574 Columbiana-Canfield Road,
P.O. Box 596
Canfield, OH 44406-0596
330-702-3000
E-mail: millcreek@cboss.com
Web site: http://www.millcreek
metroparks.com

Muskingum Watershed Conservancy District
P.O. Box 349,
1319 Third Street NW
New Philadelphia, OH 44663-0349
330-343-6647
E-mail: info@mwcdlakes.com
Web site: http://www.mwcdlakes.com

North Country National Scenic Trail
700 Rayovac Drive, Suite 100
Madison, WI 53711-2468
608-441-5610
Web site: http://www.nps.gov/noco

North Country Trail Association
229 East Main Street
Lowell, MI 49331-1711
Web site: http://www.northcountrytrail.org

Ohio Biological Survey
P.O. Box 21370
Columbus, OH 43221-0370
614-457-8787
E-mail: ohiobiosurvey@rrohio.com
Web site: http://www.ohiohiological
survey.org
Catalog of available publications on Ohio flora, fauna, and biodiversity

Ohio Department of Development
Division of Travel and Tourism
P.O. Box 1001
Columbus 43216-1001
1-800-BUCKEYE
Web site: http://www.discoverohio.com

Ohio Department of Natural Resources
Division of Forestry
2045 Morse Road, Building H-1
Columbus, OH 43229-6693
614-265-6694
Web site: http//www.ohiodnr.com/forestry

Ohio Department of Natural Resources
Division of Geological Survey
2045 Morse Road, Building C-1
Columbus, OH 43229-6693
614-265-6576
E-mail: geo.survey@dnr.state.oh.us
Web site: http://www.ohiodnr.com/
geosurvey
Catalog of maps and other resources on Ohio geology

Ohio Department of Natural Resources
Division of Natural Areas and Preserves
2045 Morse Road, Building F-1
Columbus, OH 43229-6693
614-265-6453
E-mail: dnap@dnr.state.oh.us
Web site: http://www.ohiodnr.com/dnap

Ohio Department of Natural Resources
Division of Parks and Recreation
2045 Morse Road, Building C
Columbus, OH 43229-6693
614-265-6561
Web site: http://www.ohiodnr.com/parks

Ohio Historical Society
1982 Velma Avenue
Columbus, OH 43211-2453
614-297-2300
Web site: http://www.ohiohistory.org

Preservation Parks of Delaware County
2656 Hogback Road
Sunbury, OH 43074-9561
740-524-8600
E-mail: info@preservationparks.com
Web site: http://www.preservation
parks.com

Shelby County Park District
9871 Fessler Buxton Road
Piqua, OH 45356-9602
937-773-4818
E-mail: shelbycoparks@voyager.net
Web site: http://www.shelbycopark.org

The Nature Conservancy
Edge of Appalachia Preserve
3223 Waggoner Riffle Road
West Union, OH 45693-9784
937-544-2880
E-mail:eoa@bright.net
Web site:
http://www.nature.org/wherewework/
northamerica/states/ohio/preserves

Wayne National Forest
Supervisor's Office and Athens Ranger
District
13700 U.S. Highway 33
Nelsonville, OH 45764-9552
740-753-0101
E-mail: r9_wayne_website@fs.fed.us
Web site: http://www.fs.fed.us/r9/wayne

Wayne National Forest
Marietta Unit
27750 State Route 7
Marietta, OH 45750-5147
740-373-9055

Wayne National Forest
Ironton Ranger District
6518 State Route 93
Pedro, OH 45659-8912
740-534-6500

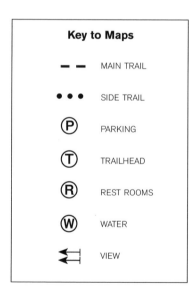

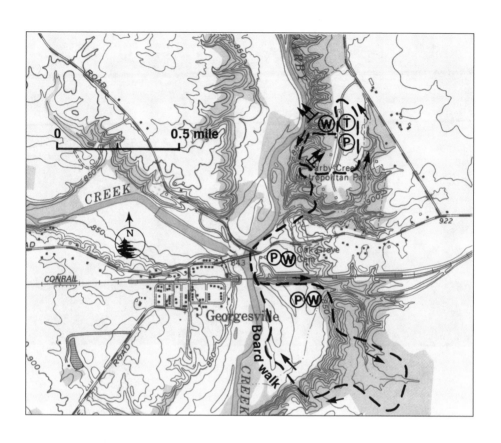

1

Battelle–Darby Creek Metro Park

Total distance: 4.5 miles (6.7 km)

Hiking time: 2.5 hours

Maximum elevation: 920 feet

Vertical rise: 90 feet

Maps: USGS 7½' Galloway; MPDCFC Battelle–Darby Creek Metro Park map

The Darby Creeks are considered to be among the finest of Ohio's streams. The Nature Conservancy designated them and their riverine environment as one of the nation's Last Great Places. They receive virtually no industrial effluent, and very little municipal, as they flow from the Darby Plains area of Madison and Union Counties to their confluence with the Scioto River just north of Circleville. Designated as a State Scenic River for many years, in the early 1990s the (Big and Little) Darby Creeks were added to the National Scenic River System. The Big Darby is a stream of pristine beauty as it passes below the high bluffs in Battelle–Darby Creek Metro Park in southwestern Franklin County.

A facility of the Metropolitan Park District of Columbus and Franklin County, this 6,633-acre metro park takes its name from the streams that flow through it and from the locally based Battelle Foundation, which provided the funds for a major expansion in the 1970s. It includes more than 11 miles of trails, public and reservable picnic areas, and a winterized meeting lodge. There is a year-round program of nature interpretation conducted by a park naturalist. Large areas of restored tallgrass prairie within the park are now open to the public, adding a new dimension to a summer or fall visit to Battelle–Darby.

How to Get There

To reach Battelle–Darby Creek Metro Park, travel 14 miles west of downtown Columbus on I-70 to Exit 75. Travel 2.5

Battelle–Darby Creek Metro Park

miles south on OH 142 to US 40, then 1.5 miles east (left) to Darby Creek Drive. Turn right and drive 3 miles south to the Cedar Ridge Picnic Area entrance on the right side of the road. The park is open every day during daylight hours.

The Trail

The 4.25-mile Indian Ridge Nature Trail starts behind the office of the park naturalist. It can be reached from either side of the building. Starting as a paved path, it becomes a gravel trail when it leaves the picnic area, heading due west toward the bluffs overlooking Big Darby Creek. The woods on the thin-soiled uplands are oak/hickory, and those in the river bottom are a typical floodplain hardwood mixture. *Note:* The Cedar Bluff Lookout Trail is now a separate trail. The bridge, steps, and trail connecting it with the rest of the trail system have been removed.

When the Indian Ridge Trail reaches the river, it turns south along the water with lots of opportunities to stop and enjoy the scenery. After dropping to a ravine and crossing a small stream, the trail emerges onto a hillside below a meadow fast filling with young trees. It then follows the contour of the land close to the river before passing beneath two new concrete bridges.

Once south of Alkire Road, the trail passes paths to the nearby parking lot and to the canoe-launching area at stream's edge, then returns to the riverbank. A large catalpa tree at this trail junction reminds me of one that stood beside my home when I was a small child. The trail now heads south to pass under a high railroad bridge coming into Columbus from the southwest. It was once a main line but now carries a largely grain-hauling, short-line railroad that serves a grain elevator at nearby Lilly Chapel. One hundred yards beyond the bridge a sign,

BEGIN LOOP, points left for a 2-mile round trip. Turn left and go upslope on what appears to be an old road. There is a picnic area through the trees to the right with drinking water and rest rooms. Old concrete fence posts mark the edge of the railroad right-of-way. Staying left at an intersection, the trail heads uphill to cross a bridge before swinging right, all the time in young oak/hickory woods. At one spot the present trail deserts the old road, leaving the water-filled ruts as good spawning areas for frogs and toads. Continuing through more woods, the trail finally reaches the mowed parkway. After entering a wet woods beyond the road, it crosses a number of obviously man-made ditches, early attempts to make this poorly drained land productive. Here grow pin oaks, good indicators of the acidity of the soil in this part of the park. Some stretches of the trail are covered with wood chips, others with gravel. There are a few places where the trail is soggy a good bit of the year. Not far off the trail lie the rusting bodies of a 1950s-era Chevy truck and some farm equipment. As the trail turns west parallel to a ravine, some great old, open-grown trees can be seen.

The trail now descends toward the river bottom, where for several hundred feet it runs on a boardwalk made necessary by the constant drainage of water across the area from the hills to the east. A side trail to the right leads to play and picnic areas, but the Indian Ridge Trail completes its loop back to the intersection via a riverside path.

Return to the northern part of the park over the same trail, but take the first trail to the right after entering the woods past Alkire Road. This trail goes up another set of steps to an overlook, then to another picnic area. As it passes through a wooden fence into the picnic area, the trail is paved once more. To return to the trailhead, cross the road and follow the trail as it loops east, then north, through young woods and shrubland. It emerges from the woods opposite the parking lot where it began.

➤ What Is a Metro Park?

Ohio's metropolitan parks are the result of legislation passed at the close of World War I that allowed the establishment of special districts for the conservation of the state's natural resources. The Cleveland Metropolitan Park District was the first, and it set the standard for the others that followed. Most important was the determination to keep 80 percent of the land within the park in a wild, undeveloped state; no more than 20 percent could be used for playgrounds, picnic areas, ball fields, parking lots, and reservoirs.

Park districts have been leaders in environmental interpretation and education, many building nature centers and hiring staff naturalists, even in the late 1930s. In more recent years, they have led the way in restoration management, using controlled burning, alien plant eradication, and other techniques to reestablish original ecosystems. They have also led the way in creating facilities for "under your own power" outdoor recreation opportunities, providing hundreds of miles of footpaths through field and forest, beside lakes and streams, and along old railroad and canal towpath rights-of-way.

There are metro parks within an hour's drive of virtually every Ohioan, providing places for many quick walks on short notice. For a brochure with the names and addresses of 63 park districts around the state, write to the Ohio Parks and Recreation Association, 1069A West Main Street, Westerville, OH 43081-1181 or call 614-895-2222.

2

Blues Creek Preserve

Total distance: 2 miles (3.6 km)

Hiking time: 1.5 hours

Maximum elevation: 971 feet

Vertical rise: 61 feet

Maps: USGS 7½' Ostrander; PPODC Blues Creek Preserve brochure

Purchased at public auction in 1993 with funds from an anonymous donor, this 138.5-acre park was first opened to the public in 2001. The former farm fields and woodlot have been developed into a nice passive recreation area in keeping with the philosophy of the young Preservation Parks of Delaware County organization. The park lies at the western edge of Delaware County on the Broadway moraine, one of many broad belts of unstratified clay, silt, and sand that were left on the land during a halt or minor readvance of melting Wisconsinan glacier. Blues Creek, a part of the Scioto River watershed, runs more or less northwest-to-southeast along the southern edge of the area of ground moraine between the Broadway end moraine and the St. Johns (end) moraine about 14 miles to the north. Blues Creek cuts through the Broadway moraine at nearby Ostrander, joining Mill Creek just south of there as it flows to the east to empty into the Scioto River at Bellpoint. According to Robert B. Gordon's map, *Natural Vegetation of Ohio at the Time of the Earliest Land Surveys,* the area was probably beech forest at the time of settlement.

Delaware Indians, led by their long-time chief Bockinghelas, were among the tribes that inhabited the area before white settlers began arriving in 1801. In 1808, the Delaware County was formed from Franklin County to the south. In the main, it prospered through the years, but the farm situated on the moraine that is now Blues Creek Park was likely a marginal producer. Probably by grazing livestock and produc-

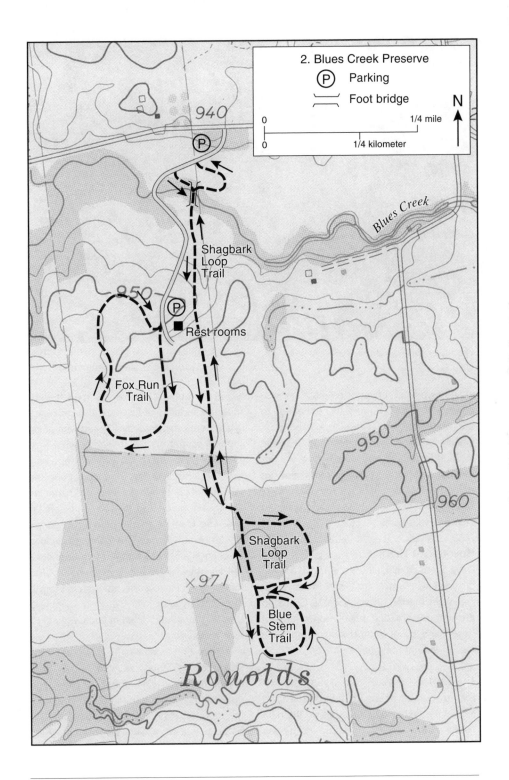

2. Blues Creek Preserve

P Parking

Foot bridge

N

0   1/4 mile
0   1/4 kilometer

940

Blues Creek

Shagbark
Loop
Trail

950

P

Rest rooms

Fox Run
Trail

950

960

Shagbark
Loop
Trail

×971

Blue
Stem
Trail

Ronolds

The Blues Creek swamp forest

ing its own feed, it supported many generations of "the family farmer." Its connection to the world was the Cleveland, Cincinnati, Chicago, and St. Louis Railroad that ran through Ostrander and what is now US 35, the Marysville Road running from Delaware to Marysville, Urbana, Piqua, and Greenville, and on west across the prairie and plains to Denver and beyond.

How to Get There

Drive west from Delaware on US 36 approximately 10 miles to Burnt Pond Road. Turn right (north), crossing Blues Creek, to the first cross road, Fontinell Road. Turn left (west) and travel to the park entrance on the left side of the road.

The Trail

Leave your car beneath the cottonwood tree at the first small lot just inside the park on the right side of the road. The trail begins

about 75 feet into the park on the left. I admire the audacity of the park administrators who posted the park road speed limit at 14 mph. It caught my eye, which is what I expect it was meant to do. When I began my walk on a hot July day, the area around the parking lot contained the usual field species like teasel, goldenrod, poison ivy, blackberries, and Canada thistle, plus a nice stand of cup plant (*Silphium perfoliatum*). A close inspection of this relative of prairie dock quickly reveals how it got its name: The leaves that encircle the main stem form a cup that collects rain. Can you imagine a tree frog hunkered down in such a comfortable hideaway?

Cross the road and hit the grass trail. Fifty feet up, the trail splits. Take your choice—they both go to the same place. I go right, planning to return on the other side of the loop. Now on gravel, the trail crossed Blues Creek on a wide steel bridge. Kids and a couple of naturalists were in the water with dip nets "creeking" (looking for anything live they could find) on the day of my visit. After emerging from the creekside woodland, the trail heads nearly due south, rising gently and continuously with woods on the right and an old field and mowed grass on the left. Ahead and to the right in the distance is the central area of the park, where there is a shelter house, rest rooms, picnic tables, and playground equipment. Soon that area disappears from view and the trail we are walking enters the woods, where it becomes the Shagbark Trail (with the appropriate trees alongside the trail).

Soon the trail makes a serpentine jog to the east side of what must have once been a fencerow. To the right, across a couple of sections of split-rail fence, you can see old field now returning to forest, perhaps by a combination of plant succession and tree planting. The park map already calls the area woodland and it is well on its way. Soon, the trail splits; I choose to go clockwise. This is a tree-learning trail, so watch for the labels on nice specimens of native hardwoods. As this is a wet woods, the trail requires bridges in a couple places and mosquitoes will be present during a good bit of the year.

After traversing three sides of this woodlot, the trail hits a T. Especially in late summer and fall, go left on the 0.4-mile Bluestem Trail through the planted prairie. You will be rewarded with the beautiful blooms of native tallgrass prairie forbs and grasses. After making the tallgrass prairie loop, the trail catches the fourth side of the Shagbark Loop Trail for the return trip to your vehicle. There's a side trail you can take to the rest room area if needed. After the downhill trip to the Blues Creek Bridge, opt for the other side of the loop entry trail to end your hike.

3

Clear Creek Metro Park

Total distance: 4.5 miles (7.24 km)

Hiking time: 3 hours

Maximum elevation: 1,100 feet

Vertical rise: 300 feet

Maps: USGS 7½' Rockbridge; MPDCFC Clear Creek Metro Park brochure

The narrow, forested valley of the small Hocking River tributary called Clear Creek has been a magnet for central Ohio naturalists for more than a century. I was first introduced to it in 1948 when I was invited to attend the annual weekend "hegira" of the Wheaton Club, a Columbus-based men's naturalist group. They gathered each year on the first weekend in June at a place called Neotoma (for the Eastern wood rat that once inhabited the rock ledges of the area), then owned by the late Edward S. Thomas, at the time curator of natural history at the museum of the Ohio Archaeological and Historical Society. The late-spring flora was at its peak and the trees were full of migrating warblers, vireos, thrushes, and the like. My eyes were opened to orchids and trilliums; lizards, salamanders, and snakes; toads and frogs; and much, much more—all new to a kid who grew up with the paved streets, storm sewers, and vacant lots of the city.

In the 50 years since, I have explored much of the Clear Creek valley in search of things that creep, crawl, sing, fly, and bloom. It is a place of splendid natural beauty where there is always a sight, sound, or smell to delight the senses and boggle the mind. In the early 1970s I played a small part in helping fend off the threat of a Corps of Engineers dam in the valley; later, I urged public officials and private landowners to preserve as much of the valley as possible in a natural state in some sort of public or quasi-public ownership.

Scientists of many disciplines have ex-

Written Rock

plored the Clear Creek valley over the years. Many theses have been written and papers delivered about the natural history of the valley at conferences and meetings. The two best-known studies, published by the Ohio Biological Survey 35 years apart, are "A Botanical Survey of the Sugar Grove Region," by Robert Griggs, and "Microclimates and Macroclimate of Neotoma, a Small Valley in Central Ohio," by Wolfe, Wareham, and Scofield. Both are still excellent references on the nature of this treasured place.

Probably the first Europeans to see this area were the 1,900 or so soldiers under the command of Lord Dunmore, Governor of the Virginia Colony, who in 1774 passed through the valley on the way west to confront the Shawnee Indians living along Scippo Creek in the Pickaway Plains. The Army of Virginia and the Indians postured and met in council but never did battle. The Mingo chief Logan delivered his eloquent but poignant speech about his life and family under what came to be known as the "Logan Elm." An agreement was reached between Lord Dunmore and the Shawnee chief Cornstalk. Though never formalized, this treaty is said to have brought some peace to the frontier. Dunmore and his troops retreated the way they came, back through the Clear Creek Gorge to the Hockhocking [sic], down to the Ohio River, then back to Fort Pitt. By the end of 1774 the army was dismissed. How many of those soldiers liked what they saw in the Ohio country and returned there to settle one can only guess.

Today, probably no one knows the valley better than Tom Thomson of Columbus, whose book, *Birding in Ohio*, extols the diversity of bird life that can be seen there. What the book does not reveal is the hundreds and hundreds of birding trips

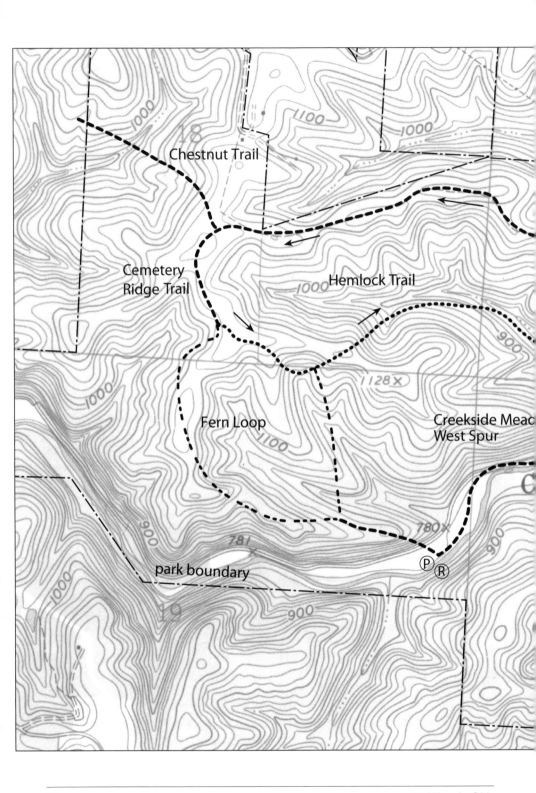

Chestnut Trail

Cemetery
Ridge Trail

Hemlock Trail

Fern Loop

Creekside Mea
West Spur

park boundary

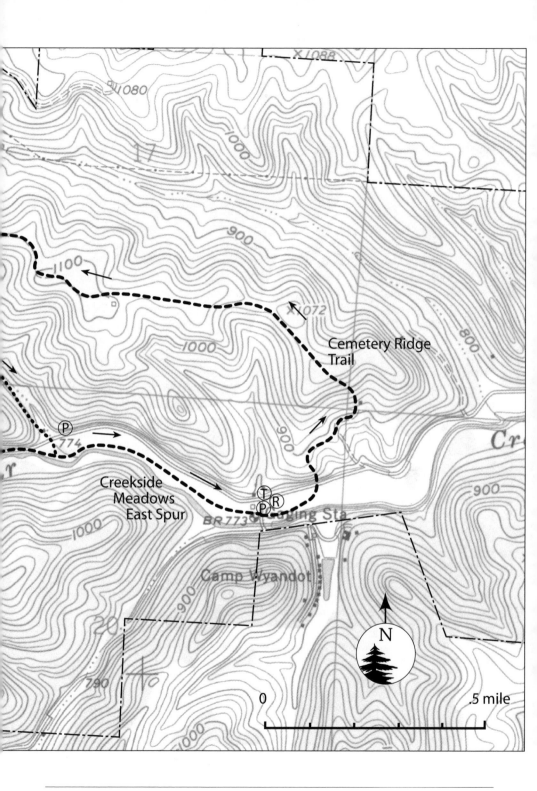

Cemetery Ridge
Trail

Creekside
Meadows
East Spur

Camp Wyandot

N

0   .5 mile

Thomson made to the valley over the course of several decades to compile what must be one of the most complete records of breeding birds made for any such area anywhere. We can all hope that Thomson publishes his observations and data someday. Attesting to the special nature of this place is the fact that most central Ohio birders, when setting out to take a "big day" bird count, jump-start their list by birding the Clear Creek Road at the crack of dawn on a May morning.

Today most of the 7-mile Clear Creek valley is in public ownership, thanks to the foresight of Edward F. Hutchins, retired director of the Columbus Metro Parks. With patience, perseverance, and persuasion, he acquired for the park district the tracts that make up the Clear Creek Metro Park. Now nearly 5,000 acres in size, the park was opened to the general public for the first time in 1996. The trail system was still a work in progress during the months I spent rewalking trails for the second edition of this book. Since then, many improvements have been made to the park and the trails. What has not changed is the beauty of fern-covered sandstone, the towering hemlocks, or the call of the wood thrush, ovenbird, or pileated woodpecker. Considered by many to be the beginning of the western edge of the Appalachian foothills, the park is known to harbor more than 800 plant species and 150 species of birds, many of which are quite rare. Walk on a weekday and you may be the only person on the trail. Even on the weekend, few people visit the Metro Park, two counties away from the core of Columbus.

How to Get There

From I-270 on the south side of Columbus take US 33 southeast, going around Lancaster on the recently constructed bypass. About 12 miles beyond Lancaster a sign will alert you to the park, which you reach by turning west (right) onto Clear Creek Road. There is a gasoline station/convenience store there. The trailhead for the park is located at the Creekside Meadows parking lot along Clear Creek Road, about 2 miles from US 33.

The Trail

Begin walking downstream on the east spur of the Creekside Meadows Trail. After leaving the mowed grass area and entering an old field that glows with goldenrod in the fall, turn left at your first opportunity, heading toward the road. Across the tarmac, a sign introduces the 2.5-mile Cemetery Ridge Trail. Climbing an old driveway below a grove of spruce, the trail soon ascends the ridge and heads west on what looks like old township and gas-line service roads. The south-facing slope holds a good mixture of hardwoods, including several species of oak. An occasional non-native white pine appears along the trail, the results of human effort to reclaim abandoned hilltop farm fields of yore. Native hemlock and Virginia pine also show up among the dominant hardwoods of the ridge.

After traveling just over a mile, look for an old cattle barn on the left. It is quite obvious when the leaves are down, but may be well hidden during the summer. There likely was once a farmhouse nearby, but its setting is not clearly evident.

The barn sits at an elevation of 1,100 feet, about 325 feet above the elevation of the Ohio State House lawn in downtown Columbus. You still have another 20 feet or so of rise to the top of the trail. After swinging north, the trail heads west, again following the gas-line road on the side of the hill. The deeply cut route of the old rural road is quite evident uphill and to the right. To this naturalist, the crushed limestone the gas company uses to fill soft spots in the trail looks out of place in sandstone country. Incidentally, most of the gas wells in this area aren't in production, but are being used for underground storage of gas piped in from outside Ohio.

As the trail returns to the ridge, the trees are especially grand. In the head of the valley to the right is a nice stand of mountain laurel. And as I walked the trail among the large white oak and tulip poplars on an early November day, a monarch butterfly flew up from the leaves. What do you suppose its chances were of staying ahead of winter's arrival long enough to make it to the overwintering roosts of central Mexico?

After crossing a narrow saddle while still in the woods, the trail soon emerges at a meadow where it heads south and the gravel gas-well service road heads north; the juncture is marked by an arrow on a 6 x 8 post. Following alongside the thicket of abandoned pasture, the trail next crosses a nice high meadow, complete with bluebird boxes, before reaching its end. With the Cemetery Ridge Trail behind, you now are traveling on the Fern Loop. A short distance farther, the trail splits. Going right will carry you around the hillside in a gentle descent toward the creek. Before reaching the road, you will have the option to turn left and ascend a valley and rejoin the Hemlock Trail or to continue to the west spur of the Creekside Meadows Trail.

If you turn left here, as I did, you will travel through young hardwoods and soon reach another juncture, where there is a sign introducing you to the 1.5-mile Hemlock Trail heading off to the left. This unimproved trail may leave you hanging onto the side of the hill, and at times walking it requires scrambling over blocks of sandstone. Suddenly the forest changes, and you are in the soft shade of a hundred hemlocks with the rustle of deciduous trees

➤ Peculiar Pollination

The mountain laurel (Kalmia latifolia) *is one of America's most beautiful shrubs. (In the southern Appalachian Mountains, where rainfall may reach 200 inches annually, it can appear somewhat treelike, reaching heights of 30 to 35 feet. Natives there refer to it as ivy.) Growing native in 25 or so counties in unglaciated southeastern Ohio, it is usually found on moist slopes, often near exposed sandstone outcrops. One look at its beautiful flower will tell you why mountain laurel is sometimes called calico bush.*

According to the pioneering plant ecologist and botanist E. Lucy Braun, the pollination mechanism of the mountain laurel is particularly interesting. In fresh flowers, the anthers (the pollen-sac-bearing structures at the end of the stamen—the male organ) lie in the concavities of the corolla (the flower petals). In this position, the filaments (the slender structures of the stamen that terminate in the anthers) are under tension. When the tongue of a bee is inserted in the crevice between ovary and stamens, the tension is suddenly released, changing the position of the stamens and causing pollen to be thrown onto the head of the bee. The bee then moves on, carrying the pollen to the stigma (the female organ) of the next mountain laurel flower visited, thus effecting pollination—an out-crossing rather than a self-pollination. Braun says this trigger-release can be effected by a pin.

left behind. The trail drops off the nose of a point of land and switches back to cross the creek on a bridge that was under construction the day I walked it. With a ravine to the right, the trail follows the contour of the land, winding in and out before climbing steeply over a ridge. Quartz pebbles in the trail are evidence of a Black Hand sandstone outcropping above, and large oblong holes chiseled near the bases of less-than-healthy trees give away the presence of pileated woodpeckers, the "cocks-of-the-woods." The stump of a long-gone chestnut remains visible alongside the trail, and mountain laurel can be seen in this cool, moist environment. Passing large sandstone slump blocks and great patches of Christmas fern, the trail makes its slow descent through the hemlock forest toward the valley floor. As I reached what looked like an old logging skid or road, I stood quietly as two yearling does moved through the forest close by—one of the rewards of walking alone.

The trail crosses and recrosses a small stream as it passes through the white oak, beech, and hemlock woods, and soon reaches a trailhead sign at Clear Creek Road. From there, it is .5 mile of hoofing to the east on the west spur of the Creekside Meadows Trail before you cross Starner Road and arrive at the parking lot. Among the many wonders of the Clear Creek valley is Leaning Lena, the huge, leaning sandstone block that you must pass under on your way back to US 33. Because neither county in which the park lies spray the roadsides, this is an especially good place to enjoy the beauty of wildflowers as you leave the park, whether you go east toward US 33 or west toward Amanda.

4

Chestnut Ridge Metro Park

Total distance: 2 miles (3.2 km)

Hiking time: 1.5 hours

Maximum elevation: 1,060 feet

Vertical rise: 150 feet

Maps: USGS 7½' Canal Winchester; MPDCFC Chestnut Ridge Metro Park brochure

A hike, a walk, or a stroll along the trails of Chestnut Ridge Metro Park will be rewarding in many ways. This is a trek through a moderate, but not overwhelming, variety of habitats. The near views, as well as those to the far horizon, can be spectacular at any time of the year. Chestnut Ridge is situated on a narrow outcropping of a sandstone resistant to weathering, the Black Hand–the same sandstone responsible for the beauty of the rock shelters of Hocking Hills, and the glory of the gorge that bears its name along the Licking River. But this time, instead of being on the hillsides, it *is* the hill. The high connected hills that make up the ridge cover only a few square miles, but they stand out on the landscape like a scene from an early western. In truth, in a state where the maximum elevation is just over 1,500 feet, the 410-foot difference between the lay of the land where US 33 crosses Big Walnut Creek 2 miles east of the park entrance and the peak of the ridge is striking: from 780 feet at the highway bridge to 1,180 feet on the highest peak. Though downtown Columbus is about 19 miles away, on a clear day it is easy to see from an overlook on Chestnut Ridge. Unfortunately, the magnificent American chestnut trees that at one time covered the ridge, and from which the park gets its name, are long gone, decimated by a deadly fungus introduced into the United States in 1903. By 1950, the forests at Chestnut Ridge were mostly empty of chestnut trees. All that is left is a few old stumps and an occasional blight-resistant hybrid along the

Homestead Trail. A few small American chestnuts have been planted along the Meadows Trail in hopes that in isolation from infected trees they will survive.

This very special place is the result of the foresight of Walter A. Tucker, the first director-secretary of the park district. He purchased the land in the 1960s, more than two decades before funds became available to open it to the public. He was truly a visionary, to whom the people of Ohio owe a great debt of gratitude.

➤ A Year on Chestnut Ridge

In his 1980 book Idle Weeds *(Sierra Club Books), naturalist-writer David Rains Wallace tells of life through the year on Chestnut Ridge. His story, which blends the largest cataclysmic events and the smallest nuances of nature as he observed and was part of them, takes the reader to a new level of understanding of life on earth. The Chestnut Ridge that Wallace describes is the Chestnut Ridge of this hike. He writes, "The ridge might even be said to have a soul, at least a place that is always beautiful, from which beauty radiates." He goes on to describe "a little grove of sugar maples on the upper west slope just below the spring-wildflower-covered mound. The maples are young, no more than sixty years old, but something about the place makes them seem venerable. A quiet emerald light plays on the slope in summer, and in autumn the crisp sunbeams that stream through the golden canopy make the grove sparkle like cloisonné. In winter the trees stand as gracefully against the snow as in those leafless woods through which knights hunt wild boar in a medieval book of hours."*

How to Get There

To reach Chestnut Ridge Metro Park, drive southeast from Columbus on US 33. After about 12 miles, at the traffic light at Carroll, make a hard right turn onto Winchester Road NW. The entrance to the park is approximately 3 miles from the traffic light on the left (west) side of Winchester Road.

The Trail

A good place to begin hiking is from the first parking lot on the left after you pass the ranger station. There are rest rooms and drinking water here. The trail leaves from the far end of the parking lot and heads for the wooded hillside. In August, both pale and spotted jewelweed bloom at the wood's edge to the left. You will find a map of the trails of the park at this intersection. Note that an oak leaf marks the Ridge Trail. Turn right under the tall trees and follow this trail as it begins its gradual ascent to the ridge. It's only about a 150-foot rise from the trail entrance to the ridge, so don't sweat it. Enjoy the beauty of the deep, mixed mesophytic woods as the large trees give way to younger growth. About halfway along this reach of the trail there is a boardwalk and a bench. Trailside interpretive signs about the trees were in place when I traveled this trail, but there was no mention of what looked like an old chestnut stump on the hillside below. Signs describing the area's history are still to come. I believe the story of the sandstone quarry on the slope below will also be told along here eventually. Around 1830, hundreds of huge blocks of sandstone were taken from the hillside quarry to be used for the construction of locks on the nearby Ohio and Erie and Hocking Canals. There were six lock chambers in Lockville, less than 2 miles away, and others up and down both canals. Where could there be a more economical source of building stone?

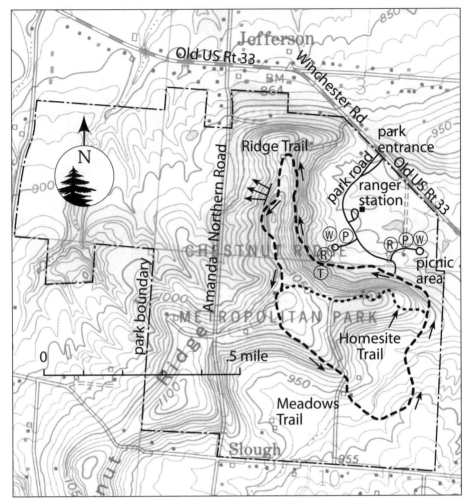

From here, the trail returns to gravel and continues uphill, making a hard turn to the left past some old fruit trees and a meadow managed for grassland birds. Reentering woods, the trail crosses over the ridge to the west side, where there is an observation deck. On a clear day you can't see forever, but you can certainly see downtown Columbus 19 miles to the northwest. Beyond the overlook, the trail continues to climb and soon levels out on the ridge where a deck protrudes into the woods to the right. This is the grove of maples that

David Rains Wallace writes about in *Idle Weeds,* and some of his words, quoted above, will be put on a sign here. Indeed, it is a good place to pause and reflect upon the beauty of the world of plants in which we animals reside.

The trail crisscrosses the ridge, soon arriving at its juncture with the Meadows and Homesite Trails. The latter goes left and leads along the ridge to a former homesite. The male and female holly trees growing in my yard started out many years ago as seedlings from hollies planted around the

---

Chestnut Ridge Metro Park trail

house that once stood here, the gift of a former resident. Beyond the obvious home garden and house area, the trail follows the high ground for a while, then drops to meet the other trails in the valley to the east to eventually join the Meadows and Ridge Trails.

I prefer following the Meadows Trail as it traces the edge of a high meadow just inside the woods. The last time I passed this way I looked to the meadow and saw 10 cabbage butterflies doing an aerial dance together in almost perfect synchrony, a sight I had never seen before and have not seen since. The trail now passes some apple trees and a planting of blight-resistant hybrid chestnuts. The American chestnut trees that originally grew in great profusion on the ridge, and from which the area got its name, died out in the 1930s when a chestnut blight swept across the country. A turn to the right takes the trail

through the woods to join what remains of the driveway that served a farmhouse of the now relocated Far View Farms on the ridge. Along this trail there are some large trees, including a sycamore that seems out of place this far from a stream, and a hackberry, a tree usually found on neutral to alkaline soil but here growing within 10 feet of a sassafras—a tree that indicates acidic soil. But seeds don't read books; they just put out a seed root and start growing if the moisture conditions are right. There is also an awesome growth of wild black cherry trees along the trail as you approach the driveway.

Turning right, the trail moves downhill alongside open meadow. I have fond memories of spending time here many years ago, photographing a female red admiral butterfly as it deposited eggs on a nettle plant in the field near the creek below. Beyond the shade of a nice maple tree, the trail heads toward a bridge over a small stream. There is a cattail wetland to the right where dragonflies hover awaiting prey, then a meadow managed for dickcissels and other grassland-nesting birds. With thicket now on the right, the trail meanders toward another bridge over the brook. Beyond, the hillside to the left is apparently being allowed to succeed from old field to woodland. Just as you enter the woods, the Homesite Trail comes down the hill from the left. It is now only a short walk through the woods to the junction with the side trail to the parking lot.

5

Conkle's Hollow State Nature Preserve

Total distance: 3.5 miles (5.6 km)

Hiking time: 3 hours

Maximum elevation: 970 feet

Vertical rise: 230 feet

Maps: USGS 7½' South Bloomingville; ODNR/DNAP Conkle's Hollow State Nature Preserve brochure

When W. J. Conkle carved his name on the face of the sandstone cliff of the hollow that now bears his name, he could not have helped but be struck by the beauty of the place. The year was 1797. The young German immigrant must have been one of the first white men to see the area, and he must have liked what he saw, for he settled there. Conkles of many generations are buried nearby, and many of his descendants still live in the region.

Conkle's Hollow truly is one of Ohio's most spectacular natural areas. A north-south-oriented box canyon about 1 mile in length, it was carved into the bedrock by a small tributary of Big Pine Creek. The light gray and buff Black Hand sandstone and conglomerate bedrock was deposited in the region as a delta from no-longer extant mountains to the south about 345 million years ago. Ranging from 80 to 250 feet thick, the rock layer is about 200 feet thick in Conkle's Hollow. Because the upper portion is structureless and well-cemented, while the lower portions are cross-bedded and more easily eroded, cliffs with one or more levels of recesses or rock shelters have formed. These features dominate the scenic gorges of the Hocking Hills region and are found to a lesser extent in Licking and Fairfield Counties.

No visit to southeastern Ohio would be complete without a walk along the trails of this very special place. To get a real feel for its grandeur and beauty, you should walk both the rim trail and the gorge trail, a hike of about 3.5 miles. Except for the 200-foot

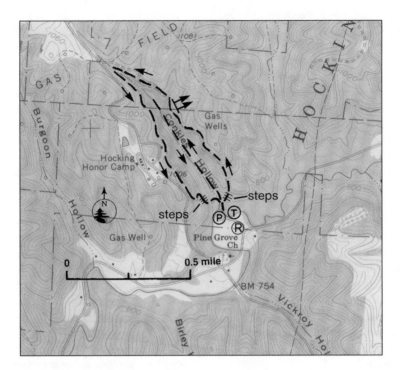

climb and descent to and from the rim trail, the hike is nearly all on flat, well-defined woodland trail. Even with stops for picture taking, the trip should not take more than 3 hours.

Though short, the Conkle's Hollow hike is very special. It is one that should be taken several times during the year to appreciate the ever-changing beauty of the area. Combined with the nearby Grandma Gatewood Trail (Hike 7), it provides a full day of hiking; by itself, it is a good walk for the end of a busy day in the city. The reward of an early-morning springtime walk might be the sound of a drumming ruffed grouse. An early-evening walk on a long summer day may serve up the haunting, flutelike call of the wood thrush or hermit thrush. Not even Michelangelo could match the colors of autumn, and the breathtaking beauty of a new-fallen snow is beyond description.

A number of improvements have been made to the trail system at Conkle's Hollow since I described it in 1989 for the first edition of this book. The latest, completed in the fall of 2004, is the paving of about 2,600 feet of the gorge trail, to within 500 feet of the end of the hollow and the addition of some boardwalk and new bridges. With the earlier upgrading of the bridges near the entrance to the hollow, this allows visitors in wheelchairs to enjoy the grandeur of this special place.

How to Get There

Conkle's Hollow is easily reached from the Columbus area by two routes. From the east side of the city, travel US 33 southeast 10 miles past Lancaster, to where OH 374 originates as a right turn from the major highway. This scenic route takes the visitor to Hocking County past all six of the Hocking Hills park and preserve sites. Follow the signs closely, as this is a twisty road in some places. Drive 13 miles on OH 374 and turn left on Big Pine Road (after passing Cantwell Cliffs and Rock House). A church adjoins a graveyard on the corner. For an interesting insight into the lives of the early residents of this area, spend a few moments reading the old headstones. The preserve entrance will appear 0.2 mile down Big Pine Road on the left. Unlike most state nature preserves, there is a rest room and some picnic tables near the entrance.

The other route from Columbus is US 23 south to Circleville, then east to South Bloomingville on OH 56. There, turn northeast on OH 664 and continue until it intersects with OH 374. Turn left and follow OH 374 about 1 mile downhill to where it intersects with Big Pine Road, then turn right to the preserve. Either way, the drive takes about an hour from the I-270 outer belt.

The Trail

Upon entering the preserve, you are greeted by an uninspiring treeless area where there are picnic tables, latrines, and a pump. Unless you need those amenities, park at the next lot. There is only one way in and out of the preserve—across Big Pine Creek on a footbridge. Beyond the bridge, the trail takes a sharp turn to the left. A gathering place off the right side of the trail about 50 feet beyond the bridge has interpretive signs, including a large map of the area and a dispenser with brochures. Shortly after the assembly area, the trail reaches a set of wooden steps to the right. If you opt to walk the rim trail first, turn and climb these stairs. The paved main trail straight ahead will take you up the valley. Regrettably, an old arched stone bridge that once stood just up the trail from here did not survive the trail-paving project. It was built by the CCC in the 1930s. After 52 steps toward the east rim, you reach a wide

landing where the first of many interpretive signs tells about the rim trail and hillside ecology. In another 37 steps, you come to about 100 yards of steep, log-lined path through an insect- and wind-damaged pine grove. The trail then curves left as it climbs about the same distance through young hemlock and hardwood. A short scramble to the left up a clearly-defined trail over bare rock brings you to the rim.

Almost immediately, the trail provides picture-postcard views of the valley, many nicely framed with scraggly pines. Upslope are more Virginia pines, oaks, mountain laurels, greenbriers, huckleberries, and reindeer lichen. Below are the tops of tuliptrees, yellow birches, hemlocks, and maples. At times the trail is on bare bedrock, and often it is near the cliff edge. Children should be kept close at hand since there are no railings. "Lucky stones"—quartz pebbles that weather their way out of the conglomerate rock—line the low spots on the trail, at some places making footing precarious. Two small footbridges span intermittent side streams set back from the gorge. In all but the driest of summers, the sound of cascading water gives away the end of the canyon. As you approach the 95-foot falls, you will see a large wooden deck at the cliff edge that affords a magnificent view. Seventy-five yards beyond, safely upstream from the edge, the stream that creates the fall is spanned by a footbridge, and signs direct you to the west rim return trail and a side trail to a nearby forest service road.

The path on the west rim lies only a short distance from the road and the forest headquarters, but it does not lose its feeling of wildness. Under towering white pines planted in 1931—legacies of the CCC and the Division of Forestry—you will likely focus on the cliffs across the valley. Canada yew grows above the edge of the cliff in this

A beautiful fall day in Conkle's Hollow

area. Wind blowing through the pines can magically obscure any intruding man-made noises. The trail takes two sweeping arcs above the rock shelters in the gorge wall. The woods above are dominated by oaks— white, red, chestnut, and scarlet—while below the forest is a blend of hemlock and hardwoods. When it's time to descend, steps in the bedrock, three steeply sloped switchbacks, and a 265-foot wooden staircase bring you to the valley floor only a few yards upstream from where you left the main trail. You have come 2.5 miles.

A left turn onto the main trail introduces a totally new environment—a deeply shaded, relict boreal forest dominated by hemlock. Although the glacial ice sheets of the Pleistocene period never reached this far (the last one stopped near Haynes, about 6 miles to the west), the colder climate of the times brought boreal forests to the gorges of the area. After the glaciers

melted from Ohio, many of these plants continued to grow in the ravines and gorges because of the colder microclimates. Many songbirds breed here, and it is home to a variety of reptiles and amphibians. The northern copperhead is indigenous, but the likelihood of encountering one is very slim. The fern- and moss-covered slump blocks (chunks of bedrock that broke away from a stratum above, rolled down the slope and eventually came to rest), the patches of Canada yew, the honeycomb-weathered sandstone, the picturesque waterfalls, and the clear-running stream all add to the ambience of the hollow. The .5 mile, 5- to 6-foot-wide paved trail crosses several small footbridges and some boardwalk before reverting to natural trail about 500 feet short of the head of the .5-mile-long valley. Most of the year, water from the stream above slides over the rock and falls about 50 feet into a plunge pool.

After drinking in the beauty of this verdant spot, head back to the parking area via the same valley trail. Note that there are different views to be had on the return trip. And, of course, remember that all things natural at Conkle's Hollow are protected as a preserve, including the critters that creep and crawl and the flowers that bloom—to be admired and enjoyed and perhaps photographed, but to be left for others to enjoy.

In the last couple of decades, a number of notable storms have left their mark on Conkle's Hollow, a reminder of nature's occasional wrath. On July 4, 1982, a small funnel cloud destroyed many of the hemlock in the front part of the valley. That area is now nicely recovered, the young growth providing good bird nesting habitat. In February 1986, a warm period followed by a heavy, wet snow wreaked havoc on the trees in the middle section of the canyon. A 20-inch snowfall on April 4, 1987, left its mark on the entire preserve, and a storm on March 4, 1988, that left the trees ice-glazed for nearly four days took down more than 100 trees on the rim trail. Since the area is a nature preserve, none of these trees were salvaged for timber. Only trees that blocked trails were removed, the rest were left to rot slowly to providing homes for creatures large and small, their nutrients eventually returning to the soil.

6

Davey Woods State Nature Preserve

Total distance: 1.5 miles (2.4 km)

Maximum elevation: 1,200 feet

Vertical rise: 100 feet

Maps: USGS 7½', Saint Paris, ODNR/DNAP Davey Woods State Nature Preserve brochure

This mature forest has numerous large tulip-trees, sugar maple, ash, and oak as well as excellent spring flora. Interestingly, the USGS 15' quadrangle map from the first decade of the 1900s shows the area with no forest cover. It is now considered one of the best woodlots remaining in this part of the till plains of west-central Ohio.

Not too many years ago, a bowhunter's camp occupied the area where the trailheads are located. In the mid-1980s it was identified as a tract that should be part of the state nature preserve system. In 1989, The Davey Tree Company of Kent, Ohio (the source of the name for the preserve), through The Nature Conservancy, stepped up to provide half of the funding necessary for its purchase with the balance coming from the Ohio State Income Tax Check-off Fund. In 1990 this 104-acre, triangular-shaped preserve was dedicated as an interpretive preserve. It sits on a hillside facing the valley of the southeast-flowing Nettle Creek, a Mad River (hence, Great Miami River) tributary. Mosquito Creek, which originates in the same valley less than 3 miles away, flows northwest through Kiser Lake and directly to the Great Miami. In the great railroad-building era of the last decade of the 19th century, the Ohio Southern Railroad (later to become the Detroit, Toledo & Ironton) routed its line across this valley on the land between the headwaters of these two creeks on what was, at the time, the longest trestle on the railroad. In 1894 the CSRR began replacing the trestle with a fill, a job which was completed by the Detroit Southern Railroad in 1905. The railroad ceased operation in the 1980s.

This preserve has been extensively studied by Dr. Ralph Boerner and his students from The Ohio State University. Though not a virgin forest, it is considered to be an excellent example of a mixed mesophytic community of the eastern hardwood forest. No endangered or threatened plant species have been identified in the preserve. Unfortunately, there are some occurrences of nuisance plants such as bush honey-suckle, garlic mustard, and barberry, but the problem is not extensive. Deer frequent the woods, but many are harvested on adjacent lands where hunting is allowed so they haven't yet been a serious threat to the flora.

Several species of owls are frequently heard in the woods and hawks have been seen nesting in the tall trees. Two trails have been developed: the short loop of less than a half mile and the longer Conrad Trail, just over a mile in length, named for a former landowner. A large parking lot at the en-

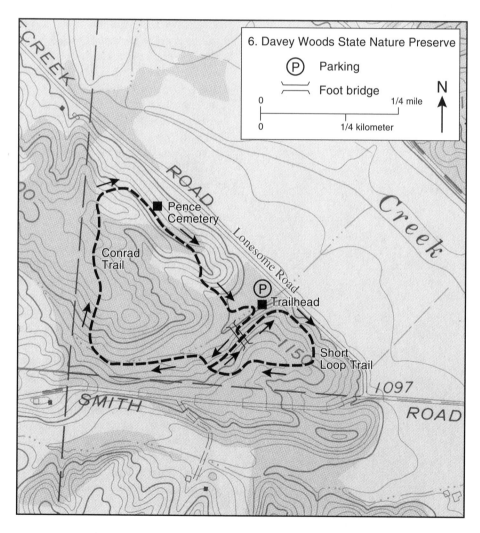

Trailhead kiosk in Davey Woods State Nature Preserve

trance to the preserve is now permanently closed so you must pull your car off the road in front of the gate. Like nearly all state nature preserves, there are rest rooms or picnic tables.

How to Get There

Davey Woods is located in Concord and Mad River townships in Champaign County about 7 miles west of Urbana and north of US 36. Turn north off US 36 on Neal Road, then go 0.5 mile west on Smith Road and northwest on Lonesome Road (formerly Nettle Creek Road) to the signed preserve entrance on the west side of the road.

The Trail

After checking the bulletin board, begin hiking by turning left off the end of the parking lot and crossing a stream on a wooden bridge. At the end of the bridge, turn left and follow the trail around the hillside above Lonesome Road, climbing most of the way. Soon the trail turns west and tops a low ridge before dropping into the valley of the stream you crossed. A trail to the right, heading downstream on the side of the hill, will return you to the bridge and former parking lot to complete the .5-mile short loop trail.

Turn left at this junction, uphill and away from the bridge, to follow the Conrad Trail around the perimeter of the preserve, in the forest all the way. Less than .25 mile up the valley the trail crosses the now much narrower stream and ascends to higher ground along the western edge of the preserve. Occasionally dipping to cross small, mostly dry streambeds, the trail continues north about .3 mile, passing under some nice large trees and by some stands of young trees reclaiming cleared land. One place near the western edge is noticeably devoid of any shrubs, possibly a "deer yard" during the winter.

Gradually the trail turns east, then southeast, and begins its descent to the trailhead. It passes a spot where there must have once been a homestead, as evidenced by old apple trees in the area. Deer likely enjoy the apples in the fall. A single cedar tree looks as if it was planted near a home rather than being a remnant of a cedar thicket. The trail passes a small graveyard where only a few headstones remain upright. The only name visible is Pence, which appears in my family several generations back in this part of Ohio. The old USGS map I referred to above shows a Pence School about a mile west of here.

As the trail continues downhill parallel to Lonesome Road, you can see some large open-grown tuliptrees and sugar maples on the slope below. They likely began life there when the hillside was used for grazing livestock. As the trail approaches the parking lot, it follows a streambed. It crosses the stream on a 3-foot bridge then turns right and left to bring you to the unused parking lot. Your car is but a short distance away.

This trail provides a not-too-challenging hike in what is usually an uncrowded setting. On the summer afternoon when I hiked it in 2006 there were very few mosquitoes and the only sounds came from katydids, tree crickets, and wood-pewees.

➤ Wolf Trees

The term "wolf tree" is applied by many naturalists and foresters to a mature, open-grown tree found among a stand of much younger trees. A tree that has grown most of its life among other trees will generally have its first branches a long way up its trunk. Not so the wolf tree. Usually such a tree has branches low to the ground, indicating it stood by itself during most of its life. Such trees avoided the logger's ax for a number of reasons. Perhaps it was deliberately left along a fencerow or at the edge of a pasture to provide shade for livestock. Maybe the lumberman saw a piece of old fence sticking out of the bark, giving him fear of the wrath of the sawyer if he hauled it to the mill. It may have even been a shade tree near a long-gone homestead, church, or school. And some lumbermen made it a practice to leave a few trees standing to provide seeds for regeneration. Sometimes when you see an even-aged stand of trees all of the same species, you can look uphill or upwind and see that the seeds came from the replanted trees the year after grazing or cultivation stopped, or after most of the standing timber was skidded down the hillside to the lumber truck. Keep your eyes open for wolf trees as you trek the Ohio countryside.

7

Hocking Hills State Park

Total distance: 6 miles (9.6 km)

Hiking time: 5.5 hours

Maximum elevation: 930 feet

Vertical rise: 183 feet

Maps: USGS 7½' South Bloomingville; ODNR Hocking Hills State Park map; BTA Old Man's Cave Section map

Old Man's Cave, Cedar Falls, and Ash Cave are among the state's best-known natural features. The caves are not actually underground but are recess caves caused by differential weathering of the nearly 250-foot-thick Black Hand sandstone bedrock of Ohio's Hocking Hills region. All three of these features are spectacular and easy to reach on foot. This hike takes you past Old Man's Cave and Cedar Falls. Ash Cave is 2 miles beyond Cedar Falls, so the round trip would add 4 miles to your hike.

Many more trails crisscross the 12,311-acre Hocking State Park and forest complex. The state began purchasing land in this area in 1924 under an early state forest law. The scenic areas were transferred to the Division of Parks upon the creation of the Department of Natural Resources in 1949. Millions of Ohioans enjoy the area throughout the year.

In January of 1998, a devastating flash flood through the Old Man's Cave gorge destroyed the original Civilian Conservation Corps (CCC)-built foot trail system, including all of the bridges. The trail was closed for more than two years, during which time the state spent more than 4 million dollars rebuilding bridges and upgrading and, in some places, rerouting the trail to make it safer and more enjoyable. The trails were reopened in May 2002. In 2003 a new park office, store, and camp office were opened at this popular park. There are class A, primitive walk-in, and group camping facilities at the park.

How to Get There

From Columbus, the Old Man's Cave parking lot is reached either by taking US 33 southeast to Logan and OH 664 south (right), or by traveling US 23 south to Circleville and then heading east (left) on OH 56 to South Bloomingville, and from there, taking OH 664 north (straight ahead where OH 56 turns right). By either route, the trip takes about 1.5 hours.

The Trail

Park at the east end of the Old Man's Cave lot, then take the wooden steps to OH 664 and carefully cross to the Grandma Gatewood Trail monument, where this hike begins. The plaque on the stone tells of Emma Gatewood, who was born in 1887, died in 1973, and began hiking after the age of 67. She walked the Oregon Trail once and the Appalachian Trail three times. This is a section of the Buckeye Trail and it was a favorite of hers. It was designated a National Recreation Trail and named in her honor in 1979. It was my privilege to have known her and to have walked this trail with her on several occasions.

Start hiking by crossing the stone arch bridge over the Upper Falls. Turn downstream and take the steps to the valley floor. For the next mile the trail travels through what is known as "The Gulf." Through the Upper Gorge area, the trail goes beneath honeycombed cliffs. It crosses a bridge by the Devil's Bathtub before climbing stairs to the level where Old Man's Cave itself comes into view on the opposite wall. Like the floor of the Upper Gorge, this recess cave was formed when the weak middle zone of the sandstone was eroded by water and wind. The cave was named after a hermit by the name of Richard Roe, a fugitive

from West Virginia, who lived there after the Civil War. It measures 200 feet wide and 50 feet high and is 75 feet deep. Roe is said to have been buried beneath rocks in the cave.

The trail next passes down a staircase inside a tunnel as it reaches the area above the Lower Falls. If you wish to explore the cave, cross the bridge and ascend a set of steps through another tunnel. Otherwise, look downstream toward the Sphinx Head profile, carved by natural forces, visible on the face of the cliff.

From here, the trail climbs to the base of the cliff before descending past the lip of the Lower Falls. It hugs the cliff before dropping down a set of steps to the valley floor below the falls. The Lower Falls is the only scenic feature in the Hocking Hills area that is located in the lower zone of the Black Hand sandstone. At the plunge pool level below the 60-foot waterfall, a deep recess cave has been carved in the underlying Cuyahoga shale, a soft stratum named for the spectacular exposures along the Cuyahoga River in the Cleveland area.

The trail now travels downstream on the left bank of Old Man's Creek. In many places it is unstable because of the seepage of water caused by the relatively impervious underlying shale, and there are places where you need to climb over rocks and roots. Large hemlock and yellow birch trees dominate the forest canopy, and Canada yew is seen in patches on the hillside, all relicts of an earlier, colder period. A 160-foot hemlock just across the small stone bridge near the Lower Falls is a state record.

At the confluence of Old Man's Creek with Queer Creek, the trail turns upstream toward Cedar Falls. The streams are not visible here but a sign points the way, and when the trail moves close to the creek you'll see that you are now going upstream. It follows the left bank, first traveling along

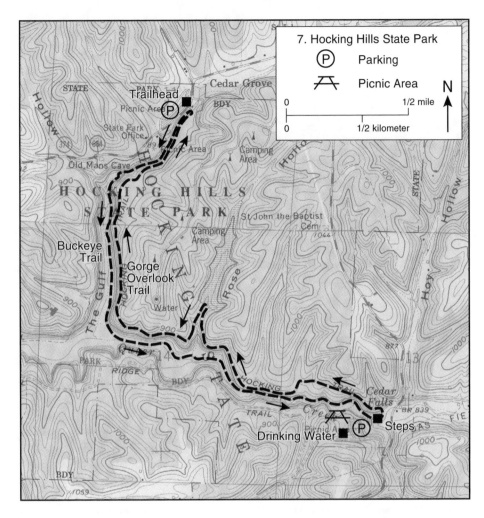

the stream, then rising to the base of the sandstone cliffs and returning to the stream several times. In some places, the trail is difficult to navigate.

An old Native American trail that connected the Kanawha River region of West Virginia with Ohio's Chillicothe area is said to have run through here. Settlers knew it as the "Road to Hell" because prisoners were marched through during the frontier wars. Huge sycamores line the stream, and in some places the ever-present hemlock give a cathedral-like feeling to the woods. The trail crosses a 25-foot bridge as it approaches a beautiful waterfall, then moves though a football field-sized grove of hemlocks before scrambling up and over lots of rock rubble. Next, it passes a lovely cave, then through another rocky area. Here, for many years the trail continued ahead on the left bank along a narrow ledge between the cliff base and the stream as it approached Cedar Falls. It could be very dangerous in the winter when icicles sometimes broke loose from above and fell on the trail, making the footing very slick. Now it crosses

The new steel bridge over Queer Creek

Queer Creek on a new steel bridge, at the other end of which there is a split in the trail. To go directly to the picnic area and parking lot, take the right fork. To visit the falls, follow the trail up the steps to the left. Another new bridge carries the trail back across the stream, bypassing the dangerous area. The sound of the falls can be heard from here, and there are several benches where you can rest and enjoy the beautiful scenery. Another bridge carries the trail to a sandbar area in front of the falls. It should be noted that there are no cedar trees at Cedar Falls. Early settlers didn't know their trees well, mistaking the hemlock trees for cedar.

After enjoying the view of the falls, take the stone steps that parallel a side stream and follow the narrow trail through the rocks to where it again branches. To go to the picnic area, rest rooms, and parking lot, follow the trail straight ahead across the creek and up the ravine to the roadway, then turn right.

There is a shelter house and drinking water there, so it is a good place for a lunch break. During the state's annual Hocking Hills Winter Hike, cornbread and bean soup are served here. If you want to hike on to Ash Cave and back, follow the blue blazes around the end of the loop road, then turn right up a forest service road. This will add about 4 miles, and probably 3.5 hours, to your hike, so before embarking on this additional leg of the trail make certain you have enough time to make it back to your vehicle before dark. The trail is well marked and easy to follow. It was first laid out and cleared in January of 1967 by my colleague Norville Hall of the Division of Parks and Recreation, me, and a group of Boy Scouts from Troop 417 of Upper Arlington.

To continue the loop hike back to Old Man's Cave, return to the split in the trail just above Cedar Falls, where a wooden staircase carries the trail above the falls.

Just beyond the top of the steps the trail leaves the woods, crossing a grassy area above the falls. This is the beginning of the Gorge Overlook Trail that will take you back to the Upper Falls at Old Man's Cave, where you began walking. The trail is marked at frequent intervals by short 6 x 6 posts with a red band near the top.

Here at the top of the falls, signs warn of the danger of leaving the trail in this cliff-top area. A kiosk tells the story of the early years of Cedar Falls when water from Queer Creek powered a mill here. Two old millstones lie nearby. An ornamental steel bridge carries the trail across the creek to where steps carry it up to a seating area under a grove of pines. A sign indicates that the Gorge Overlook Trail is 2.5 miles long. Heading west from the seating area, the trail quickly returns to a hemlock environment. It rises and falls as it crosses streams that during part of the year provide water for the falls along the Queer Creek gorge off to the right. Soon the trail begins a steeper climb and arcs to the right. In the distance a clearing can be seen and in short order the trail arrives at the east end of the dam that creates 17-acre Lake Rose, the main source of the park's drinking water. A purple bench beckons the hiker to rest at the dam. The red-banded posts indicate that the trail crosses the lake on its earthen dam and a short bridge over its spillway. At the north end of the lake, there is a wildlife observation blind built in 2006 by the Friends of Hocking Hills. Reach it via the angler's trail along either lakeshore or a trail that runs from the main park campground.

At the west end of the dam there is another bench. The Gorge Overlook Trail turns 90 degrees to the left, as indicated by a red-banded post down the trail alongside the woods. The trail quickly drops off to cross a ravine then begins climbing to a

➤ Ohio's State Trail

The Buckeye Trail is a long-distance hiking trail built and maintained by volunteers. The germ of the idea for the trail came from the late Merrill C. Gilfillan of Mount Gilead, who wrote an article for the magazine section of the Sunday edition of the Columbus Dispatch *suggesting that Ohio ought to have a hiking trail like the Appalachian Trail connecting Lake Erie and the Ohio River. Out of the article was born the Buckeye Trail Association for the purpose of providing such a trail from Mentor Headlands east of Cleveland to Eden Park in Cincinnati. Now expanded to connect the four corners of the state in a continuous loop, the 1,200-plus-mile trail passes through 40 of Ohio's 88 counties; no population center is more than 75 miles from it.*

The association was incorporated in 1959 and began to develop the trail almost immediately. In 1967, the Ohio General Assembly designated the Buckeye Trail Ohio's official hiking trail. The famous septuagenarian and Appalachian Trail–hiker Emma "Grandma" Gatewood of Thurman, Ohio, was among the early volunteers who blazed out the Buckeye Trail in southeastern Ohio's hill country. Wherever possible, the trail keeps to public lands and is off-road. Where there is no other way to make connections, lightly traveled township roads are used, but the work to get the entire trail into the woods and fields or onto abandoned canal towpaths or railroad rights-of-way never ceases. Information about the trail, the trail-building organization, and available section maps and guides can be obtained by writing to the Buckeye Trail Association, P.O. Box 254, Worthington, OH 43085.

ridge. Soon it makes a right turn to travel north along the rim of The Gulf. An overlook offers a view of the forest below and a resting spot for the hiker. A sign indicates that it is 1.5 miles back to Cedar Falls and a mile to the visitor center at Old Man's Cave. From here, the trail follows the gorge 20 or 30 feet back from the rim. It crosses a trail that leads left to Lake Rose before reaching the A-frame bridge that connects to the visitor center. A sign points straight ahead to the Upper Falls, and it's not too many minutes before the trail passes the head of the steps that lead to below the falls and the old CCC stone bridge comes into view. The hike ends as you pass the Grandma Gatewood monument and return to your vehicle at the parking lot across OH 664.

I began hiking this wondrous area in 1946, when I spent the first of three summers as a counselor/naturalist at a nearby youth camp. It has been my good fortune to be able to return to the Hocking Hills many times in the intervening years. It was a special privilege to walk them again in 2006 as I prepared to update this book. There is no other place like it in the state of Ohio.

8

Malabar Farm State Park

Total distance: 5 miles (8 km)

Hiking time: 4 hours

Maximum elevation: 1,320 feet

Vertical rise: 260 feet

Map: USGS 7½' Lucas; ODNR Malabar Farm State Park map

Author and screenwriter Louis Bromfield, born in Mansfield, Ohio, established Malabar Farm in Richland County's Pleasant Valley in 1939. He built the country farmhouse mansion to be the Bromfield family homestead. Its design reflects the native Western Reserve architecture, even to the point that it was built to look as if it had been added to wing by wing over successive generations. He immediately began applying newly developed conservation farming practices to the worn-out land. During the following two decades, Malabar gained a worldwide reputation as a model farm, largely through the books Bromfield wrote about his experiences. In the 32-room "Big House" he built, he entertained his rich and famous Hollywood friends. After his death in 1956, the farm was managed by an organization he helped form, Friends of the Land, and after it folded, by the Malabar Farm Foundation. In 1972 the foundation transferred ownership to the state of Ohio, to be operated jointly by the Departments of Agriculture and Natural Resources. In 1976 it became Malabar Farm State Park. Although the large number of livestock from the Bromfield era are gone, the buildings and crop fields have been restored. Tours of the mansion, preserved much as Bromfield left it in 1956, have been an attraction through the years. The original dairy barn, which had been built in 1890 of timbers from an old mill that dated back to 1830, burned to the ground in 1993. It was rebuilt with a barn-raising on Labor Day weekend in 1994 using mostly volunteers from the

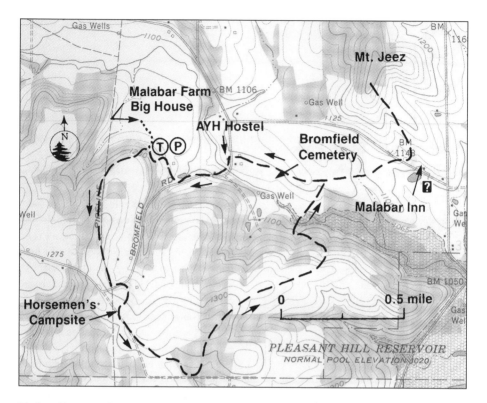

Timber Framers Guild of North America. People who have read Bromfield's books come to visit from around the world. Tours, special events, and interpretive programs help visitors understand how much Bromfield cared for the land. A new visitor center opened in late summer 2006. As this book goes to press, the Big House is closed for renovation. Plans are to restore at as nearly as possible to what it looked like when Bromfield was in residence, then reopen it for public tours.

How to Get There

To reach Malabar Farm from central or northeastern Ohio, travel I-71 to US 30, go east 3 miles to OH 603, and turn left (south). Travel 10.5 miles to Pleasant Valley Road on the right. Signs will direct the way west to Bromfield Road and the park en-

trance. Immediately after turning south into the park, make a right turn into the driveway for the visitors center and walkways to the Big House and barns.

The Trail

The trail entrance is uphill from the visitor center, across a hay field. A sign reads TIMBER MANAGEMENT TRAIL. Usually there is a mowed path around the edge of the field. Be aware of the bees moving to and from their hives to the left at the edge of the woods. The alfalfa and red clover in the field are very attractive to butterflies in late summer, when they rebloom following the second hay harvest. Enter the woods on the interpretive trail. Take time to learn the basics of small woodlot management from the signs spaced along both sides of the trail in the maple/oak/walnut woods. Within 100

The Malabar Farm Big House

feet of entering the woods, the trail is joined by an old farm lane turned horse trail coming in from the right. The path climbs the hill past sandstone outcrops on the left before opening onto another meadow. Remains of an early gas well can be seen on the left as you leave the woods. Turn right and follow the edge of the meadow, passing an old concrete stock tank, then make a sharp left turn onto a gas-line right-of-way. Sometimes deer can be seen grazing in the meadow downhill in the distance. Follow the right-of-way until it reaches the paved road. Pay no attention to the arrows on posts in this field.

This is another good area for summer butterflies since they like to "hilltop" and nectar on the alfalfa and clover. Just before reaching the end of the field, duck right and then left through the woods on the right side of the field. A sign there admonishes cross-country skiers to preserve their skis by removing them before going onto the road. Turn left (downhill) on the road, which at this point changes its name from East Hastings to Bromfield. About 150 yards downhill a driveway on the right leads you past an old barn, complete with a chewing tobacco ad, then uphill into the horsemen's campground. There are toilets located on the right, and behind Campsite 5, drinking water is available from a Baker-type pump. The well is deep, so a strong arm is required to get it flowing.

To get off the pavement and back onto natural turf, continue up the road to the far end of the turnaround, where there is a sign reading PLEASANT VALLEY BRIDLE TRAIL—HORSE AND FOOTPATH ONLY. Avoid the poison ivy as you enter, then turn left. The trail gently rises to cross a gas-line right-of-way, then passes a neatly manicured picnic area. It soon swings right through another overgrown fencerow, then turns sharply left along the edge of an old field being invaded by trees and shrubs. After 200 yards, it emerges onto a gravel road that is still in use. Turn left. About 100 feet up the road on the right stands a double-trunked American chestnut tree that has somehow avoided the chestnut blight and actually reached nut-bearing age. About 200 feet on down the road another PLEASANT VALLEY BRIDLE TRAIL sign on the left indicates that it's time to reenter the woods. Here is a fine wood, with mature oaks and hickories dominating. After a short climb to the crest of the hill, the trail descends the ridge to the right, and then crosses a brome grass field and an old tree-lined lane before emerging into a field where hundreds of young sugar maples have been planted. To protect the trees from being browsed by deer, half of them have a short piece of snow fence wrapped around them, and the other half have been planted in pieces of plastic farm tile. The latter do not seem to be surviving well.

At the end of the maple planting, the trail turns left to enter the woods, then turns immediately right on an old lane. Still moving downhill, it eventually enters tall timber, then makes a sharp left turn down a talus slope below outcrops of sandstone. It then turns west along a bench, through rich mature woods with fern-covered slump blocks. At a 4 x 4 post, it makes a sharp right turn to drop to the stream valley below. An upstream/downstream glance will usually locate a reasonably dry crossing in all but the wettest of seasons. After the crossing you will hike 100 yards or so through riverine forest with aliens such as multiflora rose present. The trail then emerges onto the farm road alongside crop fields.

A turn to the right on the lane leads you to the famous Malabar Inn, which is still serving meals. The 165-year-old structure adjoins a vegetable stand that covers the equally well-known Niman Spring. Most of the water for the farm and garden operation comes from this spring. The barn across the road from the inn was chosen as the official Richland County Bicentennial Barn in 2003, and as such has the logo designed from the celebration painted on its east side. To the west of the inn parking lot, a trail leads you up the hill that Bromfield dubbed Mt. Jeez, from the words he first uttered upon seeing the view. From the overlook at the top of the meadow, there is a great view of the entire spread. Although the temptation is to descend the hill on the vehicle road and then head for the park entrance via Pleasant Valley Road, the better path is to follow the trail back past the inn to where it emerged from the woods. A quarter mile beyond the trail entrance sign lies the country cemetery where Bromfield, his wife, Mary Appleton, and other family members are buried. Pause and reflect on the words of Bryant on Bromfield's gravestone: TO HIM WHO IN LOVE OF NATURE HOLDS COMMUNION WITH HER VISIBLE FORMS, SHE SPEAKS A VARIOUS LANGUAGE.

Continue on the farm road, past the garden, to a barnyard area where there are rest rooms and drinking water. Out the drive and across the road lies the farmstead where Bromfield lived while the Big House was being built. He didn't like the place and referred to it as the "mail-order house." It is now a hostel operated by the Columbus Council of the American Youth Hostels (AYH), Inc. Turn left downhill on the road, passing a pond and crossing the bridge. To your right is a good view of the main house and farmyard in the distance. Cows in the foreground complete the rural scene. On your left is the Doris Duke Woods, saved from logging after Bromfield's death by a contribution from the tobacco heiress, which was used to buy back timber rights Bromfield had sold during hard times. The park's sugar camp and buildings used for programs and meetings lie at the end of the road that enters the woods on the left, just beyond the bridge. The unsprayed roadside on the left between there and the Big House drive provides a show of native wildflowers in late summer.

Turn into the driveway on the right and walk by the Big House, then through the barnyard to return to the visitor center and parking lot. This 5-mile loop is a good hike to combine with the Mohican State Park hike. There is a 15-site primitive campground at Malabar, and more modern facilities are available at nearby Mohican State Park and Pleasant Mill Lake Park.

9

Mohican State Park

Total distance: 3.5 miles (5.6 km)

Hiking time: 2.5 hours

Maximum elevation: 1,240 feet

Vertical rise: 265 feet

Map: USGS 7½' Jelloway; ODNR Mohican State Park map

Two waterfalls, tall hemlocks, and the sound of rushing water lie ahead for the hiker visiting Mohican State Park in southwestern Ashland County. Located along the gorge of the Clear Fork of the Mohican River in the center of 60-year-old Mohican Memorial State Forest, the 1,294-acre park is best known for river canoeing. Yet it boasts 9 miles of foot trails and 10 miles of bridle trails, and the adjacent state forest has multiple-use trails several times that distance. The most scenic hiking trail in the park originates in its center, at the west side of the south end of the new bridge. The park is an area to avoid on holiday weekends, but it's beautiful year-round. Off-season visits reward you with peace and quiet. The Clear Fork has become popular for fly-fishing since the Division of Wildlife began stocking it with golden trout.

How to Get There

The trailhead at Mohican State Park is about a 1.5-hour drive from the Columbus, Cleveland, and Akron areas via I-71 and OH 97. Travel east from Exit 165 for 18 miles, through Bellville and Butler, to the park and forest entrance located on the left just after the Memorial Shrine on the right. Almost immediately after turning onto the park road, make a left to descend to the covered bridge river crossing, a distance of 1.5 miles. Park at the trailhead on the left side of the road just before the road reaches the covered bridge. During icy or snowy conditions, this road is impassable and will likely be closed. If in doubt, call the park office at 419-994-5125.

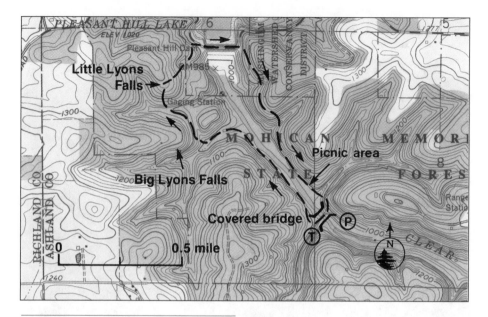

The Trail

Clear Fork Gorge is a special place. The National Natural Landmark monument at the trailhead brings that message home. How did this deep gorge get carved out in this part of Ohio? It was a product of Pleistocene glaciation. The Wisconsinan Glacier, the last one to invade Ohio, stopped less than a mile north of this gorge. During the thousands of years when the ice sheet was advancing, then melting, millions of gallons of meltwater rushed through this valley daily on their way to the sea. Since the bedrock was a hard sandstone, the rush of water resulted in this steep-walled gorge. When the glacier melted and the climate warmed, it was still cool enough in this deep, east–west-running gorge for cool-climate plants like hemlock, yellow birch, purple raspberry, and yew to continue to thrive.

Start northwest from the monument and trail entrance sign, following the Lyons Falls Trail. There is no drinking water and no rest rooms along this trail, so go prepared.

During the summer of 1988, park personnel spent many hours repairing and replacing the bridges beneath the towering hemlock trees, making the hiking easy. Just short of 0.5 mile after leaving the road, the trail divides, with a riverside trail continuing straight ahead and a side trail going left to Big Lyons Falls. Follow the latter up the ravine to see the first of the two falls that tumble over the face of the sandstone. Follow the staircase up and over Big Lyons Falls to Little Lyons Falls. Continue on the wide trail, which requires some scrambling over bare rock, to arrive at a level trail that swings right, then left near the rim of the gorge. Momentarily it comes out at the overlook area at the west end of Pleasant Hill Dam.

This earthen structure is 775 feet long and 113 feet high. It has a 199-square-mile drainage area. The permanent pool is at an elevation of 1,020 feet, and flood stage is at 1,065 feet. Like other dams in the Muskingum River Conservancy District system, it has no spillway over the top of the dam.

Covered bridge near the Lyons Falls trailhead

There are steps down the front of the dam for access to tailwater fishing.

To continue a loop hike, cross the dam on the downstream side and, at the east end, turn to the right into the woods where the trail back to the park begins. The trail passes under pines, alongside skunk cabbage, past a patch of cup plant, and past a small cattail marsh before descending to the narrow gorge and the cool shade of more hemlock. After traveling downstream .75 mile, the trail emerges from the woods near the north end of the covered bridge. Cross the bridge to return to the trailhead parking area.

While in the area, consider hiking the trail at nearby Malabar Farm State Park (Hike 8).

10

Prairie Oaks Metro Park

Total distance: 2.5 miles (4 km)

Maximum elevation: 911 feet

Vertical rise: 39 feet

Maps: USGS 7½' West Jefferson; CFCPD Prairie Oaks brochure

Before there were settlers in west-central Ohio's Darby Plains, there were bison, wapiti (elk), badger, and prairie chickens. When the migrating herds of big game moved through the area taking advantage of the warm-season grasses of the native tallgrass prairie, Native Americans seeking meat and hides must not have been far behind. (The annals of Madison County tell of the 1781 capture of eight-year-old Jonathon Alder and his subsequent removal by Indians to the land west of Big Darby Creek.) With the conclusion of the Treaty of Greenville in August, 1785, the prairie openings and oak savannahs along what came to be known as Big Darby Creek opened to settlement. White settlers of largely European origin came flooding into the country, bringing cattle to graze where the buffalo once roamed. For half a century, the cattle were driven east to market, but in 1856 a monthly cattle market was established at London, the county seat. With the coming of railroads, London became a great livestock center. A century later, the original wet prairies of the area had all but disappeared, having been drained and tilled to produce row crops. Only along the railroad tracks and in pioneer cemeteries can prairie plants such as big bluestem, Indian grass, prairie dropseed, ashy sunflower, purple coneflower, prairie dock, royal catchfly, and Sullivant's milkweed be found.

At Prairie Oaks Metro Park tallgrass prairie has been restored to more than 400 acres. In the summer, big bluestem waves in the breeze and coneflower and prairie dock

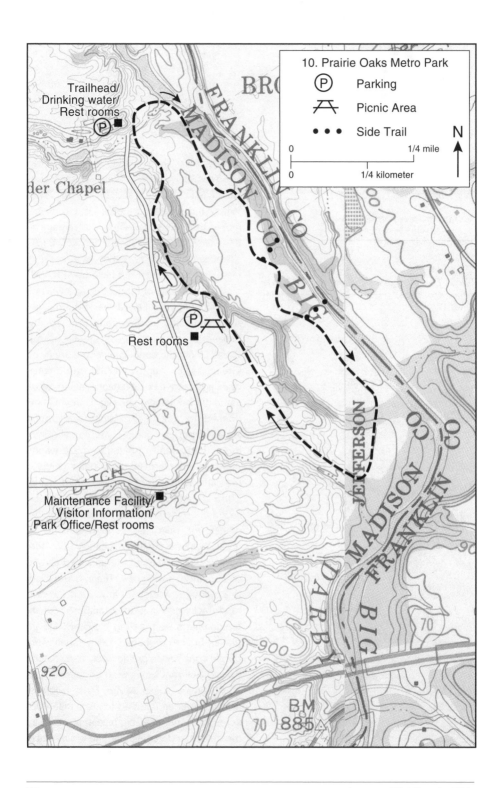

10. Prairie Oaks Metro Park

Ⓟ   Parking

🎋   Picnic Area

••• Side Trail

N

0   1/4 mile

0   1/4 kilometer

BROWN

FRANKLIN CO.

MADISON CO.

BIG

JEFFERSON

MADISON CO.

FRANKLIN CO.

BIG

DARBY

Trailhead/
Drinking water/
Rest rooms

der Chapel

Rest rooms

Maintenance Facility/
Visitor Information/
Park Office/Rest rooms

900

DITCH

900

920

900

BM
885△

70

70

hold their heads high. Butterflies nectar on the blossoms of the native forbs and grassland birds have found a place to raise their broods. More than 14 miles of trails draw the visitor to the restored prairies and the floodplain forests along the banks of Big Darby Creek, a State and National Scenic River that flows through the middle of the park. Early morning and late afternoon are perfect times for exploring this grassland environment.

How to Get There

From I-270 on the west side of Columbus, take I-70 west to the Plain City–Georgesville Road/OH 142. Go right (north) 0.8 mile to the entrance on the right.

The Trail

Once inside the park, drive to the Whispering Oaks Picnic Area. There is a shelter house, drinking water, and a rest room here. If you plan to bring a picnic, be mindful that this park operates a Carry In–Carry Out program for trash removal. Carry-out bags are provided for your convenience at the picnic area.

On the late-July day that I walked the trail the prairie coneflower (*Ratibida pinnata*) was gorgeous throughout the park. Begin walking by heading north on the wide gravel north loop of Coneflower Trail, accessible just a few yards from the picnic area. At this point, the trail is shared with the Darby Creek Greenway bicycle trail, so be alert for two-wheeled traffic. At first the trail travels through old field, not restored prairie. Soon it passes through about 100 feet of woodland, where an old stone culvert carries runoff from the fields to the west. The presence of many Osage orange trees leads me to believe that this was once the edge of field, a fencerow. Beyond the woodland a caution sign advises cyclists of a steep

grade ahead. Traveling between a split-rail fence and a limestone retaining wall, the trail curves to the right as it makes a slow descent to the Big Darby floodplain. At a trail junction, there is a bench and bike rack and a sign pointing right to the grassy Coneflower Trail. Take the trail straight ahead to circle alongside some riverine forest before reaching a wooden ramp entrance to a bridge over Big Darby. Go view the river from the bridge then return to the trail to begin hiking southeast, parallel to the river. Soon the path you're on joins the Coneflower Trail's south loop.

After cutting through some more woodland, the hiking trail intersects a horse trail. Signs help you sort out your route. The hiking trail goes right, closest to the river, with streamside woodland on the left and old field being allowed to return to woodland. About 120 feet down the trail a sign reading DARBY CREEK ACCESS points left where a path leads to the river's edge. At the end of the field, more signs sort out horse, cross-country ski, and hiking trails. After passing through another small area of trees, the trail continues through more regenerating old field. Off to the right a large clump of angelica (*Angelica atropurpurea*) indicates an area of saturated soil. At the end of this field the hiking trail almost intersects with the bridle trail just before it makes a right turn to enter the woods on a short bridge. Heading almost due south, the trail is now within hearing distance of the heavily traveled I-70. Very shortly it make an acute right turn and begins a slow 75-yard climb from the largely box elder floodplain forest to the restored prairie of the upland. About halfway up the slope, a crossing with the bridle trail is marked by appropriate symbols on Carsonite posts. At the top of the climb, the Coneflower Trail ducks between a hackberry and an oak tree to arrive at the best

Prairie Oaks Metro Park trail

area of prairie flora (including coneflowers) along the entire trail. Among a sea of coneflowers, the trail makes a T with the Darby Creek Greenway bike trail, which it joins to head northwest. It soon passes the Prairie View Picnic Area off to the left, and after dipping through a small wooded ravine it reaches the point of origin for this hike, the Whispering Oaks picnic area.

For more hiking at Prairie Oaks Metro Park, when you leave the park drive north to Lucas Road, then turn left to cross Big Darby on a very modern new bridge. Turn right where what is now called Beach Road reaches Amity Road. You will soon pass the Darby Bend Lakes area entrance on the right, where a variety of water sports are available. The next park entrance, also on the right, is the Sycamore Plains area. It provides access to three interconnecting trails that, combined, offer a woodland and meadow hiking experience of 2.2 miles, a good reason for another visit to Prairie Oaks Metro Park.

11

Stage's Pond State Nature Preserve

Total distance: 3 miles (4.8 km)

Hiking time: 2.5 hours

Maximum elevation: 720 feet

Vertical rise: 20 feet

Maps: USGS 7½' Ashville, ODNR/DNAP Stage's Pond brochure

As the Wisconsinan glacier melted from what we now know as Pickaway County, an immense chunk of it remained where Stage's Pond is today, probably protected from the melting effect of direct sunlight by a covering of sand and gravel. When the ice buried in the drift finally melted as the result of the ambient temperature, the land dropped, forming a depression in the landscape. Eventually the depression filled with water, creating what geologists call a kettle lake. Though often an outlet eventually forms on a kettle lake, or is created by people trying to drain it, the lakes develop on gravelly, sandy substrate and many simply rise and fall with the rainfall, draining into the soil to recharge the groundwater of the surrounding area. Like virtually all small bodies of water, kettle lakes eventually close in with vegetation and disappear, the only evidence of their existence being a lacustrine soil in a low spot in the field.

Stage's Pond and the smaller slough pond on the preserve were large enough to remain, perhaps 10,000 to 12,000 years, after the ice melted from the area. Doubtless mammoth, mastodon, giant beaver, elk, and bison drank from these waters during the intervening millennia. Today, they serve as resting places for thousands of migrating waterfowl each spring and fall and as a year-round home to many non-migrating species such as kingfishers, great blue herons, and Canada geese. The surrounding marsh, field, and oak/maple forest provide habitat for many other kinds of wildlife, vertebrate and invertebrate, large and small.

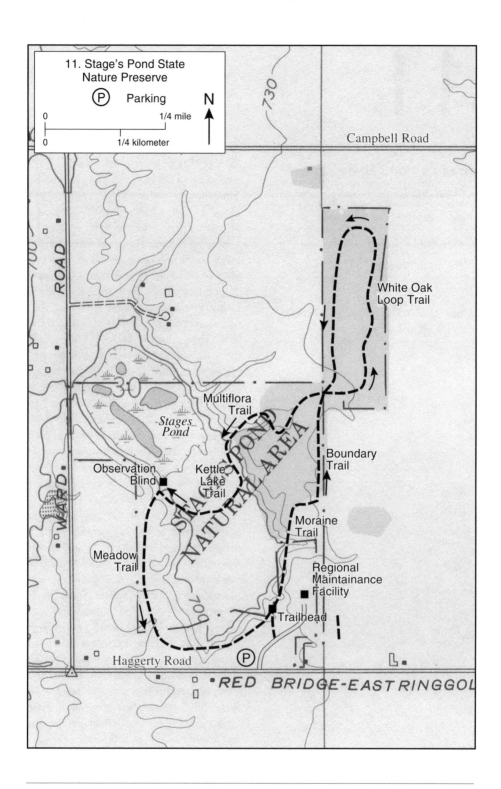

11. Stage's Pond State
Nature Preserve

Ⓟ Parking

N

0 _____ 1/4 mile

0 _____ 1/4 kilometer

Campbell Road

730

ROAD

700

30

Stages
Pond

Multiflora
Trail

White Oak
Loop Trail

STAGE POND
NATURAL AREA

Boundary
Trail

Observation
Blind

Kettle
Lake
Trail

Moraine
Trail

Meadow
Trail

700

Regional
Maintainance
Facility

Trailhead

WARD ROAD

Haggerty Road

Ⓟ

L

RED BRIDGE-EAST RINGGOL

Acquired and developed with help from the Columbus Regional Council of the Garden Club of Ohio and the Pickaway Garden Club, the preserve has been open to the public since 1974. The 3 miles of trail lead through a wide variety of open and woodland habitats, and there are two wildlife observation blinds from which to view waterfowl during spring and fall migration. The Division of Natural Areas and Preserves has a Regional Maintenance Facility on the property. No public services are provided: There are no rest rooms, drinking water, or picnic facilities. Any trash you create you must carry out. As at any wetland area, take appropriate protective measures against mosquitoes during the warmer months.

How to Get There

The entrance to Stage's Pond State Nature Preserve is located on Haggerty Road 1.5 miles east of US 23, not quite 4 miles south of the village of South Bloomfield. The entry road is closed except to maintenance vehicles, but a small parking area is provided just inside the entrance. The trails begin there.

The Trail

Begin walking north on the driveway, then turn where the sign directs you to the trail system. Straight ahead, where five trails come together, there is a trailhead sign with a map of the preserve. Some changes have been made since the map was painted, but it is essentially correct. The trail runs on mowed grass in the open and dirt or gravel in other places, with bridges and short sections of boardwalk as needed. There are a number of interpretive signs along the trail that will help you understand the ecology of the area. Take time to read them.

I suggest that you begin your hike by

➤ Great Blue Herons

The great blue heron (Ardea herodias) *is the largest heron in North America. Though primarily a summer resident in Ohio, a few are seen each winter on open rivers, ponds, and lakes in nearly every county in the state. Most arrive here from the South in early spring (males first) to mate and raise three or four young in nests built of sticks high in trees in an area where there are other nesting herons of the same species. Such a heron rookery, or "heronry," may have several hundred pairs of birds, although most are in the 10- to 75-pair range.*

Both parents help incubate the eggs, which hatch in 28 days. The parents regurgitate digested or partially digested fish to their young, who remain in the nest until they fledge in July or early August. Tall trees such as sycamore and cottonwood are often used for the 30- to 40-inch-wide nests, and there may be several nests in a single tree. In time, the trees succumb to their heavy dose of excrement and begin to come down. When this happens, returning herons will locate their rookery in a different area nearby. Though great blue herons can be seen along waterways in every county in the state, at present heronries are limited to the northern two-thirds and are most numerous near Lake Erie; they are nearly gone from the southwestern part of the state. It is always a thrill to watch an active heronry, especially in mid-spring before the trees leaf out, when adults come and go to feed their young.

going straight ahead on the Moraine Trail. Soon you will be in a tunnel of vegetation formed by young shrubs, trees, and grapevines. After crossing several short bridges, the trail reaches an intersection

Stage's Pond

where you have a choice of continuing north or turning to the right toward the eastern boundary fence. I suggest going right to where in the late-summer trumpet creeper blooms. There, turn left to reach the Boundary Trail. Turning north on that gravel trail you will almost immediately pass a very distinctive shingle oak tree well worth noting. There are other mighty nice trees along this trail and they seem to be bigger the farther north you walk. Near a sign that reads POSTED NO HUNTING, there is an elevated deer stand with a 20-foot ladder leaning against it on the other side of the fence. At another bridge, there is another split in the trail. To the right is the .75-mile White Oak Loop Trail and to the left the Moraine Trail. Follow the loop trail to explore the deep woods of the preserve. This is an excellent wildflower woods in the springtime. It is flat, poorly drained land with vernal ponds that provide breeding sites for wood frogs and salamanders. Narrow trails used by deer leaving the forest to dine in nearby farm fields are in evidence. As I walked the trail on a late-June afternoon many years ago, I was watched over by a screaming red-tailed hawk.

After completing the White Oak Trail loop, head south on the Moraine Trail to the entrance of the Multiflora Trail. Follow the latter as it takes you toward the ponds. The trail curves to the left, crosses a small draw on a 12-foot bridge, then reaches a junction where the Multiflora Trail exits the Moraine Trail to the right. Take that trail as it leaves the forest and rises and falls on its way toward the pond. At yet another trail junction, turn right on the Kettle Lake Trail. The rest of the trip will be mostly in the kind of old field habitat you now encounter. It's wonderful for summer wildflowers and butterflies. In the wet area ahead you might hear a common yellowthroat close by singing its *wichity-wichity-wich,* or see a great blue heron take wing.

The trail passes through a stand of box elder trees as it approaches Stage's Pond. In 1996, volunteers built a new bridge across the flowage in the dip between the two ponds. This trail eventually reaches the shore of the pond where there is a wildlife observation blind. The trail once continued on west to a gate, but that trail and gate have been closed. From the blind, return to the Kettle Lake Trail and immediately turn right on the Meadow Trail. This will take you close to the west and then south boundaries of the preserve and eventually return you to the five-trail junction at the trailhead kiosk. This is great butterfly country, with an ample supply of milkweed for monarch larvae and lots of late-summer flowers, such as New England aster, providing nectar to butterflies of many species. Dragonflies abound in the marshy areas near the ponds. It is also good nesting territory for bluebirds in the spring and goldfinches in summer.

Once back at the trailhead, take time to visit the other wildlife observation shelter. You may be rewarded with a glimpse of waterfowl on the water or a red fox moving stealthily on the shore. Walking and wildlife watching go hand in hand. From the trailhead kiosk, it is a short walk back on the mowed trail and driveway to your vehicle.

12

Wolf Run Regional Park/Knox Woods State Nature Preserve

Total distance: 2.5 miles (4 km)

Hiking time: 2 hours

Maximum elevation: 1,160 feet

Vertical rise: 100 feet

Maps: USGS 7½' Mount Vernon, Ohio Geological Survey Map accompanying Bulletin 59, Geology of Knox County

Knox Woods was one of earliest nature preserves to be dedicated. Located just east of the city of Mount Vernon on land owned by Knox County adjacent to the old County Children's Home, it came under the scrutiny of the county commissioners in the early seventies as they were beginning to plan for the area's redevelopment. In a conversation with the state service forester over the value of the standing timber, it was suggested that the real value to the people of Knox County might be to preserve this outstanding woods for future generations and that dedication as a state nature preserve under recently enacted laws might be the way to accomplish that. In a bold move for the times, the commissioners voted to spare the woods from the chain saw and work with the Ohio Division of Natural Areas and Preserves in protecting the woods. On October 11, 1973, the 30-acre tract was dedicated as Knox Woods State Nature Preserve. In announcing the action, the county commissioners said they "felt that the true value of this area could be more fully realized through the eyes of a child rather than the roar of the chain saw. Although this forest was marked for timbering, the commissioners acted to protect the forest and create this outdoor education area for the schools of the Mount Vernon area." By September 1975, a 1.5-mile trail had been developed along with three footbridges and a trailhead bulletin board.

In 1995, the citizens and officials of Knox County came together to form a Knox County Park District to further the task of

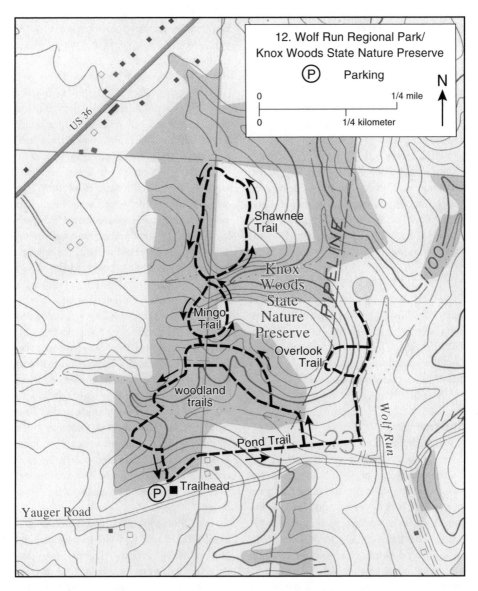

US 36

Shawnee
Trail

Knox
Woods
State
Nature
Preserve

PIPELINE

1100

Mingo
Trail

Overlook
Trail

woodland
trails

Wolf Run

Pond Trail

23

Ⓟ ■ Trailhead

Yauger Road

preserving the county's natural heritage. In 2001, the park district began acquiring a tract of forested land adjacent to Knox Woods for the establishment of the first large-scale park. With a "Clean Ohio" grant and additional contributions and partnerships, they have created the 288-acre Wolf Run Regional Park, which incorporates Knox Woods. Several miles of new trails have been built, including one that connects with those in Knox Woods and the park. Others are on the planning table and will be developed as funds become available.

The setting for the park is the rolling hills of the Allegheny Plateau. They were beyond the reach of the last glacier in Ohio, the

Wisconsinan, but were glaciated more than 100,000 years earlier by the Illinoian ice sheet; an area of ground moraine with weathered rock on the hillsides and streams cut through to bedrock. The mixed mesophytic forest contains many large trees, with their lower branches 60 feet or more from the ground, evidence that they are forest grown. Examination of maps through the 20th century confirms that this woodland remained uncleared for more than 100 years. Timber has been harvested, but the area shows no signs of ever having been clear-cut. You will gaze in wonder at the tall trees when you hike its trails.

How to Get There

Travel OH 3 or US 36 to Mount Vernon. Go east from town on US 36, past the shopping center and up the hill to Upper Gilchrist Road. Turn right (south) and travel less than a mile to Yauger Road. Turn right (east) to the park entrance, less than .5 mile on the left (north) side of the road.

The Trail

The trail begins at an opening in the woods where there is a bulletin board, park bench, and picnic table. A short way into the woods, a sign notes that the pond trail goes to the right and the woodlands trails to the left. This is somewhat confusing as the woodlands trails actually form a mile-long loop. The pond trail is a spur off the loop that goes to a small pond. Turn right to begin hiking. The trail begins a gentle descent until reaching the edge of the woods. For the next 200 feet it passes below an old barn, which is due for demolition, and a bramble-filled barn lot before reaching a large circular mowed area. Just downhill, under a large-spreading, open-grown white oak tree, are several picnic tables, a good place to eat lunch and view the valley below.

Beyond, the trail turns downhill again, passing beneath many young black walnut trees. Look uphill and you will see an old black walnut, the source for this grove.

At a split in the trail near the bottom of the hill, a sign pointing to the right indicates the route of the trail leading to the pond. Continue downhill on the woodlands trail. Beyond a short footbridge the trail turns right, then left, and left again. When I walked the trail in the summer of 2006, the crop field to the right held what I was told would be soybeans. Gravel was piled there for the start of construction on a trail up the hill along the edge of the field. Go left into the woods on what appears to be an old farm lane. It climbs gently before reaching a fork. Take the trail to the right as it climbs uphill at a steeper grade. It's a simple path made by the treading of many hikers' feet. Uphill through the very open woods you can see open land. The trail dips and climbs along the hillside, never reaching the summit. Watch for a sign pointing to the right to the Knox Woods trails. Turn right to travel about 200 feet into Knox Woods, where you intersect the loop Mingo Trail. Turn right and follow the trail uphill, then down to where it meets the Shawnee Trail above a set of steps and a bridge.

Take the steps and bridge across the small stream and turn left to continue exploring Knox Woods. During the last decade, many trees have fallen here as a result of storms. Though cleared from the trails, the downed trees were deliberately left in the woods; they were left to rot and return to the soil. The trail soon reaches a point where the original entrance to the woods was located. Two DNAP signs identify the Shawnee and Mingo Trails. Turn right beyond those signs to continue on the figure-eight trails of Knox Woods. You will

Trail fork in Wolf Run Regional Park

cross several bridges as you circle around and return to the intersection above the steps to the first bridge. There, go straight ahead to the left of the large tree and follow the trail as it arcs left to take you back to the crossover trail.

Back on the woodlands trail, turn right and go down a ridge then to the right to cross a bridge. Note the large granite boulder, a glacial erratic, partly buried in the soil just as you reach the bridge. That stone probably arrived on this land 120,000 years or so ago. Beyond the bridge the trail goes downstream a short way then climbs to the right. Continue downhill to the left to a bridge over the main stream draining this part of the woods. The trail then begins its

ascent to the trailhead, paralleling the stream through an area of many ferns. Eventually it leaves the stream course to make a steeper climb and a turn to the left to return to the trailhead.

All of the drainage in the park is via short, high-gradient streams to Wolf Run, which rises in the park and flows almost due south to empty into the Kokosing River less than 1.5 miles south of Yauger Road. It's a small watershed that drains this area of the Appalachian Plateau, which was overrun by the Illinoian Glacier so many millennia ago. (At the entrance to the park you are 403 feet higher in elevation than at the corner of Broad and High Streets in downtown Columbus.)

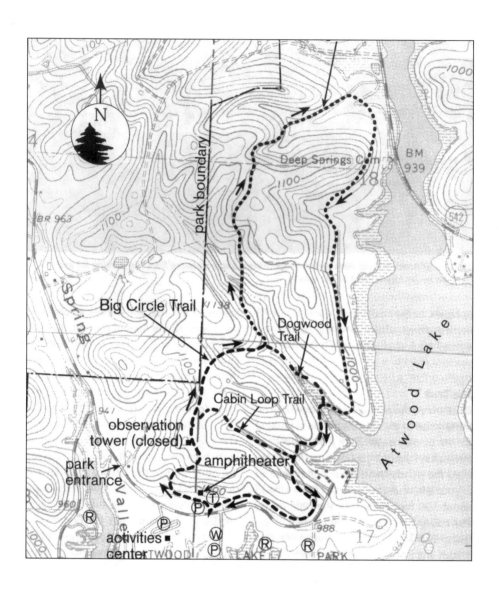

13

Atwood Lake Park (Mingo Trail)

Total distance: 3.75 miles (6 km)

Hiking time: 2.5 hours

Maximum elevation: 1,125 feet

Vertical rise: 175 feet

Maps: USGS 7½' Mineral City; MWCD Atwood Lake brochure

At 8,038 square miles, the watershed of eastern Ohio's mighty Muskingum River is far and away the area's largest. To protect the towns along the river and its many tributaries from suffering a repeat of the devastating flooding that occurred in the first third of the 20th century, the Muskingum Watershed Conservancy District (MWCD) was created in 1933. Independent from state or local government, the conservancy owns and manages 14 major flood-control reservoirs in that giant watershed, 10 with permanent lakes. Over the years the district has established multiple-use recreation facilities at many of the lakes. Such is the case at Atwood Lake, east of the city of New Philadelphia. There the conservancy has built a resort lodge, vacation cabins, campground, nature center, marina, and boat docks, as well as provided many fine facilities for walking and hiking.

Atwood Lake was named after the village nearest to the dam at the time of construction, in the tradition of the U.S. Army Corps of Engineers in the era before congressmen began putting their own names on nearly every civil works. Atwood must have disappeared under the lake, because it is nowhere to be found on the modern topographical map of the area.

Though the district owns 3,000 acres of land at Atwood, the recreation facilities are concentrated at Atwood Lake Park on the northwest corner of the reservoir.

How to Get There

The area is reached by taking OH 800 and OH 212 northeast from New Philadelphia

Atwood Lake Park trail

to New Cumberland, then County Road 93 north and east to the park entrance. There is a small fee for vehicles during the vacation season.

The Trail

Once inside the park, look for a driveway on the left side of the road that leads to parking for the amphitheater. Park there to access the trail system. As you look up the hill toward the woods and the amphitheater, turn to your left, where you will see the trailhead about 100 feet distant. To the right of the trail entrance is a large colored map of the trails; to the left is a sign that gives distances and the times required to walk them.

The trail heads into the woods and starts uphill immediately, swinging first to the right uphill from the amphitheater, then to the left to continue the steep climb through a pine plantation. As the trail nears the top of this rise, you will see an observation tower. At the time

of my visit, it was in disrepair and was closed, surrounded by a chain-link fence. One foot beyond the tower is a sign indicating that the trail goes to the left. Directly ahead is the water reservoir for the park, which explains the wide trail thus far: It acts as a service road, too. The trail follows the contour of the land north from here, still in the woods. It passes the other end of the service road for the reservoir as it continues toward the well-marked intersection with the Cabin Loop and Dogwood Loop Trails. The trail then passes under some especially tall white oak trees as it nears the corner of the MWCD property and rises to a high point. In a damp area, the papaw trees had fruit on them when I last passed by. A tiger swallowtail flew by my side as I crossed an open utility line that headed down the hill toward the cabin area. The trail next swings to the right, gently easing down a ravine. Passing under tall tuliptrees of the mixed mesophytic woods, and a lot of escaped multiflora

50 Hikes in Ohio

rose, the trail enters a pine forest perhaps 25 years old.

After you reach the bottom of the ravine, cross a creek, and begin to climb, you'll arrive at the next intersection. The Dogwood Trail goes to the right, continuing on down the ravine. The trail to the left, which is the one you want, is now the Mingo Trail. Leaving pines behind, it climbs through young hardwood, then past older tuliptrees and a magnificent, tall, wild black cherry. It is headed almost due north now, climbing to reach a long stretch of nearly flat trail past beautiful pines. A sign on a service road that crosses the trail says NO ADMITTANCE. This is the highest point on the trail: 1,125 feet.

Beyond the pines, the trail begins its long sweeping curve to the right to turn toward the lake and the return leg. After dropping a bit, you make a hard turn to the right and continue to drop, hanging on the side of the hill below more pines. After crossing a usually dry creek bed, the trail follows the contour of the hill heading south. In the summer, both pale and spotted jewelweed, or touch-me-not, fill the forest floor. Initially the park service road is downhill from the trail, but soon they merge. To the left is an oil-pump jack, and about 100 feet down the service road there is an intersection where the Dogwood Trail exits hard right (a sign also directs hikers seeking the observation tower to take the hard right).

Follow the trail labeled CABINS straight ahead. This is a narrow footpath through tall pines—and poison ivy. After turning to the right, the trail levels off on the hillside through a patch of ground pine. The trail reaches a service road and follows it a short way to where a sign hidden in the brush directs you to the right for the nature center and to the left for the waterfowl observation area. Go right on the service road, here almost at lake level. About 100 yards down

this service road, there is a vertical post labeled TRAIL with an arrow on top of it pointing left. Head for that sign, and soon you will be at the intersection where the Cabin Loop, Dogwood, and Mingo Trails all go right, up the hill toward the defunct observation tower. Another sign directs you straight ahead to the amphitheater—the trail you follow to return to your vehicle. The trail follows the contour of the land as it winds its way around the base of the hill. A well service road crosses it headed uphill. From here the trail follows an electric service line for a short way, then runs just inside a meadow, a few feet back from the mowed lawn, where the goldenrod greets you in the late summer. Your vehicle is in view.

When I revisited this area in the summer of 2006, the only real change I noticed was the size of the trees. This was especially true of areas of planted pines. It's hard to tell that a maple or an oak tree has grown taller, but when pines are growing in a nourishing environment, 10 or 20 years makes a real difference. Though this part of Ohio was not originally pine forest, through the years many pines have been planted on public lands as a way of controlling erosion and jump-starting reforestation. In most places, native hardwoods eventually invade the pine plantings, returning the area to its native cover. And that's good. As I revisit areas that I have known for many years, I'm always struck by the size of pines that I remember being planted or that were the size of Christmas trees the last time I saw them.

While you are in the area, why not visit some of the other nearby attractions? If you are interested in Ohio history, Zoar Village, Schoenbrunn, and Fort Laurens are not far from here. The New Philadelphia/Tuscarawas County Convention and Visitors Bureau (1-800-BUCKEYE) will be glad to provide brochures and maps.

14

Brecksville Reservation Metropark (Deer Lick Cave Trail)

Total distance: 4 miles (6.4 km)

Hiking time: 3 hours

Maximum elevation: 855 feet

Vertical rise: 20 feet

Maps: USGS 7½' Northfield; USGS 7½' Broadview Heights; CMPD Brecksville Reservation map

With 3,392 acres, Brecksville Reservation is the largest jewel in the Cleveland Metropark Emerald Necklace. The wooded reservation is cut by seven distinct gorges. It has a spectacular native tallgrass prairie planting. And its nature center is probably the oldest structure built for that purpose in any park system, having been constructed by the Work Projects Administration (WPA) in 1939. For the hiker, it has an extensive system of well-labeled trails, including a section of the Buckeye Trail (BT).

How to Get There

To reach Brecksville Reservation, take I-77 or I-271 to OH 82. The entrance to the park is just east of the intersection of OH 82 and OH 21, to the south off OH 82. The park is open every day of the year during daylight hours.

The Trail

The trailhead is located about 0.4 mile beyond the park entrance. The trailhead kiosk is on the right side of the road between two parking lots. This three-sided structure has a map of the park, photographs of interesting features, and announcements about seasonal activities. From the kiosk, follow the walkway into the forest and head directly toward the nature center. Throughout the park, trails are clearly marked by signposts with color-coded diamonds with symbols and arrows. A green diamond marked "NC" above another diamond with an arrow points the way to the nature center. About halfway there, the Prairie Loop Trail to the

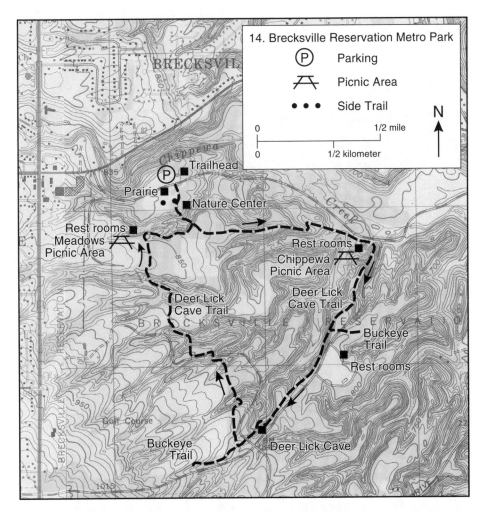

right leads to a planted tallgrass prairie. If you are hiking anytime between the first of July and the first fall frost, you should stop to visit the prairie on the way in or out of the park. There is a rest room at this trail intersection, probably the handiest one you will see on your hike.

Go inside the nature center to see exhibits about the natural history of the park and to pick up a trail map and chat with a naturalist to learn what in the way of seasonal phenomena you might want to watch for along the trail. Leaving through the front door, turn right to pass the bird-feeding area at the end of the building and begin following the tan oak leaf symbols that identify the 4-mile Deer Lick Cave Loop. Heading downslope, the trail passes an amphitheater on the left before dropping steeply on 55 wooden steps to where, in another 60 feet, the trail crosses a creek on a small bridge. There is a bench here where you may rest and enjoy the scenery, and other benches are scattered along the way. On the Halloween morning when I last walked the trail, the sun coming through

Deer Lick Cave

the golden leaves was a sight to behold.

Beyond the bridge the trail splits. Angle left to climb a set of 59 stairs. Like the earlier steps, these also have heavy hawsers as handrails. Very soon the trail reaches a T. The Deer Lick Cave Loop signs on the post indicate that the trail goes both left and right and, in fact, it does, for this is where the spur access trail meets the loop. Turn left to walk the loop clockwise. The Hemlock Loop Trail utilizes the same tread and in a short distance, Bridle Trail No. 4 joins in too. The combined trails drop in and out of a small ravine, crossing a creek on a small bridge. The mixed mesophytic forest includes some really tall hardwood trees with an occasional hemlock. Exercise caution, as this is an earthen trail with many surface roots that can easily trip you. Granite boulders of all sizes, piled in the woods or lying in a row

where there was once a fence, give away the glacial history of the area. An open field can be seen about 100 feet to the right through the woods. When the trail reaches the corner of the open field, the combined loop trails are again joined by Bridle Trail No. 4 along a wider corridor with some gravel surface. After a couple hundred yards, the bridle trail turns left and the two loop trails continue at a slight angle to the right.

The trail follows the high ground between two ravines, sometimes in the middle on the highest ground but often on the left rim of the tableland. It's relatively flat for quite a way, then dips up and down as it loses some altitude. Still to the left, the trail next descends at almost a 45-degree angle through a stand of beech trees. Following a steep downhill slope to the left and a long gentle downhill slope to the right, the combined foot trails reach the end of the ridge and make a switchback downhill toward Chippewa Creek. Bridle Trail No. 4 once again joins in. After crossing the creek on a bridge shared by a road at the Chippewa Picnic Area (where there are rest rooms), the combined trails go their own way. The Hemlock Loop Trail turns left, while the Deer Lick Cave Trail travels parallel to Valley Parkway. You begin with a couple hundred yards of uphill walking on a rocky, rooty path on a sharp spine between two fairly steep slopes. After .25 mile or so, the Deer Lick Cave Trail is joined by a connecting trail from Valley Parkway. This is the Buckeye Trail, which is coming from the Ohio & Erie towpath on the east side of the Cuyahoga River, a path it shares with the Towpath Trail. Normally marked with blue paint blazes, in the park this trail is denoted by light blue diamonds with a backpacker symbol and a directional arrow. The Oak Grove Picnic Area, with rest rooms, lies across the road just a short distance southwest of where the Buckeye Trail crosses.

Back in the woods, the combined Buckeye and Deer Lick Cave Trails drop down the hillside. For reasons only the trail builders know, the two trails separate for a short distance and then rejoin. The BT traces a "U" along the rim of a hill, while the Deer Lick Cave Trail connects its top. Soon the combined trails arrive at the side trail to the right that goes to the Deer Lick Cave(s). A set of broad stone and gravel steps arc left as they carry the hiker to the caves and waterfalls. A light rain was falling when I visited the area on the last day of October. Enough leaves had fallen that I had to kick through them along the narrow trail, yet there were still enough on the trees to make it a special time to be there.

Returning to the main trail via a couple of bridges and another set of long, wide steps,

it is time to begin closing the loop by heading north. After crossing Meadows Drive, the combined Buckeye and Deer Lick Cave Trails intersect with Bridle Trail No. 3, coming from the left. At this point, the Buckeye Trail continues straight ahead (west) along the north side of Valley Parkway, soon to leave public land. The Deer Lick Cave Trail turns right to join Bridle Trail No. 3 heading north on a broad trail that looks like it might have been a township road at one time. Crossing streams on bridges built by the Ohio Civilian Conservation Program of the 1970s, the trail weaves through the hardwood forest and old pine plantings toward another crossing of Meadows Drive. This crossing is at an angle so you need to look down the road to the left to find the entry point for the continuing trail.

Not far after this crossing, the hiking and horse trails part company for the last time. The bridle trail heads east through a ravine to where it earlier came north of Valley Parkway, essentially closing the loop. The hiking trail swings to the west, and after following high ground for nearly .25 mile it drops into a ravine and makes two stream crossings. Here the streams have cut deeply into the black shale bedrock. After rising from the last ravine, the trail moves through more forested tableland to soon reach the Meadows Picnic Area and trailhead, crossing Bridle Trail No. 4 on the way. When the Deer Lick Cave Trail reaches the driveway to the picnic area, you must look slightly to the right across the open area to find the signpost marking the continuation of the Deer Lick Cave Trail. Again traveling on nearly level ground, the trail goes straight ahead for perhaps 250 yards before making a right turn and reaching a T. A left here puts you on the loop access path for the Deer Lick Cave Trail. The nature center sign now joins the Deer Lick

Cave Trail sign in pointing hikers toward the trail and the two flights of steps that lead back out to the nature center and the parking lot.

This is an extraordinary trail. It is within a short drive of bustling downtown Cleveland, yet it offers interesting terrain entirely within a forest. There are other trails to explore within the park's nearly 3,500 acres and it adjoins the Cuyahoga Valley National Park, where there are many additional miles of hiking trails.

15

Cuyahoga Valley National Park

Total distance: 9.5 miles (15.3 km)

Hiking time: 5 hours

Maximum elevation: 850 feet

Vertical rise: 200 feet

Maps: USGS 7½' Northfield;
BTA Akron Section map

Just as the Cuyahoga National Park is a study in contrasts, so too is this 9.25-mile trail. For 6.25 miles it traverses high hills and stands witness to tall timber and deep ravines. For the other 3 miles it travels open fields, roads, and a very level canal towpath.

The Cuyahoga Valley National Park was created in 1974 as an urban park of the National Park System (NPS). It preserves 33,000 acres of pastoral valley along 22 miles of the Cuyahoga River between Cleveland and Akron. It is a diverse area, with some places of pristine beauty; others have been badly despoiled by the hand of man. The establishment of a national park has permitted the recovery of the natural values of the valley through active restoration projects and by passively allowing natural succession to occur. Preserving some of the artifacts of civilization has also been important: the company town, the railroad, and the canal with its system of hand-operated locks. Before the NPS came to the valley, both public and private agencies in Cuyahoga and Summit Counties protected many of the valley's special areas through the establishment of parks, preserves, and camps. Most of these have remained under the jurisdiction of the agencies that originally developed them, although the NPS works closely with them. The Buckeye Trail (BT) runs through the park on its way between Cincinnati and Mentor Headlands. Between Boston and Jaite it's routed on high land on the west side of the valley, making it possible to combine the trail with a section of the Ohio

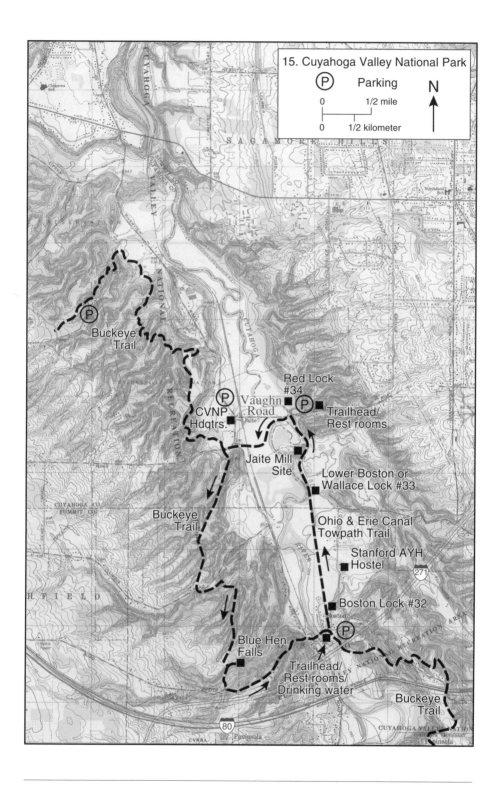

15. Cuyahoga Valley National Park

Ⓟ Parking   N

0   1/2 mile

0   1/2 kilometer

Buckeye Trail

Red Lock #34

CVNP Hdqtrs.

Vaughn Road

Trailhead/ Rest rooms

Jaite Mill Site

Lower Boston or Wallace Lock #33

Buckeye Trail

Ohio & Erie Canal Towpath Trail

Stanford AYH Hostel

Boston Lock #32

Blue Hen Falls

Trailhead/ Rest rooms/ Drinking water

Buckeye Trail

& Erie Canal Towpath Trail for a challenging and interesting loop walk.

Jaite, where one of several trailheads is located at a small parking lot east of NPS headquarters, was once a company town for the Jaite Mill located east of the river, adjacent to the canal. The buildings have been renovated for offices, and the town now looks much like it must have during its heyday. The Jaite paper mill has been razed, but many other properties of historic interest along the canal within the park have been restored. Only minimal restoration work has been done on the aging locks, but trees and vines have been removed to keep their roots from doing further damage to the old stone structures. The Canal Visitor Center is well worth a visit. It's located in a canal-era building at Lock No. 38, 7 miles north of Jaite at Hillside Road and the canal. You will also want to spend some time at the 1836 Boston Store located along this hike in Boston. It houses exhibits on the craft of canalboat building. At Boston there is also a small store where snacks are sold. Drinking water is available there too, along with modern rest rooms. There are vault toilets at the Red Lock trailhead. Be sure to carry ample drinking water on the trail.

How to Get There

To reach the Jaite trailhead, take US 271 to Exit 19, turn west on OH 82, and then travel 4.5 miles to Riverview Road. Turn left (south) and continue 3 miles to the intersection of Riverview and Vaughn Roads, where the park headquarters complex is located at the former community of Jaite. Turn east onto Vaughn Road. One trailhead is at the parking lot on the left (north) side of Vaughn Road, just beyond a railroad crossing about 200 yards after the turn. Alternative parking is located at Red Lock, about 0.25 mile east of Jaite, and east of the

Cuyahoga River on the north side of the road. Since the Red Lock lot is heavily used by bicyclists on weekends, the Jaite lot may be a good choice. Access to the trail is easy from either lot: Cross Jaite Road and pick up the trail. You could also arrive via I-77 and I-80. Watch for the signs.

The Trail

From either trailhead parking lot, cross Vaughn Road and follow the blue blazes on posts to where the trail turns south beneath the power line. After a few hundred yards, you will reach a T in the trail. The outgoing trail turns west across the railroad tracks and comes out onto Riverview Road, where it intersects with Snowville Road. Cross Riverview and head up the left side of Snowville Road; after about 100 feet, watch out for the place where the trail enters the woods to the left. Upon leaving the road the trail immediately begins climbing a steep hill to a long northeast–southwest-aligned ridge. Over the next mile, as it climbs the ridge, the trail will gain more than 200 feet in elevation. Using a combination of old lanes and a newly created trail, it travels through mixed mesophytic forest of varying age and past occasional pine plantings. Eventually the trail makes an S-curve before crossing Columbia Road.

You head northeast parallel to the road for several hundred yards beneath a stand of magnificent old white oaks. The trail then drops into a ravine, where hemlocks grow in the cool environment along a beautiful shale-bottomed stream. An occasional glacial erratic on the upland is a reminder that, unlike the hills of southern Ohio, these have seen glaciation as recently as 10,000 years ago; yet the ravines cutting through the Mississippian-aged bedrock where hemlocks grow are reminiscent of Hocking County.

Ohio & Erie Canal Lock

The trail begins to climb once more, crossing ridges and more ravines on its way toward Blue Hen Falls. Here the stream cascades over sandstone bedrock as it cuts its way to the Cuyahoga River to the east. The trail crosses the creek on a bridge just upstream from the falls, then turns upslope to emerge at a parking lot and Boston Mills Road.

Cross the road and head east, passing in front of a county road maintenance facility before making a right (south) turn to drop rapidly into a highly eroded valley close to I-271. The trail then climbs a set of steps to the top of the ridge, which it follows east as it descends to the intersection of Boston Mills and Riverview Roads. Cross Riverview and the Cuyahoga River on Boston Mills and head into Boston. You will pass an old Pure Oil/Union 76 station, now referred to as the "M.D. Garage." It serves as an events space for the park. The Boston Store, which

has fine exhibits on the building of canal boats, is just beyond the station. Behind it is the trailhead area where snacks and rest rooms are available.

Across the road from the store, begin hiking north on the Ohio & Erie Towpath Trail as it heads toward Boston Lock (No. 32). A short way up the trail, on the left (west) side of the canal, is the Boston Mills Cemetery. From this point back to the trailhead, the hike is level walking along the long-abandoned, but now restored, towpath. Be alert, because bicyclers, as well as joggers and walkers, now use the trail. Lock No. 33, which the trail passes just north of the cemetery, has not been rebuilt, but trees along its banks have been removed. Because there are no plans to water this part of the canal, it's unlikely that it will ever be rebuilt.

As the trail reaches the Jaite Mill area, it moves to the left toward the hillside to make

50 Hikes in Ohio

room for a section of the canal that carries water into the mill site, where it once was used in the milling process. In its heyday in the 1920s and 1930s, the Jaite Mill was the 11th largest multi-wall paper producer in the nation. The paper went into strong paper bags such as those used for fertilizer and cement. All of the above-ground parts of the mill have now been demolished, although in the summer of 2006 there remained some and below-ground cleanup to be done. Plans call for restoring natural habitat in this area and providing some interpretation of the mill. An impressive piece of paper-making machinery, a Fourdrinier machine, will also be left at the site.

The trail continues on the towpath as it approaches Highland Road. On the north side of Highland lies the Red Lock trailhead, an access point for people walking or riding the trail. The Canal Towpath Trail continues north through the park and on into the Ohio & Erie Canal Reservation of the Cleveland Metroparks, ending at Harvard Avenue in Cleveland. It will continue to be extended in the future.

To complete this hike, turn left (west) along the south side of Highland Road–Vaughn Road on the Cuyahoga County side of the river–and cross the Cuyahoga River. Just beyond the bridge, a connecting trail to the Buckeye Trail drops off the left side of the road, then turns right to parallel the river before swinging toward the west. At a trail intersection beneath the power line turn right to head north to the parking lot.

There are many other fine facilities in this park. A special treat is an excursion trip on the Cuyahoga Valley Scenic Railroad that travels between Canton, Akron, and Rockside Road. Write or call the park for details on this and the many other public programs they offer.

16

Eagle Creek State Nature Preserve

Total distance: 4.75 miles (7.5 km)

Hiking time: 3 hours

Maximum elevation: 960 feet

Vertical rise: 20 feet

Maps: USGS 7½' Garrettsville; ODNR Eagle Creek State Nature Preserve brochure

A walk along the trail of Eagle Creek State Nature Preserve, a 442-acre area northeast of Garrettsville in Portage County, can truly be a "walk with the wildlings." In addition to being one of the largest intact tracts of mature woodland in this area, it is home to many birds, mammals, reptiles, and amphibians infrequently seen in more intensely developed parks. Beaver, fox, white-tailed deer, raccoon, and skunk live here. Hundreds of Canada geese use the larger ponds as rest stops during migration, and the woods are full of songbirds during spring. Two species listed as rare and endangered in Ohio—the spotted turtle and the four-toed salamander—are known to live here.

There are more than 100 species of woody plants on the preserve, including many less common trees such as cucumber magnolia and yellow birch. The rich beech/maple forests on the north-facing slopes contain abundant spring wildflowers. The white oak forest communities more common on the drier, south-facing slopes have a sparser but equally interesting show of spring flowers. Over 70 species of wildflowers have been observed blooming in the preserve during May. Pin oaks are found in the swamp forest, and buttonbush swamps, small bogs, and marshlands dot the area.

Located on the eastern edge of an isolated area of terminal moraine, the preserve is mostly underlain by sandy glacial outwash. Eagle Creek meanders in a southern direction through the middle of the preserve

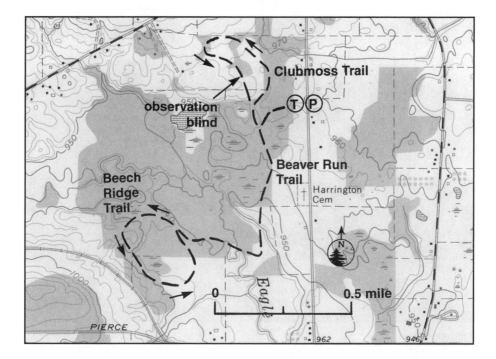

in multiple channels, and the manipulation of water levels by beavers has created more bottomland ponds.

A well-planned and well-maintained trail system allows the visitor to walk through the woods and fields past beaver ponds and beautiful wildflowers. Rather than a fast-paced recreational walk, this hike is better suited to a quiet stroll through nature's realm. The collection of any natural material is, of course, prohibited here, as are dogs, picnicking, alcoholic beverages, and camping. Bring water and other needed supplies since nothing is available at the preserve.

This preserve, with its easily-hiked trails, is one of those special places that can be visited throughout the seasons. It is open from dawn to dusk year-round.

How to Get There

Garrettsville, near which the preserve is located, is about equidistant from Akron, Youngstown, and Cleveland on OH 82. The preserve entrance is on Hopkins Road, which runs north and south about 2 miles east of Garrettsville. To reach it, travel OH 82 or OH 88 to Garrettsville, then take Center Road 3 miles northeast to Hopkins Road. Make a hard right turn onto Hopkins Road and go less than 1 mile to the entrance on the right, just north of Harrington Cemetery. The preserve is within an hour's drive of the Akron, Canton, Cleveland, and Youngstown areas.

The Trail

Shortly after leaving the parking lot, the trail enters the woods. A small buttonbush swamp is to your left. At the T in the trail, go north (right) on the 1.25-mile Clubmoss Loop Trail. After passing a sphagnum bog on the left, the trail divides to make its loop. Turn right. This trail passes another bog and a skunk cabbage patch, and then goes

---

Information kiosk

through an old field area and young woods before turning south and east alongside a large beaver pond. An observation blind beckons you to spend a few minutes scanning the area with binoculars in search of wildlife. Since the blind faces southwest, great photographs can be taken shortly after sunrise or, for spectacular backlit pictures, just before sundown.

Now traveling south, the trail completes its loop. Continuing beyond the side trail to the parking lot, the Beaver Run Trail stays on the high ground overlooking the East Branch of Eagle Creek and many small beaver ponds and dams. A half mile after passing the trail to the parking lot, the Beaver Run Trail drops down the slope to cross both branches of the creek. A trail up the slope beyond the second bridge is the connection with the .75-mile Beech Ridge Loop Trail. Walk it in a counterclockwise direction. Tall beech trees provide shade for the vernal flora of the forest floor. The trail circles, but does not pass through, a wetland. In this corner of the preserve, former agricultural fields are being allowed to return to woodland.

After completing the Beech Ridge Loop, return to the parking lot via the Beaver Run Trail.

17

Fernwood State Forest

Total distance: 4 miles (6.6 km)

Hiking time: 2.5 hours

Maximum elevation: 1,120 feet

Vertical rise: 220 feet

Maps: USGS 7½' Steubenville West (OH and WV); ODNR Fernwood State Forest map

At 2,107 acres, Fernwood is one of Ohio's smaller state forests. Located in the coal belt of southern Jefferson County, it did not get its name from its plant life, but from a nearby community that no longer exists. Unlike the large state forests of the southern part of the state that were acquired primarily to ensure a continued source of timber, Fernwood was purchased mostly for its recreational potential. So-called "pre-law" land, it was strip-mined by earlier methods that left standing highwalls with ponds at their bases.

The forest is in three units. The central section, which is also the largest, has a small picnic ground known as the Little Round Area and a well-developed and well-maintained foot trail. There are three parking lots here, including one at an overlook where there is a good view of the Cross Creek valley.

The western unit, which is the smallest, has a camping area known as Hidden Hollow, an area designated for handheld trap shooting, a rifle and pistol range, and a short nature trail known as Hidden Hollow Trail.

The third area, to the south, has not been developed and is accessible by road at only one corner. All three areas are open for public hunting. Deer, turkey, squirrel, and ruffed grouse are the most frequently sought-after game.

The view from Fernwood State Forest

How to Get There

To reach Fernwood from the Columbus area, take I-70 east to I-77. Turn north on I-77 and travel to OH 22, where you turn right (east) to Wintersville. From northeastern Ohio, travel I-77 south to US 250, where you turn east to Cadiz. There, go left on OH 22 and continue to Bantam Ridge Road. Take Bantam Ridge Road right (south) 3 miles to County Road 26, turn right, cross a railroad, and go over Cross Creek. Go up a hill to Township Road 181, where you make a left turn and immediately arrive at the forest service center. There is no office maintained there, and no fee for camping. A patrolling ranger will write you a permit. The area is remote, with very few visitors during most of the year. The trailhead for the foot trail is at the second parking area, about 0.7 mile east of the service center.

The Trail

The trail starts south from the parking area, rising at first but then dropping to follow the contour of the land. Beaver ponds lie between the trail and the base of the highwall. The timber is regrowth oak hickory with black locust. After ½ mile, a spur goes to the left. The main trail continues straight ahead, eventually dropping to Long Run. There was formerly a side trail to the left across a small footbridge that led to several small ponds about ½ mile downstream, but it is no longer maintained. If you can get through, these ponds are worth exploring for views of wildlife. I carried a pack rod and reel with me and spent some time fishing, but had little success. The loop hiking trail makes a right turn upstream past several beaver ponds.

After another ½ mile, the trail turns north and passes the right side of a small, man-

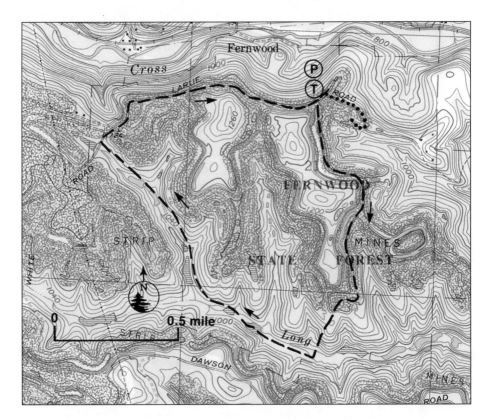

made lake. It does not cross the dam but continues up the right side of the valley, passing more beaver ponds before ascending to the township road just west of the service center.

To complete the loop requires that you hike .75 mile out the road to the parking lot and trailhead. A walk along the nature trail at the Hidden Hollow campsite would be a worthwhile venture while in the area. It is located on the north side of County Road 26, about 3 miles west of the service center.

18

Findley State Park

Total distance: 3 miles (4.8 km)

Hiking time: 2.5 hours

Maximum elevation: 915 feet

Vertical rise: 24 feet

*Maps: USGS 7½' Wellington;
ODNR Findley State Park map;
BTA Norwalk Section map*

Findley State Park's origin as a state forest is evident from the moment you enter the area. Row after row of tall pine trees greet you. These trees were probably planted in open fields shortly after the area was purchased. Named for the late Judge Guy Findley, an early advocate of protection for the area, the original 890-acre tract was transferred to the Division of Parks and Recreation shortly after its creation in 1949. An additional 107 acres have been added since that time. Virtually all of the park's 9 miles of trails, which include about 1.3 miles of the Buckeye Trail, are within woods. The park includes a modern 275-site campground, several picnic areas, and a 93-acre lake with a public beach and boat ramps.

How to Get There

The park entrance is off OH 58, not quite 2 miles south of Wellington in Lorain County. For this hike, turn right just after entering the park and follow Park Road No. 3 to the camp check-in station. If there is an attendant there, tell him/her that you want to hike, but not camp, and that you want to park on the lot inside the campground. You will be allowed to enter at no cost. Use the lot just northwest of the check-in station. If you want to stay overnight, make arrangements for a campsite as you come in.

Findley Lake is well stocked with fish, and only electric motors are permitted. It is a good place for some lake canoeing, perhaps "plugging" the shores for bass or using catalpa worms, red worms, or crickets for bluegill. It is a pleasant park for an

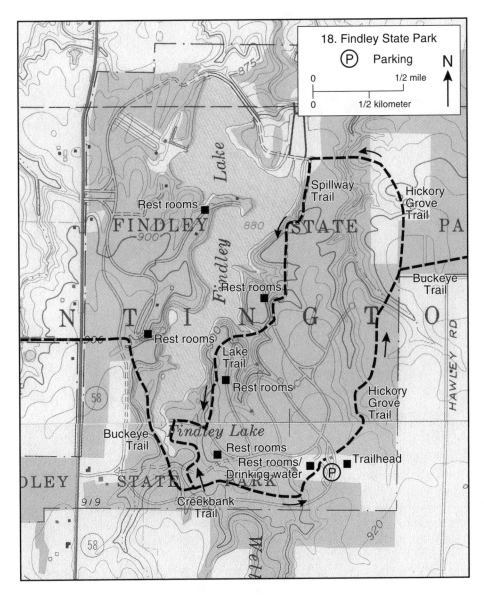

outing within an hour's drive of Cleveland, Akron, or Mansfield.

The Trail

Nearly the entire hike at Findley State Park is in woods. At many times of the year the trails are damp, so be certain you have adequate footwear and are prepared for mosquitoes. The route suggested here is different than in earlier editions of this book. The change was made to avoid conflict with mountain bikers and to take the trail out of high-use recreation areas.

Begin your hike by starting out on the 1.1-mile Hickory Grove Trail as it enters the woods just north of the check-in sta-

The author's camp in Findley State Park

tion on the right side of the road (No. 3). This is also a section of the Buckeye Trail, and as such is marked with blue blazes. After about .5 mile of walking you see an almost parallel trail, the Wyandot Trail, join the Hickory Grove Trail from the right. Ignore it. Not far beyond, the Buckeye Trail exits to the right to leave the park and head east toward its northern terminal at Headlands Beach State Park. Ignore this too, and the mountain bike path that will twice cross your path as you twist and turn your way to the east side of the Findley Lake spillway. There you will intersect the Mountain Bike and Larch Trails coming across the spillway. The Mountain Bike is a one-way trail and any traffic will be coming toward you from the spillway. To continue hiking, turn left on the Spillway Trail and head south. (You can, of course, circumnavigate the lake if you wish, but the trail will take you past the beach and through several picnic areas—not my favorite walking spots.)

About .5 mile of walking on the Spillway Trail takes you back into the camping area on Road No. 3 between campsite 112 and 113. At this point, I suggest turning right on the Lake Trail located behind the campsite across the road. This .5-mile woodland trail comes out on Road 10, just uphill from a boat-launching area near the upper reaches of the lake. Turn toward the lake and walk past the natural debris dump area on the right, watching for the entrance to the Creekbank Trail on the left (south) side of the launching area parking lot. Take the Creekbank Trail upstream through the woods to where it intersects the Mountain Bike Trail and the Buckeye Trail in less than .25 mile. Turn left on the shared foot and bike trail. After a few hundred yards a short-cut foot trail to the left goes to Road 10 in-side the campground. Ignore it and continue uphill toward the amphitheater and naturalist program area. The Mountain Bike Trail splits off to the right before you get there. Once at the naturalist building, you will see your vehi-cle in the distance across the mowed area. There is a small store in the check-in area. Enjoy a night at the campground or drive carefully on your way home.

19

Hinckley Reservation Metropark

Total distance: 5 miles (8 km)

Hiking time: 3.75 hours

Maximum elevation: 1,225 feet

Vertical rise: 304 feet

Maps: USGS 7½' West Richfield; CMPD Hinckley Reservation Trails map

Like the swallows returning to Capistrano in California, the turkey vultures are said to return to Hinckley, Ohio, right on schedule each spring. On the first Sunday after March 15, the return of the buzzards is celebrated in this metropark and in the nearby community of Hinckley. The timely arrival of the large black scavengers is usually reported on the wire service news. People come from far and wide to see the birds ride the thermals as they pass over the high ridge that runs through the park.

The land for this southern anchor of Cleveland's Emerald Necklace park district was purchased in 1925, and in 1926, 90-acre Hinckley Lake was built by damming the East Branch of the Rocky River. Hinckley is the only reservation in the Cleveland Metroparks System located entirely outside Cuyahoga County.

How to Get There

Located about 30 miles from downtown Cleveland in Medina County, 2,288-acre Hinckley Reservation is reached from north or south by traveling I-71 or I-271 to the OH 303 exit (Center Road). Head east 4.5 miles from I-71 or west from I-271 to OH 606 (Hinckley Hills Road). Turn south and drive 0.5 mile to Bellus Road. Turn left (east), go 0.25 mile, and enter the park by turning right (south) on West Drive. After about 1 mile on West Drive, you reach a road labeled BOAT HOUSE and JOHNSON'S PICNIC AREA. Enter to the left and drive to the boathouse parking lot. Park here and look for the trailhead kiosk. Though Hinckley

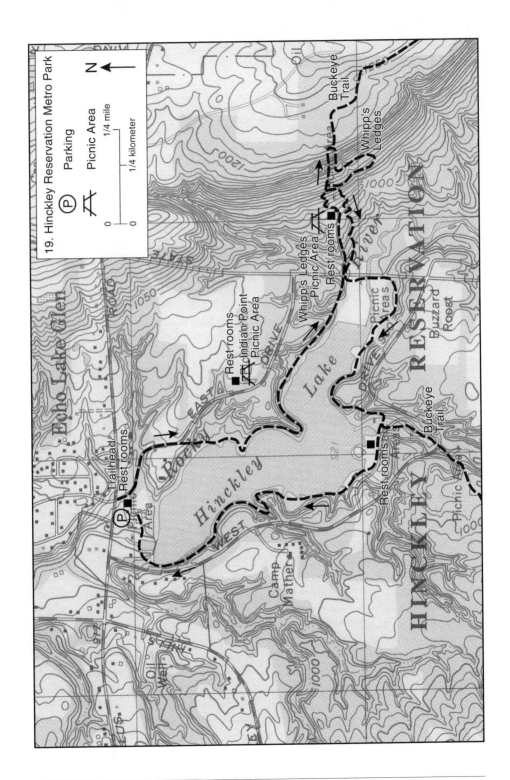

Reservation is located within 50 miles of several million people, it offers good hiking in a natural setting. By virtue of being in park district ownership for over 60 years, those areas that were young secondary succession woods at the time of purchase are now mature forests. As an island of green in an increasingly urban area, it is a haven for wildlife.

The Trail

To begin walking the Hinckley Lake Loop Trail, park in the lot adjoining the ranger station on the north side of Bellus Road just east of Hinckley Hills Road, or at the lot at the spillway trailhead on the south side of Bellus Road just east of the ranger station. If you want to carry a trail map, there is generally one available in a box on the front porch of the ranger station. The trailhead sign has a map of the area, a display about the park system and this park in particular, and announcements of upcoming activities. There are rest rooms throughout the park, including one just west of the trailhead kiosk. Like other Cleveland metroparks, the trails are well-marked with colored diamond-shaped medallions and designs, usually with markers of the same shape and color and an arrow pointing in the direction of travel below the trail symbol. Most are located on meter-high posts along the trail at entry points and intersections. The trails utilized on this hike include the Hinckley Lake Loop Trail, identified with a great blue heron on a light blue diamond; the Whipp's Ledges Loop Trail, which sports a white oak leaf on a tan diamond; and the Buckeye Trail, with a backpacker symbol on a light blue diamond. You will also interact with the All-Purpose Trail, which is marked with a jogger on a maroon diamond. I have chosen to hike this trail clockwise, but it can be traveled in either direction.

Hike north on the sidewalk to where it makes a T with the All-Purpose Trail. Turn right and follow this blacktopped trail with a green center line through the spruce grove to East Drive. Turn right there, and join the combined All-Purpose and Lake Loop Trails as they begin climbing toward the southeast. Initially there is a ravine to the left of the trail, but soon the road and trail curve to the right, leaving the ravine behind. You will shortly see the East Drive Scenic Overlook through the woods, although it isn't shown on the map. At a point where the combined trails move left away from the road, you will see an opening in the woods on the right side of East Drive where a trail angles off toward the lake. Though not marked as such, this is a shortcut to the Hinckley Lake Loop Trail. You can walk under the spruce trees to cautiously cross the road and then join this trail to continue hiking. The alternative is to continue on the combined trails along the north and south ballfields and out the drive and across East Drive to the Indian Point Picnic Area, where you will find a Hinckley Lake Loop Trail marker on a post at the head of a trail leading to the lake.

In either case you will soon find yourself hiking a shoreline trail. There are benches placed at good viewpoints, and short docks are set at convenient spots for the bank fishermen who use the lake quite heavily. Though the map would lead you to believe that Hinckley Lake is all open water, the presence of emergent vegetation reveals that it is actually the victim of heavy siltation and some industrious engineering by beavers. The hillside vegetation appears to be mixed mesophytic, with some nice oaks along the trail. Many specimen trees through here are identified with informative multicolored interpretive signs. Unfortunately, they have been placed high on the trees, evidently to prevent vandalism, so if you aren't

The Hinckley Reservoir dam

looking for them you may miss them. After twisting and turning up the hillside away from the lake, at a labeled sugar maple tree, the trail begins its drop to State Road. It reaches it directly opposite the roadway to the Whipp's Ledges Picnic Area and trailhead. Cross State Road and head up the entrance road to where you see a Buckeye Trail (BT) marker on the right. As an alternative to road walking, use the BT to work your way up the hill through the woods to the Whipp's Ledges Picnic Area.

The BT emerges next to the rest room opposite the trailhead kiosk at the upper end of the parking lot. A classic stone picnic shelter, probably built during the Great Depression, overlooks the hillside area. This is close to the halfway point on this hike, a great place to break out the sack lunch and take a bit of R&R. After filling your water bottle and using the facilities, it will be time to make an assault on Whipp's Ledges.

Take the trail that begins on the steps near the shelter. Go easy and enjoy the special feeling of walking through the bedrock slump blocks and up and over the ledges. The trail gains over 200 feet in elevation as it winds up the steep hillside. Once you are above the ledges and the Buckeye Trail has come in from the right, continue due east on the combined trails. At the Top O'Ledges Picnic Area there is another rest room.

The Whipp's Ledges Loop Trail makes a right turn, leaving the BT to continue east to exit the park and follow Parker Road. The Whipp's Ledges Loop Trail doubles back around and meets the incoming trail. Make a left turn on the combined trails, and when the BT quickly exits left, follow it to experience a different sensation as it drops into the upper end of the valley of another small Rocky River tributary. When it nears the rest room, you can opt to continue following the BT to State Road, or walk out the blacktopped park road. Note that the hollow through which the BT travels has been designated an Important Bird Area by the National Audubon Society.

In either case, when you reach State Road cautiously cross the road, then turn left on the All-Purpose/Hinckley Lake Loop/Buckeye Trails. As the merged trails approach the steel footbridge over the East Branch of Rocky River, there is a designated boat launch area on the right. If you are like me, you will make a mental note to return next spring with a kayak or canoe to explore the environment of the beaver impoundment. Once across the bridge, the Lake Loop and Buckeye Trails leave the paved All-Purpose Trail, turning right to closely follow the lakeshore.

The trail continues along the shoreline for a short distance, then climbs the hillside and passes along the bottom of a clearing beneath the deck at the West Drive Scenic Overlook. Dropping back to the lakeshore, the trail soon rounds a corner to the left and leaves the lake to pass between a hillside on the left and a picnic area across a creek on the right. As the combined foot trails approach the boathouse access road, the Buckeye Trail joins the All-Purpose Trail to head south. The Hinckley Lake Loop Trail takes a sharp right along the All-Purpose Trail as it travels northwest toward the boathouse trailhead, the docks, a launching ramp, and the boathouse. Where the All-Purpose Trail follows the road uphill, stay to the right and take the blacktopped path to the left of the boathouse. Just beyond it you will see the sign with a heron on a blue diamond, indicating that you are still on the Hinckley Lake Loop Trail. The graveled path climbs the hillside among young hardwoods. Then it drops close to the lake as it crosses an area of swamp forest. As it leaves the wetland, it rises to the right about halfway up the hillside among young white oak trees, then returns to the shoreline.

As the earthen dam comes into sight in the distance, there is a fork in the trail. Ignore the left fork that ascends the hillside. The Lake Loop Trail continues along the shore. Again there are small fishing docks jutting out into the lake. Continuing the hike is now a matter of staying on the lakeshore trail as it approaches the west end of the spillway. Upon reaching the dam, take the 52 steps toward the swimming area. Cross the tailwater on a footbridge. At the east end of the bridge, the trail returns to sidewalk. The right sidewalk leads to the park concession building. The left one passes among some spruce trees and past a downed redwood tree to carry you back to the spillway trailhead and your vehicle.

20

Mill Creek Park

Total distance: 6 miles (9.6 km)

Hiking time: 4.5 hours

Maximum elevation: 986 feet

Vertical rise: 121 feet

*Maps: USGS 7½' Youngstown,
MCPD Mill Creek Park trail map*

Founded in 1891 as Ohio's first park district, Mill Creek Park encompasses a unique combination of natural and cultural features. Volney Rogers, a man with vision beyond his century, determined that owning the valley of Youngstown's Mill Creek could enhance the quality of life in the community. On the leading edge of the industrial revolution, the burgeoning steel town needed a place for its mill-weary people to stretch their legs and breathe fresh air. His vision was for a community park where all people could shed their worries and rest their souls in the presence of nature. Almost single-handedly, he accomplished the mission he set out for himself. On the Volney Roger monument at the Memorial Entrance to the park is the inscription: CONCEIVED IN HIS HEART AND REALIZED THROUGH HIS DEVOTION. In 1989, the township park that Volney created became the Mill Creek Metropolitan Park District. In 2005, Mill Creek Park, with the exception of areas younger than 50 years, was placed on the National Registry of Historic Places as the Mill Creek Park Historic District. The total park system, which started with 400 acres, now covers 4,300 acres in seven townships and three cities in Mahoning County.

For more than 10 years, Mill Creek Park naturalist Ray Novotny had been pitching his park to me as a place I just had to visit. It's a long way from Columbus to Youngstown and somehow I just never made it. But during a hot week in early July 2006, when I was camping at Beaver Creek State Park, I finally took the plunge. It turned out to be a wonderful walk along a mostly babbling stream in the shade of tall hemlocks all the way. Where else in Ohio, other than in the Hocking Hills, can that be done?

I left the Ford Nature Center at shortly after 1 P.M. and returned to my car hot but happy at about 5:30 P.M. Though the Mill Creek valley has been shaped and reshaped many times and in many ways during its century-plus as a park, it still retains a unique natural character. There are many man-made features such as dams, picnic shelters, steps, playgrounds, goldfish ponds, gardens, and much more, but none of that bothered me as I trod the trails here. There are at least 34 named trails totaling more than 15 miles in Mill Creek Park. Even for a park that encompasses approximately 2,600 acres, that is a lot of trails.

The Mill Creek watershed is small, draining just 68 square miles of land. The stream begins in Columbiana County and flows almost due north for fewer than 20 miles to empty into the Mahoning River in the middle of Youngstown. Unlike most streams in northern Ohio, the Mahoning does not flow to Lake Erie. Rather, it flows southwest into Pennsylvania where it meets the Shenango River to form the Beaver River, which continues south to the Ohio River. Located in the glaciated Allegheny Plateau region of Ohio, the area was covered with ice more than once with the last advance, the Wisconsinan, about 10,000 years ago. The deep gorge of Mill Creek could have been created by post-Wisconsinan erosion. Or it might have been cut after earlier glaciers, filled again during each new ice advance, and then re-excavated after the Wisconsinan to its present configuration. Of course, it continues to be cut but, dammed as it is, not with the ferocity of the past. The Mississippian-aged sandstones through which it cut are quite massive and well cemented, producing high cliffs and rock shelters. The gorge's depth and north-south orientation provide a cooler, moister microclimate than the surrounding uplands, allowing remnant populations of plants from a cooler time to persist. Hemlocks line the gorge and farther up the slope there is mixed mesophytic woods instead of the mixed oak found on most uplands in the area.

If your vision of the Mahoning Valley is one of only abandoned steel mills in the heart of Ohio's "rust belt," think again. Mill Creek Park is a "beauty belt,"—a natural treasure that is worth a trip from anywhere in the state.

How to Get There

The parking lot for this hike is at the Ford Nature Center, 840 Old Furnace Road, in Youngstown. Coming from the north, I-680, the "loop" around Youngstown, is accessible from I-80 via Exit 218; coming from the west, reach I-680 via I-76; and from the south, get on I-680 from OH 11. Once on I-680, take Exit 5 (Glenwood/Mahoning Avenues). This puts you onto High Street. Travel to the three-way stop sign and continue straight ahead to the traffic light at Glenwood Avenue. Cross Glenwood and enter Mill Creek Park on East Glacier Drive (the lake is down in the valley on the right). Bear right at the stop sign and go downhill. Pass up Slippery Rock Bridge and then Slippery Rock Pavilion on the right. Go up a hill to a stop sign, and turn left onto Old Furnace Road. Immediately look to the left where you will see the Ford Nature Center. It's the big old mansion set back from the road. The parking lot is to the left of the building. Note that along this route there are several brown park signs with a list of facilities, including Ford Nature Center, and directional arrows.

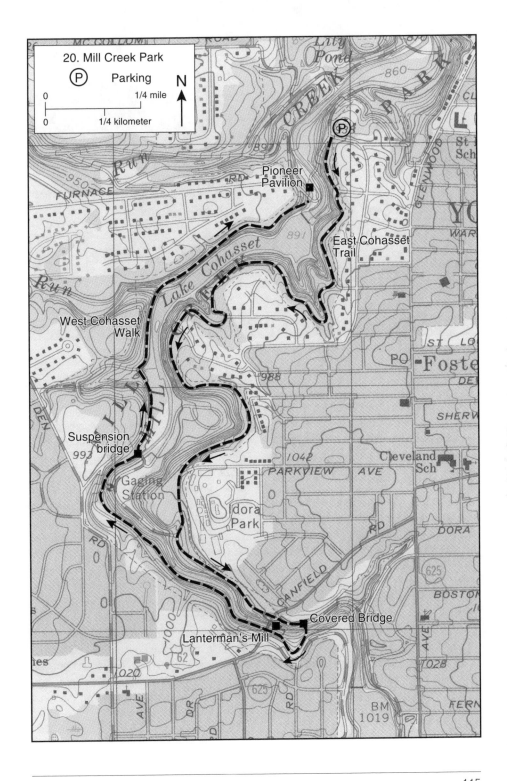

20. Mill Creek Park

Lanterman's Mill

The Trail

Begin walking from the Ford Nature Center parking lot. Head out the drive to Old Furnace Road, turn right, and then carefully cross the road to a walkway between the road and a steep bank on your left. Move to the left off the berm onto a narrow trail about 10 feet above the road. It carries you downhill and into the forest along Mill Creek. You will immediately hear the sound of rushing water, but not for long. There are three major impoundments on Mill Creek within the park. Lake Cohasset is the oldest, built in 1897 using stone quarried in the park for most of the construction. The name is said to be an Indian word meaning "place of pines" or "place of hemlocks." It was originally a mile long and covered 28 acres. The foundation is a hard, fine-grain sandstone, and the lake was excavated by pick to a depth of 18 inches to 4 feet. It has been dredged at least once since it was built.

The 1.5-mile East Cohasset Trail follows an old road in places, crosses several bridges, is joined by a side trail coming from the left, makes a U-turn in and out of a side cove, and climbs a few steps as it follows close to the east shore of the lake–all the while under stately hemlock trees. Every nook and cranny and large stone along the way has acquired a name in the 100-plus years of use by the trail's devotees. Sites of early structures have been identified and have also acquired traditional names of their own. Dr. John C. Melnick's wonderful book, *The Green Cathedral, History of Mill Creek Park,* documents all of these. The Civilian Conservation Corps is said to have had a camp in the area and helped with construction in the park. When they pulled out, the Works Progress Administration put 300 local men to work on building shelters, bridges, and retaining walls.

Eventually, the East Cohasset Trail

emerges from the woods onto an area known as Hiawatha Flats. Before you come out of the woods, you will get a glimpse through the trees of a magnificent suspension bridge over the creek. It was built in 1895 by the American Bridge Company as an authentic suspension bridge, 86 feet long and 32 feet wide. It has seen many modifications and repairs over the years, with the most significant in 1973 when the roadbed was strengthened and a concrete support in the creek bed was added for support. The bridge still carries traffic.

A trail runs from the Hiawatha Flats to a natural amphitheater just to the north. There is not a conspicuous trail across the flats. To continue walking, head for the far left corner of the open area, then carefully cross Valley Drive and pick up the trail alongside the road. This is the beginning of the East Gorge Trail. As the name implies, the valley of Mill Creek does narrow into a gorge. For some distance you will still be hiking along the upper end of the lake. As on the East Cohasset Trail, you will be walking uphill gradually, again under hemlock trees. This .5-mile trail is narrower and there are more rocks to scamper over because the valley is narrower too. There are benches upon which to rest at strategic places. Eventually the trail reaches a place where it is better served by a boardwalk up against the rock wall.

Shortly, the high US 62 bridge comes into view, and beneath it the falls of Mill Creek. Just beyond is historic Lanterman's Mill. This structure is believed to be the third mill at this location: the original mill operated from 1799 until 1822, a second mill from 1823 until 1843, and this mill built by German Lanterman from 1845 until 1888. Following its closing, the park purchased it in 1892. Before renovation began in 1982, the old building was used for many pur-

poses—dance hall, boat storage, nature museum, concession stand, bath house. In 1976 the mill was entered in the National Registry of Historic Places. Since its reopening it has been an operating mill, a historic museum, and a gift/book store. Be sure to spend some time there.

Continue hiking upstream past the mill to the covered bridge across the creek. The bridge was built in 1989 on the site of an earlier bridge. It carries the trail across Mill Creek where a trail that curves uphill to the right starts you on the return trip downstream to where you began. The trail ducks under the US 62 bridge high upon the hillside. From there it goes up and down the hillside on a sometimes-narrow path. Occasionally it reaches near to water's edge and sometimes it uses steps to gain elevation in a tight spot. This is the 1-mile West Gorge Trail. It's considered to be of moderate difficulty with only slight grades. The trend is generally downhill as the creek is heading for its confluence with the Mahoning River. Once away from the US 62 bridge, traffic noise disappears and, imperceptibly, so does the murmur of the creek below. Then you are once again alongside Lake Cohasset. When you come down the side of the road to the suspension bridge, take time to listen for a phoebe calling. They like to use bridges for nesting sites.

North of the bridge, you begin the last leg of your hike, now on the 1-mile West Cohasset Walk. There is an active road between the trail and the lake north of the suspension bridge, so the trail occasionally moves onto higher ground, away from the hemlocks trees, but they are nearly always in sight below. At one place it is necessary to walk for some yards along the road, but the trail soon drops over the retaining wall between the road and lake. It finally leaves the forest at the Pioneer Pavilion, a stone building built in 1821 as a woolen mill. Like other structures in the park, it has seen good times and bad, but it now appears to be in good repair and is seeing use as a program facility. A state historic marker tells the tale of its nearly two centuries of influence on the valley.

Beyond the pavilion are the remains of a 19th-century charcoal-fired iron furnace, probably built by one of the Heatons (later changed to Eatons) who owned the woolen mill and other iron furnaces in the area. The furnace was excavated in the early 2000s and is in rather poor condition. There is a historic marker here, also. Beyond this early industrial site, it is time to cross the creek on the concrete bridge that in 1973 replaced the steel-and-wood bridge that had spanned the creek since 1885. (I doubt that the new bridge will see 97 years of service.) Walk carefully up Old Furnace Road to the Ford Nature Center parking lot. There are many more things to see and places to explore in the streamside park.

21

Tappan Lake Park

Total distance: 9 miles (14.5 km)

Hiking time: 5.5 hours

Maximum elevation: 1,210 feet

Vertical rise: 310 feet

Maps: USGS 7½' Deersville;
MWCD Tappan Lake Park trail map

The watershed of the Muskingum River, which runs to the mighty Ohio, covers one-fifth of the state. The people living along that river and its many tributaries suffered many decades of seasonal floods that destroyed their homes, farms, and businesses. In 1933, the Muskingum Watershed Conservancy District (MWCD) was organized to provide flood control, conservation, and recreation in that eastern Ohio area. By 1938, 14 reservoirs were established, and permanent lakes were being retained behind 10 of the dams. The other four dams would be closed only at times of high water. Since 1939, the Army Corps of Engineers has been responsible for flood-control operations, but the MWCD is totally in charge of conservation and recreation throughout the district's 16,000 acres of water and 38,000 acres of land. At five of the reservoirs, the conservancy district operates parks. These are not state parks, but they fill that function in their respective areas, providing campgrounds, lodges and cabins, interpretive programs, picnic areas, beaches, marinas, and miles of hiking trails.

Tappan Reservoir is a 2,350-acre impoundment of Little Stillwater Creek in western Harrison County. The district owns 5,000 acres of land surrounding the lake, including the fully developed Tappan Lake Park on its southwestern side. Food, water, and rest rooms are available in the camping area but nowhere along the trail. This area makes for a good weekend family outing that meets the interests of everyone. The campground includes facilities for many

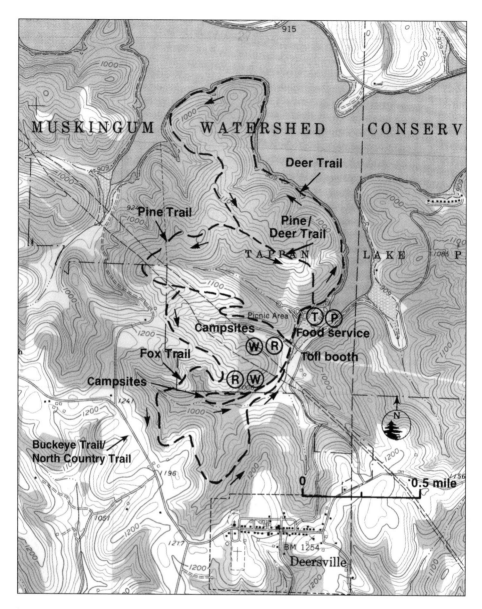

recreational activities such as basketball and horseshoes, and the lake allows for water sports.

Tappan Lake Park has six hiking trails, five of which originate at, and return to, the campground. Three of these are combined for this hike. The Deer Trail is 4 miles long, the Pine Trail is 2 miles long, and the Fox Trail traverses 6 miles. Since they overlap in some places, a combination of the three makes a 9-mile trek. Although directional signs on the trail are the reverse of the way described here, I prefer walking this direction because parking is available at the

Pine Tree Trail entrance

campground marina where the Deer Trail comes out, but not in Campground 4, where the Fox Trail starts. Two additional trails, the Cabin Beach Trail and a nature trail, are located elsewhere in the park area. A new trail, the Turkey Ridge Trail, is accessed outside the park entrance. It links the park to the Tappan Wetlands and Nature Study Area.

How to Get There

The park is easily reached from the northeastern Ohio metropolitan area by traveling I-77 south, then US 250 east. It can be reached from central Ohio by traveling east on I-70 to I-77, then north to OH 36 (New-comerstown exit), then east to US 250. To get to the park from US 250, travel south on County Road 55 near the eastern end of the lake. Turn right (west) on County Road 2. The park is 3.5 miles from US 250 on the right. During the summer vacation season

there is a charge for admission to the park. If you tell the person at the camp check-in station that you want to take a day hike on the trail, you will be admitted without paying a camping fee.

After passing the check-in station, turn left into the campground, then take the first road to the right. At the next left, turn to drive beyond the campsites to the campground marina parking area.

The Trail

Walk straight ahead on the left side of the embayment past the amphitheater to begin the Deer Trail. After it enters the woods, the trail stays at about the same elevation, 100 feet back from the shoreline, for a little over 2 miles. This part of the trail is a section of the Buckeye Trail that passes through the park. Secondary succession oak/hickory forest covers the hillside above the trail, while rows of 30- to 40-year-old white pine

Tappan Lake Park

fill the hillside below it clear to the shoreline. Now and then there is an old "wolf tree" with a large bole and low-growing branches alongside the trail.

When you approach the upper end of another large embayment, turn to the left on what must have been a township road. After climbing for about .5 mile, the trail reaches a pine-covered ridge, where it travels about 100 feet below the summit. It arcs gently to the left at that level for several hundred feet, then climbs steeply to the right to meet the Pine/Fox/Deer Trail coming up the valley from the campground.

Your trail now turns to the right into another white pine plantation. Pine Trail is certainly a good name for this trail, which runs from Campground 1 to 3, because the ridge here is planted with white pines nearly all the way. The Fox/Pine Trail travels on or just off this ridge for less than .5 mile, where it meets the Fox Trail coming in from the right.

At this point the trail is close enough to the lake that the noise of boats can be heard. Take the Fox Trail downhill along a white pine planting, crossing a pipeline and passing through more pines. The trail goes straight, crosses another utility right-of-way, then goes uphill to the left with white pines on the right. After making the ridge, the path makes a sharp curve to the left downhill past poor second-growth hardwood. Returning to white pines, the trail goes along the hillside close enough to Campground 4 that you can hear campers.

The pines disappear as you veer left. A couple of handsome old oaks stand along the right side of the trail. Climbing again, the path turns left as it hits the ridgetop, where there is an old, spreading white oak and more pines. The trail takes a steep drop into the pines. The road at the end of Campground 4 is visible downhill to the left. The trail goes right through medium-aged hardwood, down to a fill crossing over a culvert. From there, it climbs steeply to a junction with a trail coming in from the right. Go left, climbing gently, dip, and then rise again. This time, turn to the right at another trail junction. The path climbs gently through more pines at the top of the ridge, after which it quickly begins to drop. Making a hard right, it continues to drop, levels off, rises, then levels off again among some old wolf oak trees. It then crosses a culvert, turns uphill, and finally descends among sandstone slump blocks and large beech and tuliptrees on its way to Campground 4. There it drops behind a culvert, passing the Red Fox trailhead sign and Campsite 526 on the left.

When you arrive at the campground road, turn right to leave Campground 4. Then turn left, walking past the trailer dumping station and the activity center to return to the camp marina parking lot at the far end of Campground 1.

22

Marie J. Desonier State Nature Preserve

Total distance: 2.5 miles (4 km)

Hiking time: 2 hours

Maximum elevation: 920 feet

Vertical rise: 220 feet

Maps: USGS 7½' Alfred and Coolville

A walk on a woodland trail sometimes brings totally unexpected pleasures. Who would think that a 490-acre forested tract close to the Ohio River in Athens County would include an isolated high meadow full of butterfly weed and busily nectaring butterflies, "wildflowers of the air"? But that is the case at Marie J. Desonier State Nature Preserve. Three hundred and one acres of this remote preserve were given in 1975 by Henry I. Stein in memory of his sister, Marie J. Desonier. The remaining 189 acres were purchased by the Department of Natural Resources with federal dollars that were a match for the value of the gift. No money came out of Ohio taxpayers' pockets. The nature preserve's remoteness has kept visitors away, but not scientists. Two Athens-area entomologists have caught, identified, cataloged, and published on the butterflies of Desonier preserve. The preserve is open every day of the year. As in all nature preserves, pets are not permitted.

This is a trail of the Appalachian oak country of eastern Ohio. I do not remember seeing a single evergreen on the entire trail, and the high meadow, probably created by a farmer to grow hay for livestock in an earlier time, is on its way to becoming hardwood forest. In time it will be a marvelous unfragmented tract of old-age forest where the neotropical songbirds that spend their summer in Ohio can breed. The flash of red, yellow, orange, brown, black, and blue butterfly wings in the fields will be replaced by the sights and sounds of beautiful birds such as the scarlet tanager.

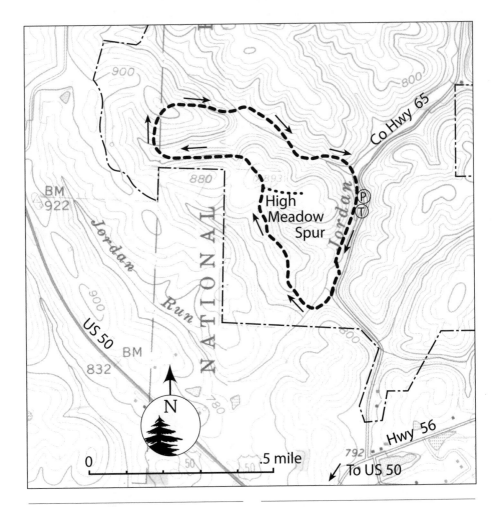

How to Get There

Reach the preserve by traveling east from Athens on US 50/OH 32 approximately 23 miles to County Road 65. This road goes left (north) and is easy to miss. After 0.3 mile, turn left on Deep Hollow Road (County Road 65). The preserve entrance sign can be seen on the right side of the road after just over 0.5 mile. The entrance is just beyond the sign. If it's open, drive in and use the lot. If it's closed, park in front of the gate as far off the road as you can.

The Trail

The Oak Ridge Trail begins at the south corner of the parking lot behind and to the left of the bulletin board. A short way from the parking lot is a borrow pit on the right side of the trail where gravel was taken for the parking lot. It is now well hidden by vegetation. The trail follows Jordan Run for perhaps .5 mile, crossing the main and side branches of the stream on plank bridges as the need arises. This trail can be very slippery after a rain.

Trail marker and bench

Walking in late June, I was serenaded by singing northern yellowthroats; the damp air was full of damselflies and dragonflies; and bergamot, milkweed, tall boneset, and mountain mint were in evidence. When I again walked the trail in September 2006, ironweed, both species of jewelweed, joe-pye weed, and other flowers of summer wafted their aroma into the air to attract nectaring butterflies. A large patch of the amber-colored, twinning, chlorophyll-less common dodder spread itself over a group of milkweed plants. The hum of female mosquitoes looking for a blood meal was not far off in this creek-bottom environment, but that is the tradeoff we make in order to enjoy the flora and fauna of wetlands. A school of minnows swimming in the stream below is not an unusual sight along this trail.

About 100 feet beyond the third bridge, the trail has been rerouted to the left and along the hillside then back to the bottom-land onto a boardwalk approach to one more bridge across Jordan Run. The reason for the new route is obvious when you look up the valley from the bridge. Beaver have built a dam and water seeping from beneath it keeps the trail wet most of the time. In the late summer, cardinal flower blooms at the right side of the approach to this bridge. Beyond the bridge, the trail heads uphill into a young mixed oak woodland. With sandy soil underfoot and an occasional chunk of sandstone alongside, the trail winds its way up the slope through woods and an occasional opening. Blooming white snakeroot plants filled one opening when last I hiked here. This is the plant associated with milk sickness, an often-fatal poisoning that occurs in humans when they drink milk from cows that have eaten this common forest-edge plant.

At one point, the woods are composed of almost a pure stand of aspen, perhaps indicating that there was a fire here in the past. After .25 mile the trail reaches a T, where you'll find a bench. A sign directs you right to the High Meadow spur or left to continue on the Oak Ridge Trail. Take the spur downhill to the right and you will be rewarded shortly with sunshine and, in summer, lots wildflowers of field and forest edge. I was greeted by a profusion of mist flower, the native plant that looks like garden ageratum, on my last visit. This trail at one time circumnavigated what was then a large meadow, but it now runs down the middle of the rapidly-filling field. In 2006 there were still areas of open fields, but the dogwood, sumac, sassafras, and tuliptrees were taking over. The late-June flight period of the single-brooded great spangled fritillary butterfly seems guaranteed to provide you a glimpse of this orange and brown beauty on the common milkweed and butterfly weeds that grace this meadow. It won't be many years before this old field will be hardwood forest, the normal climax vegetation for this part of Ohio.

Returning up the trail to the intersection, take the moss-covered Oak Ridge Trail as it starts out downhill, then shortly begins to climb once more around the hillside amid a beautiful bed of several species of ferns. Now rising and falling to cross the heads of small streams, the trail soon climbs to reach the high point in the preserve, all the time circling to the right. The vegetation becomes more lush, with many large beech trees. The land to the right drops off steeply and the streams the trail crosses are cut deeply into the bedrock, headed towards waterfalls as they tumble into the valley below. Eventually the trail heads downhill quite steeply on what looks like an old logging road. It makes one switchback before dropping straight down the hillside toward a tributary of Jordan Run. It was in this valley that a ruffed grouse and I surprised each other. The trail utilizes more bridges to stay out of the streambed as it winds toward the parking lot. The flowers of the forest edge once again line the trail, which passes large sycamore trees on its final reach to the parking lot.

23

Dysart Woods Outdoor Laboratory

Total distance: 2 miles (3.2 km)

Hiking time: 1.5 hours

Maximum elevation: 1,340 feet

Vertical rise: 180 feet

Maps: USGS 7½' Armstrongs Mills and Hunter; Ohio University Dysart Woods Laboratory brochure

A walk through Dysart Woods is a walk among the giants; there is no other way to describe it. It is home to the largest number of 36-inch-diameter trees (at breast height) that I know of in Ohio. Acquired by Ohio University over 30 years ago with the assistance of The Nature Conservancy, it was one of the first natural areas in the state to be designated a National Natural Landmark by the federal government. Ohio University, whose Belmont campus is less than 12 miles to the north, uses the woods as an outdoor laboratory, with busloads of students and their teachers frequently visiting the area. There are no facilities here, but it is open to the public. Note that smoking is not permitted while in the preserve. Picnicking and camping facilities are available at Barkcamp State Park just a few miles to the north. Dysart Woods has experienced a number of severe storms in recent years and there many downed trees, some lying across the trail. When I walked here in 2006, the bridges were in need of replacement, though I was able to use them. Exercise caution when you do so.

Dysart Woods has been the subject of much controversy during the first decade of the new century. Like much property in mineral-rich Appalachia, the ownership of surface rights and the mineral rights have been separated. Ohio University does not own the mineral rights to Dysart Woods, and the people that do would like to extract coal from beneath the land. Several efforts have been made to prevent the mining, but they were unsuccessful and the mining is sched-

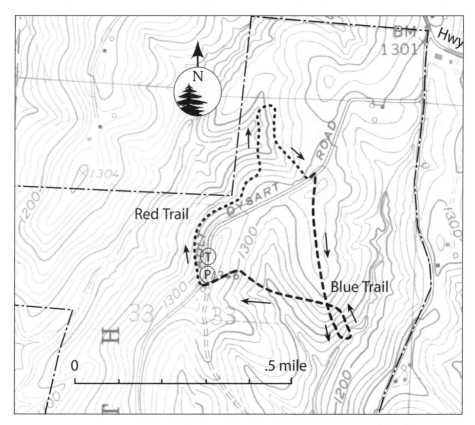

Red Trail

Blue Trail

0   .5 mile

uled to take place. As I understand it, the coal is to be removed using a subsurface technique called long-wall mining with the hope that no subsidence of the land and, hence, no disturbance to the forest, will take place. Only time will tell. Perhaps this is an even more compelling reason to put Dysart Woods high on your list of places to visit soon.

How to Get There

Finding Dysart Woods is not difficult. Travel east of Cambridge on US 70 to Exit 208, OH 149. Take this road south 3.5 miles into Belmont. There, take OH 147 out of the southeast corner of the community and travel 5 miles until you see the Dysart Woods sign on the right side of the road.

Turn right onto Township Road 234, then right again immediately onto Township Road 194 (Ault Dysart Road). The preserve headquarters is at the farmhouse on the right (east) side of the road. A brochure that includes a map is usually available from a self-dispensing box there. The trailhead is at a grassy area labeled DYSART WOODS PARK-ING on the left side of the road about 0.75 mile beyond the house.

The Trail

There are two connected trails: the Red Trail on the west side of the road and the Blue Trail to the east. Their routes are marked with posts and/or blazes of the appropriate color. I prefer to begin to the west, crossing the gravel road to enter the woods

---

A one-rail bridge

past a red blaze, and then traveling downhill. You are soon struck by the size of the trees around you, including tall, forest-grown beeches and maples. The plaintive call of a wood-pewee greeted me as I walked this way on a hot July afternoon. This is a dirt trail, with an occasional water bar to reduce erosion. The relatively wide track the trail starts on soon leaves to the left, and the red-post-marked trail becomes a narrow footpath and continues to wind around the hillside.

As the larger trees give way to much younger ones, you can look through the woods to the left to a large hillside pasture beyond the boundary fence. A well-kept barn stands out on the horizon uphill from the fence. As a red-tailed hawk screamed overhead, a female black rat snake appeared on the path in front of me. It was docile, as are most of its species, and it al-

lowed me to lift it off the trail with my walking staff.

Beyond the opening in the young trees that affords a view of the farm, the trail enters a growth of much larger trees while moving gently downslope toward a small ravine. There the trail turns left before hitting the bottom of the ravine, where it turns right. Stay left at a split in the trail, following the red posts. Here the large trees stand about 15 feet apart with small sugar maples in the understory and spicebush in the shrub layer. Beechdrops can be seen beneath a large beech tree that appears to guard the approach to a very narrow footbridge across a seasonal stream. Beyond the bridge, the trail turns upstream and winds its way up the hill, then turns right around the hillside to pass giant white oak trees, as well as a beautiful, straight, wild black cherry. It finally arrives at the fallen giant of the forest—a huge tuliptree that succumbed to a windstorm in the summer of 1995. Somewhere in my files is a slide of me standing in front of this tree in 1972. That was the first of many visits I made to Dysart Woods, and the tuliptree was magnificent to behold. I had to use binoculars to see the leaves on its lower limbs to identify its species. Even in death and returning to the earth, it is an impressive specimen.

The trail continues to make its way though the open forest of huge white oak and tuliptrees as it drops downslope to the creek. Down the valley, at a fork in the stream, the trail crosses the streambed on another picturesque but rather unsubstantial 2-foot-wide bridge with a single handrail. There is a small but photogenic waterfall downstream from the bridge. Fifty feet beyond is another footbridge that looks even less durable. The trail winds and dips, but mostly climbs as it makes its way toward the township road. As the trail makes an oblique approach to the road, multiflora rose begins to appear in the understory. At the road, a sign suggests crossing over to take the Blue Trail, the entrance to which is about 60 feet up the road to the left.

The Blue Trail begins between a poison ivy-covered black walnut tree and a hawthorn tree, then heads toward the woods on a wide, grassy trail. The grass runs out as the trail enters a young wood of maple, ash, tuliptree, and other hardwoods. Soon the trail reaches an area of open forest with good-sized trees. A wood thrush broke out in song as I passed through here in the summer of 1996. At a trail junction you have the option of exploring more deep woods by taking a short loop trail to the left or continuing straight to the parking lot on this trail. Take the loop trail, of course. A less-traveled trail, it winds among large

⮞ Storm Damage and Renewal

Severe storms can strike Ohio at any time of the year. They are viewed with alarm by the public because of their potential damage to life and property. To the naturalist, they are considered an important element of the ecosystem. Prairie fires set by lightning strikes from autumn storms contribute in many ways to the health and vigor of the prairie grasses and forbs. Heavy winter snowstorms effectively prune or even bring down dead, dying, or weak trees, allowing stronger, healthier trees to take their place in the canopy and creating openings where creatures that need brushy habitat can live. Springtime tornadoes or heavy wind- and rainstorms likewise bring trees crashing down, allowing more light to reach the forest floor, thus creating new habitat. Untold numbers of species of invertebrates and vertebrates make their homes in, around, and under downed tree trunks and branches, and cavity-nesting creatures soon go to work on the dead snags left standing by such weather events.

beech and maple trees where spicebush makes up the shrub layer. It looks as if it would be a great spring wildflower trail. At a large blank sign, designed to tell you that this is as far as you can travel up this valley, turn right and hang onto the side of the hill as the trail returns to where it began.

Turning downhill and then downstream, the trail soon reaches a bridge over a small stream. At the far end of the bridge there are steps poorly carved into the hillside, and there was once a handrail here to help the hiker up a short steep place. Once over this hurdle, the trail climbs steeply up a ridge between two streams. The trees along here are of incredible dimensions. At the top of the slope, the trail turns left to follow a fairly level terrace for about 100 feet before breaking through the edge of the woods onto the parking lot.

This extraordinary woodland is a place to cherish, as are your memories of a walk along its trails. It strikes me as a place to return to—at different seasons of the year and at different times of the day. It's a place to share with the other living creatures whose presence makes it so very special.

24

Lake Katharine State Nature Preserve

Total distance: 4.5 miles (7.2 km)

Hiking time: 3 hours

Maximum elevation: 800 feet

Vertical rise: 170 feet

Maps: USGS 7½' Jackson; ODNR Lake Katharine State Nature Preserve map

More species of plants have been recorded in Jackson County than any other county in Ohio. This fact can most likely by attributed to the late Circleville farmer and botanist Floyd Bartley, who spent decades collecting in the area and depositing his specimens in university herbaria. The area also served as a refugium for plants of the Teays River Basin during Pleistocene glaciation. And, because of its deep, cool ravines, it retained relict communities of boreal plants after the last glacier melted. Bigleaf magnolia, a tree of the southern highlands whose northern limit is only a few miles to the north, is found on the preserve. The rare round-leafed catchfly grows on the slopes below the sandstone cliffs of the preserve, and the small, thorny tree known as Hercules'-club can be found in the mixed mesophytic woods that dominate the area.

Though unusual plants and spectacular cliffs reaching as high as 150 feet in places are the main features of Lake Katharine Preserve, wildlife also abounds. Deer and wild turkey are seen often, and bobcats have been reported in years past. Needless to say, the spring wildflowers are spectacular, and for many years the Division of Natural Areas and Preserves has conducted a wildflower workshop here at the peak of the wildflower season. Information on this and other programs is available on the bulletin board at the main parking lot or from the division office in Columbus. There is a regional maintenance facility near the parking lot, but it offers no public services. There is also a private residence occupied

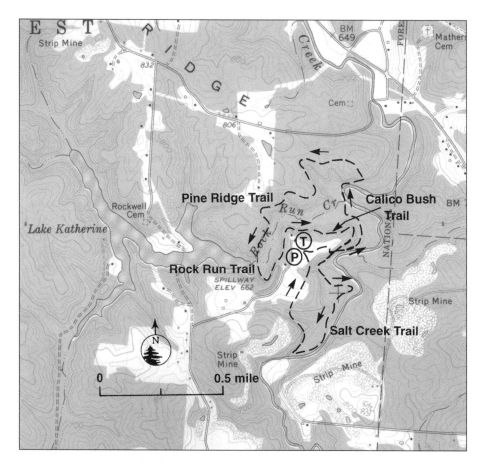

by people who aren't ODNR employees. Please do not disturb them.

There are no facilities for picnicking or camping at Lake Katharine, but both are available at Lake Alma State Park about 12 miles to the north off OH 93, just above Wellston. For the person interested in industrial archaeology, there are a number of old charcoal-fired iron furnaces located in the area around Jackson. A map giving their locations is available from the Ohio Historical Society in Columbus.

There is a small impoundment known as Lake Katherine on the preserve that was created by the damming of Rock Run when, during the Great Depression, the area was Camp Arrowhead, a summer youth camp for children of Jackson County. It offers good fishing for bass and panfish, but fishing is on a written-reservation basis only. Restricted to five boats per day, with no motors of any sort allowed, fishing is permitted Monday through Friday between April 1 and October 31. To obtain a permit, call 614-286-2487 during normal working hours on the last Friday of the month before the month for which fishing permission is desired. To reach the lake, you must haul your boat down a 110-foot slope, which, of course, you must clamber back up as you leave. As you drive into the preserve you will see another vestige of the area's youth camp days, a small block-house located to the right of the road just before you reach the parking lot. The camp lodge that for many years sat just beyond the parking lot was removed after many years of deterioration.

How to Get There

The preserve can be reached from Chillicothe by traveling US 35 to Jackson. Turn right (east) onto County Road 84 and follow it 3 miles into Jackson to State Street. Follow State Street out of town—it becomes CR 76—for about 2 miles, then turn right onto CR 60. After traveling a little over I mile, this road ends at the location of old Camp Arrowhead, where the preserve office and trailheads are located. It takes about 2 hours to reach the preserve from the Columbus area.

From the Cincinnati area, travel OH 32 to the OH 93 exit on the south side of Jackson. Turn left and take OH 93 north past downtown Jackson to State Street, where it turns right. You turn left though, and follow the directions above.

The Trail

At the right end of the parking lot, three trails head toward the woods' edge: the Calico Bush Trail, the Pine Ridge Trail, and the Salt Creek Trail. This hike uses all three in a figure-eight pattern. You will travel the top loop counterclockwise and the lower loop clockwise.

About 200 feet from the parking lot, the combined trail passes through a stand of young tuliptrees, then encounters Virginia pines before entering mature oak woods. The trail turns right when the old road it has been following continues straight. Rock outcroppings begin to appear on the right, with hemlock and mountain laurel now being seen. Not far down the trail you will see a sign for the Salt Creek Trail pointing to the right. Fifty feet beyond is another sign that points to the right for the Pine Ridge Trail, and one that points left for the Calico Bush Trail. Take the Pine Ridge Trail. (After hiking the Pine Ridge Trail you will arrive back at this point from the left on the Calico Bush Trail. Then you will need to go up the hill a short way on the combined trails and leave to the left, or south, on the Salt Creek Trail to complete the hike.)

Going right, the Pine Ridge Trail heads down an old logging skid, with cliffs on the left. At the bottom of the slope the trail turns left, then right, then traverses bottomland before crossing a bridge across Rock Run close to where it empties into Little Salt Creek. The latter gently curves to the right. Cliffs appear on the left, with tall hemlock at their base, and tuliptree, bigleaf magnolia, and wahoo on the talus slope. The cliffs seem to run out, then reappear. The trail heads up the valley. There is a good spice-bush understory in this area. Large slump blocks of the Sharon conglomerate, the exposed rock of the preserve, lie between the trail and the overhanging cliff. A small arrow indicates a turn from the old road uphill to the left. In wintertime you can see US 35 traffic and a farmstead from here. The trail climbs on multiple switchbacks, reaching the Virginia pine-covered summit shortly. It then winds its way through young hardwood, with an occasional young white pine and ground pine on the forest floor. The trail next drops to the hardwood-covered hillside above Rock Run, where it follows the hillside just above the steep, hemlock-covered slope. It then climbs back to the pine-topped ridge, for which the trail was named. There is an interesting invasion of young hemlock under the pines in this area. The trail along here can be particularly lovely after a light snow-fall. Two short boardwalks cross a wet area

The Lake Katharine shoreline

above the cliffs. The woods include a lot of red oak, white oak, and chestnut oak, with an occasional scarlet oak. Leaving the ridge, the trail drops into the hemlock-filled valley to a small footbridge below a rock face. Moving along the cliff, it drops further to the bridge over the Lake Katharine spillway before emerging from the woods to cross the lake's earthen dam.

Beyond the dam, the path enters a hemlock woods, heading uphill past a cliff on the right that shows evidence of having once been quarried. Bore holes for blasting charges are visible. About two-thirds of the way up the slope, a sign indicates that the Pine Ridge Trail leaves the roadway to the left. Take the five wooden steps to the left and follow a lovely trail through young hemlock trees below low cliffs. After 100 feet, a sign indicates that the Pine Ridge Trail goes upslope to the right toward the road, that the parking lot is straight ahead, and that

the Calico Bush Trail goes left. Unless you need to cut your hike short by returning to the parking lot, continue hiking on the Calico Bush Trail. (Calico Bush is an alternative common name for the late-spring-blooming mountain laurel, *Kalmia latifolia,* of Ohio's Allegheny Plateau.)

The trail travels among the calico bush and hemlock just downslope from rock outcroppings. Here you can easily see the layers of quartz pebbles in the Sharon conglomerate. In early summer you may be able to catch a glimpse of the uncommon scarlet-flowered, round-leafed catchfly in bloom in the nooks and crannies of the cliffs above the trail. (This is one of only a half dozen or so bright red native Ohio wildflowers. Red flowering plants are, for some reason, much more common in the tropics. Hummingbirds have a special attraction to red flowers. They seem to show up in Ohio in the spring when the columbines begin to bloom, and they are known to be the principle pollinator of the royal catchfly of the west-central Ohio prairies.)

Shortly the trail meets up with the Pine Ridge Trail, completing a loop. After a right turn, 50 feet up the combined trails the Salt Creek Trail originates at a fork, going to the left down the hillside. Should you want to end your hike, the trail to the right leads up the hill to the parking lot. To continue hiking, follow the Salt Creek Trail downhill on old road to where it turns right up a set of wooden steps between a cliff and a slump block. There are lots of pebbles in the rock wall here. The trail next descends to the valley floor where it continues beneath the base of the 75-foot-tall cliffs along the bank of Little Salt Creek. Then it climbs another set of steps to travel along the middle level of the Sharon conglomerate. Where the cliff meets the stream, the trail climbs nearly to the cliff top via the stairs before returning to the valley floor on still more steps. The sheer cliff face shows centuries of erosion, which has taken place here as the stream cut deeper into the valley. At a boardwalk beneath a cliff overhang, the layer of quartz pebbles in the conglomerate lies about 6 feet above the ground. There are usually antlion holes in the dry sand below the overhang. This is a good place to observe vertical fractures and horizontal bedding in the rock, a quartz pebble lens, and honeycomb erosion.

A sign points left to the long loop and straight ahead to the short loop. I suggest going left to where you cross a wet area on several hundred feet of boardwalk, passing beneath umbrella magnolia, sweet gum, red oak, black oak, spicebush, and hemlock. Reaching a nearly pure stand of hemlock, the trail goes up and then back down the slope, with the cliffs above disappearing and reappearing. It bears left to cross a

➤ Wildflowers

The common name "catchfly" is used for two of the most attractive wildflowers of the state: one a plant of the woods, the other of the prairies, although the two are closely related. There are only five native wildflowers that are scarlet in color: Oswego tea (Monarda didyma), a mint; cardinal flower (Lobelia cardinalis), of the bellflower family; and three members of the pink family, fire-pink (Silene virginica), round-leafed catchfly (S. rotundifolia), and royal catchfly (S. regio). The name catchfly is used for a number of other members of the genus Silene, including some from Europe. Where did that strange name come from? All three of these bright-red-flowered Silenes of our Ohio flora have what could best be described as sticky stems. They have a viscid sap that exudes from the stem. If you touch them, they feel tacky, but it does not come off on your skin. Most botanists believe that this sap prevents crawling insects from stealing the nectar without pollinating the flower.

The Latin name is also derived from this sticky characteristic. Most sources say it comes from the Greek word sialon, which means "saliva." Another opinion is that it is named for Silenus, who was Bacchus's foster father in Greek mythology and was said to have been found with sticky beer all over his face. Believe what you wish, but do gently touch the stem of the next fire-pink or round-leafed catchfly you come across on a southeastern Ohio hillside, or the next royal catchfly you encounter in a prairie preserve in Madison County. Don't pick it, though. Let it live in your memory, not die in your hand.

Little Salt Creek tributary on a bridge, then swings right to once again follow the right bank of Little Salt Creek. Cliffs and hemlock are visible across the stream, and magnolia along the trail. Passing through another hemlock stand, this time on an old sandbar, the trail moves at floodplain level through sycamores, cottonwoods, and willows before passing more magnolia. As the stream moves back toward the cliff face on the right, an arrow on a post indicates that the trail goes to the right and up an old road. After a steady climb of several hundred yards through hardwood forest, the trail turns right to cross streams on bridges at the heads of ravines. It then follows the hillside to the left, rising and falling as it crosses more small streams that parallel the hemlock/hardwood ecotone (an ecological community of mixed vegetation formed by the overlapping of adjoining plant communities). Moving back into hemlock and then uphill into the mixed mesophytic hardwood community, the trail continues to climb, passing an especially handsome shagbark hickory. A hard left turn and a gentle left curve take you just inside the edge of the woods. In a few hundred feet, the trail emerges from the woods just below the aging blockhouse that is about the only remains of the old youth camp. It then passes through a pine planting and an old meadow being rapidly overgrown with shrubs and trees to return to the parking lot.

25

Shawnee State Forest (Backpack Trail)

Total distance: 6.75 to 27.5 miles (10.8 to 44 km)

Hiking time: 1 to 7 days

Maximum elevation: 1,280 feet

Vertical rise: 682 feet

Maps: USGS 7½' Buena Vista; USGS 7½' Otway; USGS 7½' Pond Run; USGS 7½' West Portsmouth; USGS 7½' Friendship; ODNR Shawnee State Forest and Backpack Trail map

The hills of Shawnee State Forest, in the rugged Appalachian Plateau country of western Scioto County, have been called Ohio's Little Smokies. From the highest points in the forest, you see ridge after ridge rolling away to the horizon in a gentle blue haze. The color comes from the moisture in the air, generated by the thousands of acres of forest.

At 59,603 acres, Shawnee State Forest is Ohio's largest public landholding. Lying as it does just north of the Ohio River, to which all streams in the southern two-thirds of the state flow, it also has the greatest relief of any state forest. The area was hunting ground for the Shawnee Indians, one of the last tribes to occupy Ohio as the frontier was being pushed ever westward. Having migrated from the south into the Ohio valley, the Shawnees called themselves the Shaawanwaaki, literally "the Southerners." They established a major village, known as Lower Town, near the confluence of the Scioto and Ohio Rivers. As pressure from white settlers mounted, they moved northward up the Scioto Valley and then northwest into the valleys of the Little Miami, Mad, and Great Miami Rivers. Eventually they were defeated and driven from the state.

Prior to pioneer settlement, a mixed oak forest covered these ridges. The valleys and coves were mixed mesophytic forest, with good stands of beech on some of the gentler slopes. Game was abundant, including deer, black bear, wolf, beaver, and river otter, and bird life was plentiful. These resources housed, heated, fed, and clothed the settlers trying to survive in the wilderness. By the

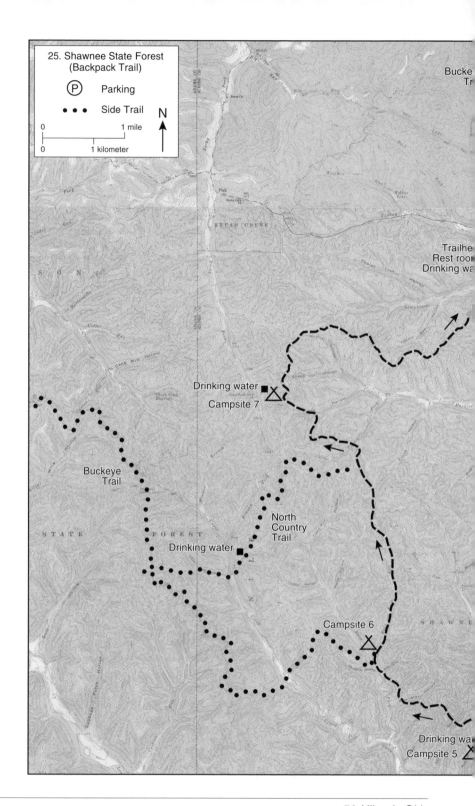

25. Shawnee State Forest
(Backpack Trail)

Ⓟ   Parking

• • •   Side Trail   N

0 _____ 1 mile

0 _____ 1 kilometer

Bucke
Tr

Trailhe
Rest roo
Drinking wa

Drinking water
Campsite 7

Buckeye
Trail

North
Country
Trail

Drinking water

Campsite 6

SHAWNE

Drinking wa
Campsite 5

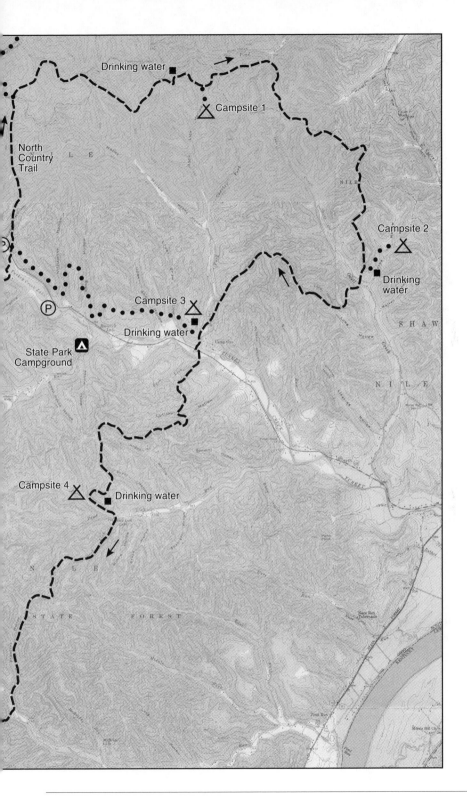

Drinking water

Campsite 1

North
Country
Trail

Campsite 2

Drinking
water

Campsite 3

Drinking water

State Park
Campground

Campsite 4   Drinking water

SHAW

NILE

NILE

STATE   FOREST

Serviceberry in bloom

early part of the 20th century, the virgin timber was exhausted and the big-game animals gone. The land was too rugged to provide a living from farming, so many descendants of the early settlers abandoned the land for homes and factories in the big cities. The production of moonshine was one of the last profitable enterprises of the area, and the federal "revenuers" did not take kindly to that activity. Shawnee State Forest was established in 1922 with the purchase of 5,000 acres of land that had been cut over for timber and ravaged by fire. During the same year, acquisition was begun for the Theodore Roosevelt Game Preserve. These were the first of many purchases made to assemble the large state forest and park complex of today.

In 1973, a 22 .75-mile loop foot trail was constructed north of OH 125. A year later, nearly 40 more miles of foot trails were opened south of the highway, completing

what is called the Shawnee Backpack Trail. The 29-mile south loop was later reduced to 23 miles and the number of campsites reduced by one in order to keep inviolate nearly 8,000 acres designated as the Shawnee Wilderness Area. I scouted the entire trail, taking copious notes, but due to space limitations of the book, only the south loop of the Backpack Trail is described here. You can easily add the 9.8-mile Shawnee Wilderness Area side trail to make a 36.4-mile trek.

The campsite that formerly existed in the wilderness area has been closed and camping is not permitted along the wilderness side trail. Along the Backpack Trail you must camp in designated areas. Each is complete with an outhouse, a fire ring, and, except for Camp 6, a source of drinking water. The water supply sites are along forest service roads, where Division of Forestry tank trucks can reach them. They consist of buried tanks

50 Hikes in Ohio

with a spring-loaded, frost-free hydrant located about 25 feet downhill. The Division of Forestry may not service water tanks in the winter due to bad road conditions. If in doubt, inquire at Forest Headquarters before starting out on the trail.

A word of warning: This is copperhead and timber rattlesnake country. It is unlikely that either will be encountered, but you should be mindful that these creatures share the forest. Be especially careful when stepping over logs and through deadfalls and brush. It is also wise to use caution when scrambling over rocks. Vigilance is the best snakebite prevention. Do not kill any living thing along the trail, including poisonous or nonpoisonous snakes. Given some space, they will always move out of your way. In addition, black bear have returned to southern Ohio. (Read and heed the "Living with Bears" sidebar elsewhere in this book.) In bear country, I hike with a "bear bell" jingling merrily from my pack. Ticks and deerflies can also be a nuisance at certain times of the year, so be prepared to deal with these pests.

The Shawnee State Forest is one of Ohio's most precious resources. It is home to many species of amphibians, reptiles, and mammals and, because of the vast tracts of forest, to a great many bird species. Deer and wild turkey are seen frequently. Many rare or endangered plant species live on the ridges and hillsides and in the ravines of the forest, protected so that future generations of Ohioans may know their natural heritage. It is a special privilege to be able to hike in this vast preserve where, except for the passing of an occasional airplane, the only sounds are those of the natural world. When I scouted the trail, I did so alone. I chose the period from the last weekend or April through the first weekend of May, figuring that this was when I could see the most wildlife and the most wildflowers in bloom. I was amply rewarded with everything from orchid to scarlet tanagers. Unfortunately, it was the time of spring rains and as I crossed from the north loop to the south loop, I cached my pack and hiked round trip from Camp 3 to my car at the trailhead to get a pair of dry boots. Ah, but what memories. In a state as densely populated as Ohio, how fortunate I and my fellow citizens are to have such an area in which we can get completely away to backpack and explore.

How to Get There

From central Ohio, go south on US 23 to Portsmouth to reach Shawnee State Forest and Park. Then travel west on US 52 and OH 125. The distance from Columbus is 120 miles, requiring about 2.5 hours traveling time.

From Cincinnati, the trip via OH 125 takes 2 hours and covers a little over 90 miles. There is a large state park sign on the north side of OH 125 about midway into the state forest. The turn leads to the resort lodge, park office, housekeeping cabins, and the Turkey Creek Lake beach. You also turn here to reach the Shawnee Backpack trailhead. Immediately after the turn onto the park road, a driveway to the right leads to the trailhead parking lot. A sign along the right side of the lot reads SHAWNEE FOREST BACKPACK TRAIL PARKING. Another on a wooden kiosk reads SHAWNEE BACKPACK TRAIL INFORMATION. PLEASE REGISTER. One box on the front of the kiosk holds maps, and another contains self-registration cards. It is important that every hiker register. Registration cards are checked daily, and if you do not return to your vehicle close to the time and date indicated on the registration card, rangers will begin a search. The hand-out map includes trail tips, Backpack

Trail rules, and a list of emergency telephone numbers. At one time it was suggested that hikers could pick and choose segments of the trail to hike, leaving their vehicles parked at spots in the state forest where the Backpack Trail intersected forest roads. But with less frequent patrolling of the roads and an increase in vandalism, that is not a safe thing to do. You should plan to start your hike from the main trailhead at the highly visible lot along OH 125.

The Trail

Day 1: Trailhead to Camp 3
Distance: 5.3 miles (8.5 km)
The trail begins with 13 log steps on the north side of OH 125, across the road and slightly to the left of the trailhead shelter. This is the starting point for hiking the entire trail or just the north or south loops. It is also an access point for the North Country Trail and the Buckeye Trail headed east or west. The routed wooded signs of the past have been replaced with Carsonite posts; brown on the main trail and white on some of the connecting trails. You will see a symbol of a tent representing the word "camp," then a number for the next campsite on the trail, then an arrow indicating the direction of travel to that camp, and finally the distance in miles. One note: the distances provided here differ from those in earlier editions of this book, and on the Division of Forestry's earlier maps. These are thought to be much more accurate.

Thus, to begin walking on the north loop, take the trail to the left labeled CAMP 1, 6.2 MILES. To hike the south loop as described in this book, turn to the right, following the sign CAMP 3, 5.3 MILES. The main trail is blazed with orange paint. White paint is used for the side trails, including the segment from the trailhead to Camp 3. Blue blazes are used on the Day Hike Trail, which overlaps the trailhead-to-Camp 3 segment. All of the blazes are well spaced, with one almost always in sight. If you do not see blazes after a few minutes, backtrack and check to see if you missed a turn. The Buckeye Trail and the North Country Trail (NCT) utilize 14 miles of the Backpack Trail (BT). BT and NCT decals on Carsonite posts are used to designate the route of these two long-distance trails. Since the eastbound routes of these trails use the Backpack Trail from the trailhead to Forest Road 6, you will see the signs at the entrance to the trail.

Soon after heading out on the trail to Camp 3, you cross over three washes and a 5-acre area that was burnt over by a human-caused fire in 1981. The trail parallels OH 125 on the end of a ridge, and then drops into Williamson Hollow. At this point, a trail makes a T with the blue-blazed, 7.2-mile Day Hike Trail coming up from a trailhead across OH 125 from the Shawnee State Park Nature Center. The Day Hike Trail and the trail from the trailhead to Camp 3 share the same path for about .5 mile going up Williamson Hollow. The white-blazed trail to Camp 3 leaves the Day Hike Loop Trail turning to the right (east). Since this is the other end of the Day Hike, it is marked with both blue and white blazes. This combined trail soon gains almost 200 feet as it goes nearly straight up to reach the crest of the next ridge to the east, then turns south to angle down the side of the slope into Long Hollow. After the trail crosses the stream, you will soon see a "wild" trail, which goes downhill to OH 125 to access the Roosevelt Lake campground.

The trail to Camp 3 climbs toward the north then drops toward another stream. Next it nears the phone-line right-of-way and turns to follow the ROW clearing to near

OH 125. A switchback to the left takes you down the ridge. The trail travels along a side ravine until it crosses the small creek and heads downstream, where it crosses the main stream of Upper Shaw Hollow. After climbing over the end of a ridge, the trail meets an old road coming in from the right. Together, they head down Lower Shaw Hollow and cross the streambed. The blue-blazed Day Hike Trail exits left, leaving you with only white blazes to follow. Once across the creek, the trail leaves the old road and begins climbing to a rock-strewn side wash. A quarter mile later, you reach the water source for Camp 3 and a sign directing you to the campsite. It's located on a wooded point about 200 feet above Turkey Creek, so it's wise to fill your water containers before you take the white-blazed side trail uphill to the campsite.

Day 2: Camp 3 to Camp 4

Distance: 5½ miles (8.8 km)

Begin the next leg of your hike by heading downhill from Camp 3 to the water supply. Just beyond, the main trail—now blazed with orange paint, as the main Backpack Trail will be for the remainder of the hike—enters an open field, which it crosses to the left, heading for the water supply service road. Then it turns right onto Forest Road 1, almost immediately crossing Turkey Creek. Next it crosses OH 125, onto which it turns left. About 25 feet beyond a group of mailboxes it leaves the highway through an opening in a rose hedge. After crossing an open field the trail goes through another rose hedge, then enters the forest. Beyond an abandoned road crossing it skirts the left end of a small pond that has a rock cliff hanging above it and hemlock trees overhead.

The trail climbs to the right to get above the cliff, then heads left uphill. Soon it is paralleling the beautiful Buck Lick Gorge below

it on the left. The trail drops into a sandstone gorge, where it crosses the creek and heads briefly upstream. It then angles up the left slope, headed for the corner of state property. (State forest boundaries are blazed with yellow paint.) For a short distance it follows an old wagon trail, but it soon exits to the left and, after crossing the heads of several ravines, begins a slow descent into Cutlipp Hollow. This valley abounds in wildflowers in the spring. When the trail reaches the creek, it turns left, downstream, to the first side stream on the right. It climbs rather steeply beside this stream to a knob at 950 feet in elevation. Turning left at the knob, the trail continues a gentler but steady climb up the ridge and the left flank of Cutlipp Hollow. There it passes through a magnificent stand of large oak trees with many wildflowers, including the rare spotted mandarin, scattered on the forest floor. Passing to the right of a 1,160-foot knob, the trail joins the fire access road utilized by the Pond Lick Bridle Trail and reaches a saddle on the ridge. The bridle trail and hiking trail separate and rejoin twice, with the Backpack Trail taking the higher ground to the right and the road to the left. The downhill slope to the left is covered with an even-aged stand of mixed oaks and hickories, the result of a clear-cut operation made several decades ago. Quite a bit of mountain laurel grows here, even under the secondary-growth forest.

Where the road goes to the left, the trail turns right over a high knob that is more than 600 feet above the benchmark at the entrance to Cutlipp Hollow. Beyond that high point the trail rejoins the road, and Mackletree Bridle Trail comes in from the right. The hiking trail once more drops off the ridge to the right of the bridle trail, and then comes back up to the ridge to cross the bridle trail and leave it for good. The Backpack

Trail swings left to follow a ridge and cross over or pass around knobs to the south for about .75 mile. The trees are large here and the forest rather open. Greenbrier once again can be an annoyance along the trail. When the ridge ends, the trail drops in .5 mile from 1,160 feet to 760 feet, the elevation of Camp 4.

Where the trail reaches the valley bottom, there is a "T." Camp 4 is across the creek to the right. In contrast to previous camps, there is no long side trail to this one. Apparently because of its closeness to the road, the campground appears to be heavily used. The sound of the nearby rippling water is conducive to a good night's sleep.

The water supply is beyond the camp along the main trail. The tank is slightly up the left flank of the valley and may be partially obscured by wildflowers in late summer. Locate it by looking for the access road used by the tanker that keeps it supplied with water.

Day 3: Camp 4 to Camp 5

Distance: 4.6 miles (7.4 km)

The orange-blazed trail leaves Camp 4 by heading downstream out of the valley and past the water supply. Following an old logging road, it then goes toward Pond Lick Run. A cable blocks vehicular access to the valley. The trail leaves the road to the right to cross the creek just upstream from Pond Lick Lake. This crossing usually requires removing shoes and socks to wade. The trail continues on to the paved road. The distance from the point where the trail crossed OH 125 to where you're now standing is about 5.5 miles. The only structure remaining at the site of the Vern Riffe CCC Camp, which was located a few hundred yards down the valley beyond Pond Lick Lake, is the old log cabin made from American chestnut logs that was the headquarters building. All the other buildings have been razed.

The trail next goes to the right on the paved Pond Lick Road for about 15 feet before turning left to enter the mouth of the Rock Lick Creek valley. This is a damp section of trail. A half mile from Pond Lick Road, the trail passes a hillside on the left that was clear-cut in the late 1900s. After traveling below this timber-harvest area for .3 mile, the trail climbs and turns left onto a ridge where you get a different view of the regenerating forest. The trail then crosses Forest Road 2, about .25 mile from its intersection with Forest Road 13, the McBride Road. When you reach that point, you will have traveled about 2 miles from where you hit the road near the CCC camp.

After crossing the road, the trail reenters the woods, travels a ridge for a short distance, then descends into Pheasant Hollow. How this hollow got its name is a puzzle, because this is not pheasant country. These big alien game birds do not survive in the hill country of southern Ohio, even if stocked there. Perhaps the native ruffed grouse was mistaken for pheasant. The trail reaches Pond Run Road (Forest Road 1) after 1.5 miles along a stream, which it crosses frequently. The trail now follows the road to the left, stopping just before the bridge that crosses the branch coming out of Pheasant Hollow. There it turns right across a meadow to the riverine forest along Pond Run, where a stream crossing is required. This can be difficult, if not impossible, if the water is high. It is a good idea to have a strong walking stick in one hand to maintain balance when you're fording the stream.

After the crossing the trail turns left, following a terrace above the stream. It then turns to the right into the mouth of a ravine, crosses a small stream, and comes back out to the terrace. Next it heads downstream for a short distance before entering another ravine to begin a long climb to Forest Road 5. This valley is very narrow and rocky and is filled with ferns and wild-flowers. At the head of the valley, the trail ascends via four switchbacks to a ridge that carries it out to the road. A tenth of a mile after the trail turns right onto the road, you will see a white-blazed side trail exiting to the left. It follows a ridge to Camp 5, less than .5 mile away. The water supply is just off the gravel road to the left of the white-blazed trail. Since Camp 6 is only 3 miles away, some hikers skip this campsite to re-duce their time on the trail by a day. The de-cision to do this requires careful thought, for the next 2 miles of trail are difficult and Camp 6 is the only site with no supply of fresh drinking water.

Day 4: Camp 5 to Camp 6
Distance: 3 miles (4.8 km)

Though only 3 miles long, the next section of trail may take as much as three hours to cover. After filling your water containers, re-turn to the orange-blazed main trail. Turn right onto the trail and go a short distance up the road to a point just before where Forest Road 5 begins to curve to the right. There you see a sign and orange blazes in-dicating that the trail is leaving the road to the left. It can be hard to see this exit when the tall summer wildflowers are at their peak. The trail heads west on a ridge, then drops off steeply to the left into a small ravine. It then turns right to descend 200 feet into Stable Gut Hollow. After crossing a stream, it begins a 400-foot climb. Quite steep at first, the trail soon makes three switchbacks to gain elevation with a lower gradient, hence less effort. After crossing a 1,060-foot saddle in the ridge, the trail turns left to descend on an angle into Blue Clay Hollow. Be careful not to slip, as I managed to do, on the steep sections of this trail.

Eventually a couple of switchbacks slow the rate of descent on the way to the bottom, where the trail crosses the creek near the mouth of the hollow.

Next it travels up the valley of the East Fork of Upper Twin Creek, which is out of sight off to the left. Follow the orange blazes. One stream crossing goes over a sandstone ledge, with a lovely low waterfall just to the left of the trail. In the springtime, treasures such as pink lady's slipper, showy orchids, and whorled pogonia can be seen along this section. Soon after passing through this pic-turesque area, the trail turns left downslope to come closer to the East Fork. Then it turns right up the valley on an old road. The deep cut this old track has made into the earth in-dicates that it has seen much use over many decades. On the rainy day that I hiked here, the trail was more of a stream. After follow-ing this track for a short distance, the trail exits left and drops close to the stream. Still on the right bank of the East Fork, it skirts the left edge of an open brushy area and then returns to the old track to enter a nice stand of hemlock.

At the edge of this evergreen grove, a side trail goes left down to the stream. This is the trail to the Shawnee Wilderness Area and one possible route to Camp 6. Be warned that this would add 9.8 miles to your day's trip. It is possible to get special permission to camp along this side trail, but you must do it through the Division of Forestry office in advance of your trip. The orange-blazed main trail goes straight ahead under the hemlocks to near the con-fluence of the East Fork and Bald Knob Run. Camp 6 is just across Pine Run, at a point where it is cutting its way through the sandstone bedrock. This is the most remote campsite, and one you won't soon forget. Reaching it requires a short ford, but it is well worth it. The outhouses are downstream about 100 feet on the camp side of the East Fork.

Day 5: Camp 6 to Camp 7 (formerly Camp 8)

Distance: 5 miles (8 km)

Assuming that you have not chosen to include the Shawnee Wilderness Area in your hike, follow the orange-blazed main trail from Camp 6 as it exits the area on the other side of the East Fork. You can either ford the stream at the campsite or go downstream beyond the outhouses to the trail fork to cross and then return on the other side of the creek to pick up the trail opposite the campsite. The trail follows the valley of Bald Knob Run along the right fork of the stream for its entire length. Eventually the trail arcs up the slope around the head of the valley, making one switchback. It comes out on the ridge just short of a road now closed to traffic that once was part of the Panorama Loop, which tourists drove while admiring the fall leaf coloration. (There is no longer a Panorama Drive in the area of the forest south of OH 125. A new route in the northern half of the forest has been given that designation.) There the trail turns left and stays just below, and several hundred feet to the left of, the road. Although the trail has gained several hundred feet in elevation, it has done so gradually.

After going directly across the road, it travels downhill along the center of a sloping ridge, then drops steeply off to the left before swinging around to the right in a more gradual drop, headed for the upper end of a small hollow. You cross several side streams before crossing the main stream to the left, just before its junction with the Shawnee Wilderness side trail. The orange-blazed main Backpack Trail, now joined by the blue-blazed Buckeye Trail and the North Country Trail, goes out a hollow,

through a small weedy area, and then intersects with Mackletree Road.

The trail then turns right for 50 feet of road travel before entering the woods to the left, just opposite a parking spot used by hunters and mushroom gatherers. Twenty-five feet after leaving the road, the trail crosses Plummer Fork, and then turns left to begin a gradual 320-foot ascent to the ridgetop. After dropping in and out of one saddle, the trail enters a second saddle, from which it descends to the right into a small ravine that empties into Long Hollow. (Perhaps an early inhabitant's name was Long, for this hollow certainly is not long.) Turning to the left, upstream, the trail crosses the main stream once and a small side stream twice. It then enters a headwater ravine to climb rather easily to the ridge. The trail follows the ridge to the left and then swings to the right, passing a grassy area on the left. The path continues on the ridgetop until it drops into a saddle that was once crossed by a wagon trail.

The white-blazed side trail to Camp 7 goes to the left down the old wagon road. Descending the hill, the trail to the campground leaves the track to the right. At first glance the area around Camp 7 appears to have been recently timbered, but a closer inspection reveals the charred remains of a devastating 500-acre arson fire that occurred in April 1981. What looks like logging was actually a salvage cut designed to recoup as much of the loss as possible by taking out the large trees killed by the fire. This cutting also helped prevent an infestation of forest insects and disease in the area, since injured trees are highly susceptible to such pests.

The water supply for this camp is 10 minutes away. Instead of turning right off the old road to Camp 7, follow the track downhill to where it makes a T with a logging road. Turn left and follow the logging road toward the paved road. The tank is on the hillside to the left of the logging road and can be spotted by the muddy track that swings up over the hill. The campground is on a gentle slope in a rather sparse stand of hardwoods. Two latrines are located around the hillside beyond the old road. Although it is about 4.5 miles from the Camp 7 side trail to the trailhead parking lot, the easy walk takes no more than 3.5 hours. With enough daylight, you can bypass Camp 7 and reduce the length of your trip by a day if you need to.

Day 6: Camp 7 to Trailhead
Distance: 4.5 miles (7.2 km)
The hike back to the trailhead on OH 125 is easy. From Camp 7, the trail continues out the ridge for a little less than 1 mile, then leaves the right side of the ridge to drop to Forest Road 16. Along the way, it crosses the Lampblack Run Bridle Trail. After crossing the road, the combined foot paths climb immediately to a ridge, which the trail more or less follows for 2.5 miles. The drop to the Lampblack Run valley and the end of the hike begins when the trail hits an old wagon trail, which it follows for a short distance. Then it begins its descent by dropping off the left side of the ridge. Sometimes following a rock-strewn wash, and several times using switchbacks, the trail soon reaches a hillside terrace that it travels for a short distance. Using more switchbacks, it drops to the valley floor opposite the park service center. Blazes seem to end as a paved road near the beach comes into view. A wooden bridge to the left leads across an embayment of Turkey Creek Lake, beyond which a smaller bridge crosses another stream. A concrete staircase carries the trail up to the lodge driveway. To complete your 27.5-mile hike, follow the blacktopped road to the right, across Turkey Creek and on to the parking lot.

As you travel home, you will likely start planning a return trip to Shawnee State Forest, perhaps to do the 4-day, 23-mile North Loop of the Backpack Trail, or to put them both together for eight days on the trail.

➤ Minimum-Impact Camping

Campsite etiquette has changed dramatically in the 60 years that I have been hiking the trails of the Buckeye State. Gone are the days of the wax-treated cotton canvas army surplus pup tents with hastily dug trenches around them to carry away the runoff. So too is the practice of doing your business over a fallen log in the woods, leaving toilet tissue to "weather" away. Big, roaring evening fires just for the sake of the ambience no longer make good sense.

Backpackers are now expected to practice extremely low-impact camping. That means no damage to trees, and minimal damage to the ground cover; no open fires for cooking, and fires for warmth only in emergencies. Plan to carry out all empty food containers. Bury human waste many yards away from the trail and any water, deep enough that animals won't unearth it. Use little or no soap for washing up, and dig a hole in which to dispose of your gray water. Don't forget to fill it in before you leave. Respect the desire of other campers for space, quiet, and privacy. When you pack up your gear to move on, return the leaf litter to the footprint of your tent to make the area appear as natural as possible. Trite though it may sound, "Let no one say unto your shame, all was beauty here until you came."

26

Tar Hollow State Park and Forest

Total distance: 12 miles (19.3 km)

Hiking time: 9 hours

Maximum elevation: 1,200 feet

Vertical rise: 498 feet

Maps: USGS 7½' Hallsville; USGS 7½' Laurelville; USGS 7½' Londonderry; USGS 7½' Ratcliffburg; BSA Troop 195, Columbus, Logan Trail map; ODNR Tar Hollow State Forest map

Tar Hollow State Park and Forest lie just east of where the glaciers ended, close to the intersection of Ross, Hocking, and Vinton Counties. When the area is approached from Circleville, the unglaciated hill country can be seen to the east from the high hills of the Marcy Moraine located about 5 miles east of that city. The country is rugged, with little mineral wealth. Its major asset at the time of settlement was the trees that covered the steep hillsides and narrow ravines. Now dominated by several species of oak, the forest once included the native American chestnut and, on some of the ridges, pitch pine. When cleared, the rocky hillsides of the area could barely grow enough crops for a family to eke out a living; so, in addition to cutting the virgin hardwood for lumber, the settlers distilled pine tar from the pitch pine. Pine tar was commonplace on the shelves of many 19th-century households. It was blended with grain alcohol and used as an expectorant or, in viscous form, as an antiseptic salve. It also served as a sticky lubricant for the wooden gears and axles of early implements. With the advent of petroleum distillates, pine tar fell into disuse. What probably was never a very lucrative enterprise died out, leaving only another place-name derived from a long-gone economic activity—in this case, Tar Hollow.

Tar Hollow is a special place for wildlife. Turkey, deer, squirrel, ruffed grouse, pileated woodpeckers, and many species of woodland songbirds abound. So do reptiles and amphibians like the northern copperhead and timber rattlesnake, though in far

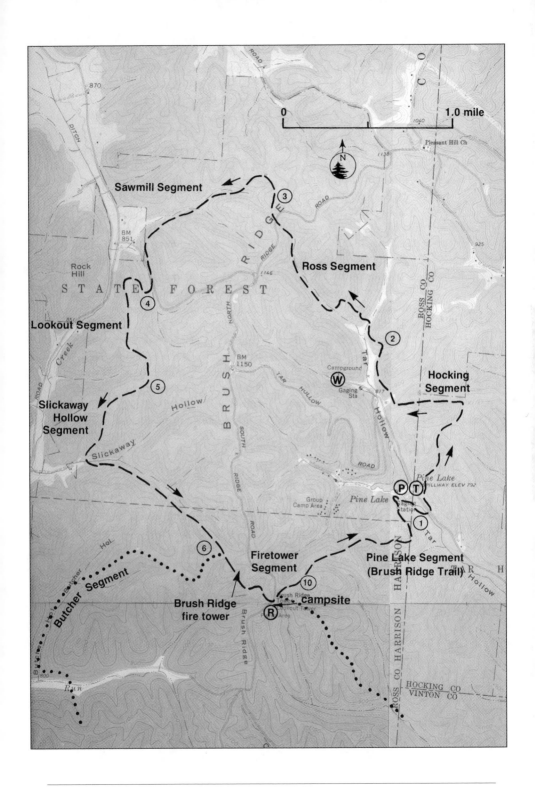

fewer numbers. The rattlesnake is listed as a threatened species in Ohio. The capture of reptiles is tightly regulated. Since all but the park area is open to public hunting, it is a good idea to avoid coming here during the week of deer gun season in the fall and turkey season in the spring. The wildflowers are beautiful during the last week of April and the first two weeks of May, and dozens of species of mushrooms can be seen after a rain during the warm months of the year. Tar Hollow should be visited often, for despite its size and nearness to the well-known Hocking Hills parks, it is not very heavily used. It deserves to be better known, for its excellent Logan Trail if nothing else.

Unlike many other parks in the region, the hiking trail at Tar Hollow owes its existence to neither the Civilian Conservation Corps nor the Department of Natural Resources. The present-day Logan Trail, with its north and south loops originating out of the park area, was developed and is maintained by Boy Scout Troop 195 of Columbus. Named for the famous Mingo Indian chief, the trail was originally opened in 1958, using park and forest roads. It was not popular with Scout units, however, who felt that in a state forest hiking should be on woodland trails. Completely shut down and carefully rerouted off roads and into the woods, the trail was reopened in 1965. I walked the trail with my Scout troop shortly after its reopening. Like most Scout trails, a badge is available to Scouts who complete the hike. Unit leaders can get more information about the trail from Roy Case, Logan Trail Treasurer, 643 Weyant Avenue, Columbus, OH 43213. He can also be reached by phone at 614-235-7026.

The hike described here utilizes only part of the 21-mile Logan Trail. Because of the rugged nature of the terrain, hiking the entire trail requires 15 or 16 hours of daylight. The Logan Trail is well marked. There are directional and checkpoint number signs on 4 x 4 posts at road crossings and other appropriate points along the trail. In some places, red metal arrows are nailed to trees. The trail is blazed with red paint, but because it is designed to be walked in one direction only, it is blazed only in the direction of the numbered checkpoints. If you do not see a blaze after 100 feet or so, retrace your steps, as you probably missed a turn. Although road crossings are minimal on this neatly laid-out trail, the few that there are allow you to walk shorter loop hikes utilizing the forest roads. The trail is divided into named segments between numbered checkpoints. Most of the checkpoints are at road crossings.

There is no potable water along the route, so you must carry a supply for the full trip or cache some at one or more of the checkpoints. Camping is not allowed along the trail. A primitive, pack-in camping area known as Camp N. A. Dulen, located about a mile south off the south loop of the trail, is available for Scout units only. Troops or posts planning to camp there must inform the park ranger in advance. There is a drive-in campground in the park for family camping by the general public and there is an area designated for group camping that can be used by groups before or after hiking the trail. Backpackers are permitted to camp at the fire tower area, but they must self-register at a registration box on the porch of the general store beyond the beach at the upper end of Pine Lake *before heading up the trail*. This is a matter of safety, so rangers can locate you in the event of an emergency.

How to Get There

Tar Hollow is reached from the Columbus area by traveling south on US 23 to Circleville, then east 28 miles on OH 56 to

50 Hikes in Ohio

The Tar Hollow State Park trading post sign

OH 180. There, turn right (south) and travel 0.7 mile to Adelphi. Next turn left (south) onto OH 327 and travel 7.5 miles to the park entrance on the right side of the road. The trip takes about 1.5 hours. From Cincinnati, take either US 50 or I-71 and US 35 to Chillicothe, then continue on US 50 east 12 miles to OH 327 at Londonderry. Take OH 327 left (north) 9 miles to the park entrance. From the Dayton area, use US 35 to reach Chillicothe and the route described for Cincinnati travelers. The parking lot for the trailhead is located about 1.2 miles inside the park, below the dam at Pine Lake. A sign at the entrance to the lot reads LOGAN TRAIL PARKING.

The Trail

All the signs along this trail have been made and put in place by volunteer Boy Scouts and/or their adult supervisors. They are not uniform in design and, since they are almost always near park or forest roads, they are subject to frequent vandalism. Paint blazes on trees are the most dependable indications that you're on the correct path. Do not attempt to walk this trail in reverse as the signs and blazes have been placed to be read in one direction only. When you reach a road crossing, the continuation of the trail is not always directly across. It may be a short way to the right or left and may not always be easily recognized. A sign may be missing. Be certain that you are on a red-blazed trail before proceeding.

The north loop trail begins on a hard-to-recognize gravel service road at the southeast corner of the parking lot, opposite the launching area near the dam. The trailhead sign is frequently missing, but the red blazes on the trees to the right of the trail indicate the correct route. Just before the trail reaches a small creek, there is supposed to be a CHECKPOINT 1 sign pointing left to the beginning of the Hocking Segment of the trail. It too is sometimes missing. In any event, the trail goes to the left before the service road reaches the creek crossing. Follow the trail along the streambank uphill to the park road. There is a large paint blaze on a tree here instead of a checkpoint sign, and perhaps a small sign across the road indicating the continuation of the trail. After crossing the road the trail climbs sharply, making a left turn through the pines. Beyond the pines, the trail enters deciduous forest as it drops to a creek crossing. It then turns right up a ravine, climbing smartly up the left slope. This difficult climb of over 300 feet to the ridge is just over .5 mile long and is the only such climb on the north loop.

After following the ridge for a short distance, the trail turns left to descend on the spine of a side ridge. A red arrow points right as the trail drops off the ridge and into a hollow, where it makes a T with another trail. The red-blazed trail turns right, then left across a stream, and then left again as it begins climbing the hillside. Partway up the slope, it levels off to follow the hillside above the group camping area driveway. At a fork in the trail it goes right, still in the woods above the campground. There are a number of "wild" trails in this area, so it is especially important to keep the red blazes in view. Turn right at another T, this one with a trail coming in from the campground. Eventually the trail drops to the valley to cross a small stream. The number on the tree here identifies Checkpoint 2, almost 2.5 miles from the start of the trail.

The 1.75-mile Ross Segment begins by climbing out of the streambed. The trail leads up the slope a short distance before turning to the left to round the end of a ridge. There are more wild trails here, used by hikers starting from the campground. Shortly thereafter the trail drops to the bottomland, goes straight across the streambed, and then heads uphill. It eventually levels off, turns left, and curves to the right around the end of a ridge. Drop into a small ravine to cross a side stream and cross another stream after 125 feet. At yet another T, the trail turns right to start a moderate climb up the valley to a crossing with the blacktopped North Ridge Road. The trail reenters the woods across the road, slightly to the left. Look for a red arrow on a tree along the road. The post announcing Checkpoint 3, where the trail turns to the right, is about 30 feet off the road.

Going north, the trail occasionally uses an old wagon road as it passes through a brushy area and then to the right of a small pond. Reentering the oak/hickory woods, the trail leaves the old road and turns left to begin dropping into a hollow. Now headed in a westerly direction, it moves back and forth across the streambed and up and down the valley wall, then passes near an old dump and a rotting slab pile. Moving down the hollow, the trail hugs the left slope as it approaches Swamp Hill Road (Forest Road 16). Instead of dropping to the road as it draws near, the trail swings left around the hillside to parallel it for several hundred yards before turning toward it. This approach detours around a private inholding at the mouth of the valley and keeps the trail on state-owned land. Just across the road is Checkpoint 4, the end of the 2-mile Sawmill Segment.

After reentering the woods the trail crosses a stream, then turns right, angling up the slope on what may have once been a logging skid. At an easily missed left turn, the trail begins its steepest climb. Fortunately the climb is short, and at the top there is a nice grassy spot under oaks that begs to be used for a respite. For the next mile the trail follows the ridge in heavy forest.

➤ The American Discovery Trail in Ohio

If you are out and about on the trails of southern Ohio sooner or later you will see a slightly bulging triangular sign that reads AMERICAN DISCOVERY TRAIL (ADT) on a tree or a post. From the beginning, the creation of the ADT was a grassroots volunteer venture. Like the Appalachian Trail, the Buckeye Trail, and the North Country Trail, the ADT is a work in progress. Its 6,300-mile route passes through 15 states. It leads to 14 national parks and 16 national forests and visits more than 10,000 sites of historic, cultural, and natural significance along the way. Tens of thousands of hours of volunteer effort have gone into its making and thousands of folks "under their own steam" have traveled sections of it in forest, field, mountain, and prairie across this great land. The 11 sections of the ADT in Ohio cover 511 miles, using public lands and private lands with landowner permission. It enters the state from the east at Belpre. Before leaving Ohio for good, a southern route crosses into Kentucky via the Roebling suspension bridge to allow exploration of sites in the Covington area. It returns to Ohio by way of historic Anderson Ferry then, after passing the tomb of President William Henry Harrison, enters Indiana on State Line Road near Elizabethtown. The Northern Midwest Route of the ADT also enters Indiana on State Line Road, but east of Richmond. On its last gasps in the Buckeye State it passes Miami Whitewater MetroPark, through Governor Bebb Park, Hueston Woods Park and State Nature Preserve, and Indian Creek Preserve, and finally passes through Harshman Covered Bridge.

On the hikes detailed in this book, you will tread on the ADT on the Archers Fork Trail in the Wayne National Forest, on the Gorge Trail at Fort Hill State Memorial, at Tar Hollow State Forest, at Hocking State Park, at Shawnee State Forest, at East Fork State Park, and at Hueston Woods State Nature Preserve, and you will come within a whisker of it at Wildcat Hollow in the Wayne National Forest. When you see the red, white, and blue symbol on post or tree, it's an invitation to explore beyond state boundaries on a trail like the one on which you're walking, built by hands like yours and mine for those of us who want to explore the world using what my mother used to call "shank's mares."

Turning left onto an old wagon road, it shortly reaches Checkpoint 5, where a sign on the right indicates a right turn off the old road. Here ends the appropriately named 1.5-mile Lookout Segment. Next, the trail follows the ridge for another .5 mile then begins a steep descent into Slickaway Hollow. There are no switchbacks, and the trail is badly eroded and quite rocky in places. Exercise due caution. At the bottom, the trail crosses the hollow and turns to the left to begin a mile-long climb back to the ridge.

The trail crosses the stream several times and occasionally follows an old road that once came all the way up the valley. Toward the head of the ravine the trail follows a fork to the left, hugging the right slope as it makes a gentle climb. Just before reaching the ridgetop and the edge of the woods, the trail hits a T. A sign identifies Checkpoint 6, the junction with the south loop, which goes to the left. The trail to the right goes to the fire tower area and the continuation of your north loop hike. A sign also points to the right to Camp Dulen for Scouts, who are now about 5 miles away from that overnight spot. The Slickaway Hollow Segment has covered 2.3 miles.

At this point you have traveled a total of 10 miles. Another 2 miles of easy hiking will complete the north loop. Proceed via a left turn at the T. The trail climbs a few feet and emerges from the woods onto a logging road, which takes you to the left. Shortly up the logging road, your red-blazed trail exits to the right. It goes down and around the head of a ravine, then up and over a knob. After you cross a stream, you climb steeply and then more gently to the Brush Ridge fire tower. The trail emerges onto Forest Road 3 (South Ridge Road) directly west of the tower. This is the end of the .5-mile Firetower Segment. The "official" trail through the woods can be bypassed for a slightly longer but less rugged route by continuing on the logging road until you reach pavement, where you turn right to the fire tower.

Checkpoint 10, the beginning of the Pine Lake Segment, is identified by a red-topped 4 x 4 post, but this sign is also subject to frequent vandalism and is not always there. Normally it is to the left of the fire tower across the gravel loop driveway. There is also a forestry sign there identifying the trail as the 1.5-mile Brush Ridge Trail, which the Logan Trail uses to complete the loop.

Here the Logan Trail comes close to the Buckeye Trail (BT), which passes through the area both on and off the road. The entrance to a short, white-blazed connecting trail is marked by a round post near where the fire tower loop drive meets the paved road just south of the tower. About 100 feet beyond the post, there is a T where the blue-blazed BT leaves the Logan Trail, going to the right. The Brush Ridge Trail is easy and well defined. It is probably the most used trail in the park/forest, since many day-hikers travel it between Pine Lake and the fire tower.

After rounding the head of a ravine, the trail rises gently to go out to a ridge. After .25 mile, there is a fork. The left branch goes to a resident camping facility in the valley below. The Logan Trail continues on the right fork, where it rises gently to and over a 1,100-foot knob before starting its descent to the Pine Lake area. Near the bottom of the hill it crosses a power-line right-of-way. Beyond is the Brush Ridge Trail sign pointing back the way you came. The red-blazed Logan Trail continues along the hillside past another sign that announces the end of the trail and the location of the trailhead. Yet another sign points back up the trail to the BT, 1.5 miles away. The trail comes out at dam level and follows the spillway downhill, which it then crosses on a bridge. The trail ends on the mowed lawn of the earthen dam within sight of the Pine Lake parking lot, where there are rest rooms and a shelter house. Having sampled the rugged terrain and the solitude of Tar Hollow State Park and Forest on the north loop of the Logan Trail, you will want to plan for another day, perhaps in another season, in the area. Before you leave, pick up a state park and/or state forest brochure with information about other hiking and camping facilities in this 18,026-acre public area.

27

Wayne National Forest (Archers Fork Trail)

Total distance: 9.5 miles (15.2 km)

Hiking time: 7 hours (day hike) to 2 days (backpack trip)

Maximum elevation: 1,125 feet

Vertical rise: 375 feet

Maps: USGS 7½' Rinard Mills, OH, and Raven Rock, WV; USFS Wayne National Forest hiking and backpacking trails map

On a warm spring morning I made the long drive from my home in the Columbus area to eastern Washington County to walk my last unwalked section of the Archers Fork Trail. The hike could not have been nicer. Though the trees were still bare, spring peepers were calling, mourning cloak butterflies (which overwinter as adults) were on the wing, and a dozen wild turkeys crossed the trail about 75 feet in front of me. I saw not another soul the entire time I was in the forest. It was a wonderful wilderness retreat for me. I returned to Columbus late in the evening, buoyant after my walk on this forest path. As in other Wayne National Forest areas, I could have camped overnight along the trail if I so chose.

The Archers Fork Trail is a loop trail in an Appalachian oak forest area of southeastern Ohio. Along the route there is a beautiful natural rock arch, many rock shelters, early oil-pumping rigs, and lots of tall timber. The North Country Trail (NCT) uses part of the Archers Fork Trail as it crosses the state; there are connecting trails to the Ohio View Trail to the east and the Covered Bridge Trail to the west should you want to make an extended backpacking trek.

How to Get There

To reach an Archers Fork trailhead—there are two other parking sites—travel east from Cambridge on I-70 to Exit 202 (OH 800). Turn south on OH 800 and follow it through Barnesville and Woodsfield to its intersection with OH 26. Go south on OH 26 to the OH 260 intersection. Turn east and drive

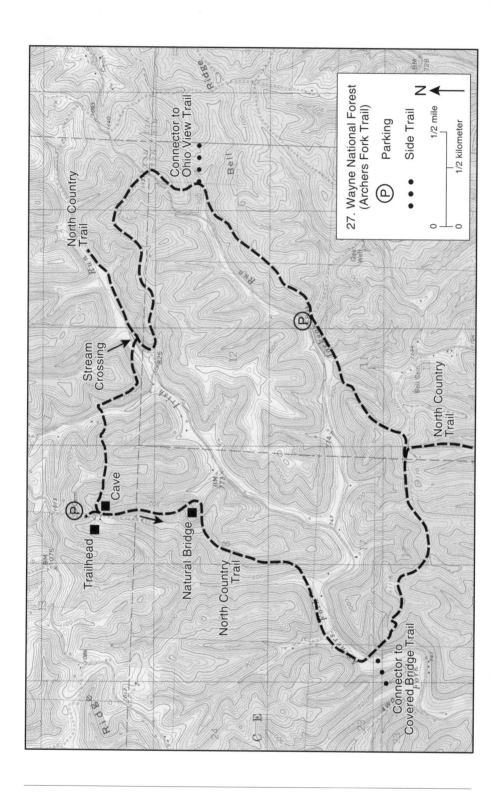

27. Wayne National Forest
(Archers Fork Trail)

Ⓟ Parking

• • • Side Trail

N ←

0 ————— 1/2 mile

0 ————— 1/2 kilometer

Connector to
Ohio View Trail

North Country
Trail

Stream
Crossing

Cave

Ⓟ Trailhead

Natural Bridge

North Country
Trail

North Country
Trail

Connector to
Covered Bridge Trail

approximately 4 miles to Hohman Ridge Road (Township Road 34). The road goes to the right just as OH 260 turns sharply left, so it is easy to miss. Turn right (south) and follow this gravel road 1.3 miles until you see a NORTH COUNTRY TRAIL PARKING sign on the left side of the road. Enter here and drive past the front of St. Patrick's Cemetery to the parking area. A sign directs you down an abandoned road to where you pick up the Archers Fork and North Country Trails. If you started in the Columbus area, you will have driven about 165 miles.

The Trail

The trail begins just a few hundred feet due south from the parking lot. Blue diamonds with arrows on them indicate you are headed toward the NCT. The combined NCT/Archers Fork Trail will come in from the left and continue straight ahead and will be blazed with two different signs: a white diamond with a blue disk for the Archers Fork Trail, and a solid blue diamond for the NCT.

Archers Fork is the name of the principal stream that drains this area, along with two small tributaries, Irish Run and Jackson Run. Archers Fork empties into the Little Muskingum River and thence to the Ohio. It is also the name of a small community downstream, a little over a mile from where the trail crosses the stream.

The bedrock nearest the surface in this part of Ohio is Permian, the youngest in the state, thought to date from 280 million years ago. As you walk the rutty old road toward the trail, the fine-grained Permian sandstone is visible underfoot and the cliffs and rock shelters of the area are of this same stone. The presence of oil in the deeper bedrock of the area is indicated by the number of wells you will pass along these trails, including one to the right as you walk toward the juncture of the trails.

Turn left at a sign on a tree on the left side of the old road that reads HIKER. Just down the trail is the corner where the combined trails go both east and south. There is a sizable cave (really a rock shelter) located near here. To visit it, walk east across the dip in the trail and scramble down the east side of the ravine. The cave is virtually under the trail you just traveled.

You can, of course, hike either direction on the Archers Fork Loop Trail. Since the day I was walking was "cloudy-bright," a good day for taking photographs without hard shadows, I wanted to get to the natural bridge. So I began walking south, counterclockwise on the loop. The trail travels at a fairly constant elevation on the hillside above the ravine for .75 mile before rising to the right, then turning left to where a sign says BRIDGE. There is an open area along the trail just prior to the bridge that would make a good campsite. The natural bridge, or arch, is up against the hillside, and it takes a bit of scrambling to get into position to take a picture. (Though the forest service map calls it a natural bridge, most geologists save that term for a feature that water flows under, or has in the past. The preferred term for a structure such as this one is "arch.") This one has been called by two names: Irish Run Natural Bridge and Independence Arch. Take your choice. When the forest service map was created, the authors knew of only four natural bridges in Ohio. Since then, Tim Snyder, formerly of the Ohio Division of Natural Areas and Preserves, has scoured the countryside for such features. He now has a list of 63 confirmed locations of arches and natural bridges, and he is still looking.

The forest is not what anyone would call old growth, the area having been logged many times since settlement. Nevertheless, it has been more than half a century since it

The Archers Fork Trail crosses this large natural arch not far from the trailhead

was last clear-cut, and it provides a nice environment for walking. Beyond the arch, the trail turns west and rises more than 100 feet before crossing a hilltop, making a downhill arc to the right, and then crossing the ridge to begin its descent to Archers Fork. Over the next .5 mile the trail drops about 300 feet on a path that angles gently down the hillside. After crossing a small side stream, the trail stays above the valley floor on the right side of Archers Fork for another .25 mile before crossing an old farm lane, then dropping to the floodplain. This bottomland is subject to periodic flooding, which sometimes leaves debris or washes out a bit of the trail. There is a trail junction here where a connecting spur goes to the right toward the Covered Bridge Trail along the Little Muskingum River.

Continuing this hike requires fording the stream (many township roads of the area do that, too) before leaving the floodplain to cross Township Road 14 and heading on a

right oblique up the hillside. The rise over the next .3 mile is from the 740-foot elevation of the road to 1,100 feet. An uninterrupted climb of short steps with a slow pace brings you alongside a small old hilltop field. From there, the trail heads southeast to drop into a saddle, then rises again to the same elevation before turning east to follow a winding ridge for .5 mile and passing another 1,100-foot knob. This is the country of ancient oil wells and pipelines. Lots of Ohio crude oil from this Washington County well field helped fuel an oil-hungry nation before low prices for foreign oil made further development here uneconomical, although it never gushed from Ohio wells as it did from wells in the American Southwest or the Middle East. Some oil is still pumped from the area, but not nearly as much as in the past. (The Macksburg oil and gas field, one of the earliest in the nation, was in the northwestern corner of county.)

After about a mile of ridgetop travel on an old well service road, the trail reaches a junction where the NCT goes straight ahead and the Archers Fork Trail heads through a gap between two hills to the left. Follow the white diamonds with blue dots as the trail arcs right and begins its slow descent toward the 800-foot elevation of the valley of Archers Fork. Once in the valley, the trail stays a couple of hundred feet back from the road, crossing first one stream, then another. It is at this second side stream's valley that a gas-well road connects the trail to a forest service parking lot along Township Road 14. This is a grassy parking area cut in among young trees and, unlike the other two parking lots, has no sign. If you want to make an overnight trip using camping gear that you don't want to carry, this might be a good place to cache your supplies. However, during hunting seasons, especially those for turkey and deer, there will likely be hunters in pickup-truck campers parked here.

Beyond this access point the trail heads northeast and makes a steep climb, gaining 300 feet in .5 mile. After reaching the 1,100-foot level it hangs on the hillside to drop gently, and then more steeply, to the upper reaches of Jackson Run. (Another connector trail exits the loop, headed right (east) to carry you to the Ohio View Trail.) From here it is a short climb on the Archers Fork Trail to reach a nearly flat section of trail and the crossing of TR 14. The third forest service parking area that serves this trail is but a couple of hundred feet up the road to the right (east). Continue hiking by climbing the steps across the road and following the trail through the woods. It soon joins a wide old service road to head northwest, rising and falling along a ridge for less than .5 mile. The trail crosses gas lines that may confuse you—watch for the blazes. This is

➤ The Wayne National Forest

The Wayne National Forest has its roots in the Weeks Law of 1911, which allowed the federal government, with the concurrence of state legislatures, to purchase land to create national forests. Ohio approved such action in November 1934, and between 1935 and 1942 approximately 77,000 acres were acquired in the five purchase units in southeastern Ohio. During the 1930s the Civilian Conservation Corps planted trees, halted erosion, and built much of the infrastructure of what, in 1951, officially became the Wayne National Forest. In 1983 it was targeted for disposal, but strong public reaction saved it. In the late 1980s and early 1990s, the Wayne (as it is generally referred to) received strong support from Congress and Ohio's citizens.

Though scaled back in the number of purchase units, the forest service has worked hard to consolidate its holdings and reduce the checkerboard pattern of ownership. As of the last accounting, it comprised 237,529 acres in twelve Ohio counties. There has been a steady increase in the number and mileage of high-quality hiking trails in the Wayne during the past decade, to the benefit of those of us who enjoy the deep woods of southeastern Ohio's hill country.

where I saw the 12 wild turkeys I mentioned above. Just beyond a point where the trail stays on high ground and the road (or gas line) that the trail was following falls off the left side, the old road turns left and the trail goes a short distance straight ahead. Where the gas line/road heads steeply downhill ahead, the trail ducks through a hole in the woods to the left to stay on high ground. This is an easy turn to miss. Again, look for the blazes. The trail then begins to drop off the point of the ridge, soon catching an old logging skid to head down a valley to Irish Run. There are very picturesque small rock shelters above the trail here and a wonderful carpet of moss underfoot. One of these rock shelters would surely protect a lone hiker from a sudden thundershower and might even provide cover for a night's sleep.

The trail reaches the road and although the NCT map makes it appear to go directly across, it does not. Turn right and go the length of a football field, then look for a trail dropping off the left side of the road. On the floodplain next to the creek there is a sign marking another juncture with the NCT, which goes to the right back up onto the road to head northeast, then north, eventually crossing OH 260 a couple of miles to the east of Hohman Ridge Road. The Archers Fork Trail, combined once again with the NCT, heads across the creek. Be prepared to wade.

The trail is now about a mile from closing the loop. After crossing the creek, it heads uphill about 150 feet, curving left to follow the hillside. Next it drops gently down to cross Township Road 40. There are wonderful tall trees up this valley, and the forest service has considered designating this a Special Interest Area. Across the road, the trail drops down to ford a small unnamed headwater creek of Irish Run. Heading up a small ravine, the trail curves right, then left to head almost due west toward the cave and the service road to the parking lot at St. Patrick's Cemetery. May the luck of the Irish, who pioneered this area many years ago, travel with you on the trail and your years of hiking be many.

28

Wayne National Forest (Lamping Homestead Trail)

Total distance: 5 miles (8 km)

Hiking time: 4 hours

Maximum elevation: 1,010 feet

Vertical rise: 290 feet

Maps: USGS 7½' Graysville and Rinard Mills; USFS Wayne National Forest hiking and backpacking trails map

It is hard to say why the Lamping family chose to settle in the valley between Pleasant and Haney Ridges near the Clear Fork of the Little Muskingum River, but they did. As far as we know, they were the first to put down roots and build a cabin on the land this trail traverses. The land had been part of the first seven ranges surveyed in 1786 in what was to become Ohio in 1803. Though initially part of Washington County, in 1813 it became part of Monroe County. There was a land office to file patents on unclaimed land as close as Marietta. During those first two decades of the 19th century, a steady flow of Americans, mostly from the Mid-Atlantic states, headed to Ohio, Indiana, and Illinois. In 1816, on just one turnpike in Pennsylvania, 16,000 wagons rolled past a tollbooth on their way west, carrying families eager to carve new homes from the wilderness. Even so, by 1840 there were only 533 people living in Washington Township, where the Lampings had settled. One of my great, great, great-grandfathers, Thomas Farson, an Irishman, settled only a few miles to the west of here in the 1820s in what was then Washington County.

No one seems to know where the Lampings came from—or, for that matter, where they went when they left here—but they did not stay long. We will never know why they left, but perhaps the graves in the Lamping Cemetery, located on a knoll along this trail a couple of hundred yards from the site of their home, might provide a clue. At least two young Lamping children are buried there, victims of who knows what

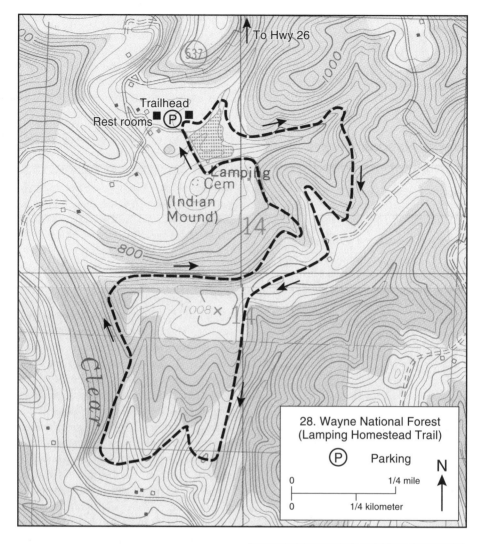

To Hwy 26

Trailhead
Rest rooms
Lamping Cem
(Indian Mound)

28. Wayne National Forest
(Lamping Homestead Trail)

Ⓟ   Parking

N

0   1/4 mile

0   1/4 kilometer

sort of malady. In moving on, the Lampings would not be the first family, nor the last, to uproot themselves to leave behind sad times. In any case, the house and barn of what more than 100 years ago had been the Lamping homestead were removed when the forest service acquired the land in 1971. Over the next two years, the Youth Conservation Corps aided the forest service in developing the Lamping Homestead Recreation Area on the shore of a new lake.

How to Get There

The Lamping Homestead Recreation Area can be reached by driving east from Cambridge on I-70 to Exit 202 (OH 800). Turn south on OH 800 through Barnesville and Woodsfield to its intersection with OH 26. Turn south again on OH 26. One mile beyond Graysville, turn west on winding OH 537 and follow it about 1.5 miles to Township Road 307. Turn left onto this

The Lamping Homestead Trail

gravel road, and then almost immediately left again into the parking lot. There are picnic shelters and rest rooms overlooking Kenton Lake and several lakeside campsites are available. As with other forest service land in Ohio, you can camp along the trail after you get away from the developed recreation area.

The Trail

The Lamping Homestead Trail is well marked with white diamond-shaped plastic blazes nailed on trees and fence posts. It is a loop trail and the blazes for outbound and inbound routes are visible from the lawn between the dry hydrant and the lake. Before I began hiking on a warm August day, I took my camera and a 100 mm macro lens and walked along the expansive patches of joe-pye weed, milkweed, and ironweed, taking pictures of tiger swallowtails, red-spotted purples, and other scale-winged beauties

sucking up nectar with their proboscises.

To begin walking, head to the left of the lake through the pines that shade picnickers. There is a white diamond with a hiker on it and another with an arrow pointing toward the trail. At the far end of the picnic area the trail passes more pines, these planted too close together for good growth. The trail turns left to cross a bridge over one of the very small tributaries of the Clear Fork of the Little Muskingum River that was dammed to create the lake. Beyond the bridge the trail goes around the lake past more pines, then makes a left oblique turn to climb the hillside and head up the other headwater valley. Leaving pines behind, it hangs on the side of the hill as it enters a stand of young hardwoods and follows the creek upstream. It then continues around the hillside clockwise before climbing the hill at an oblique angle headed almost due south. After .5 mile or so of travel, the trail reaches 1,000 feet in elevation and the edge of the forest service land. When it reaches an old road, it makes a right turn ,then a second right to travel gently downhill before nearly reversing itself to head south-southeast back to the same old road. Just before reaching that road, there is a very short side trail to the right that goes due west to connect with the return route of the trail, allowing for a 1.2-mile loop hike.

Unless you need to cut your hike short, ignore the crossover trail and continue on the main Lamping Homestead Trail, keeping watch for the white-diamond trail markers. A hundred or so feet beyond the cutoff the main trail turns to the right, heading due southwest out and over a ridge at the 1,100-foot level. Turning now to the south, the trail has left the Lamping Homestead Lake watershed behind. From an overlook, you see the steep-sloped valley with drainage directly into the Clear Fork of the Little Muskingum River. Now heading just a bit west of straight south, the trail drops nearly 200 feet in the course of .3 mile. Next, it turns to the right to drop again in and out of the heads of two small ravines prior to circling right around the end of a promontory to begin its return trip to the homestead area. Traveling the hillside to the north, the trail gains 120 feet in 0.4 mile. Turning right (east), it follows a nearly level path for 0.5 mile before turning north, then east to its junction with the crossover trail.

At one point, you are in a really nice Appalachian oak woods, much like it might have been when the Lampings roamed these parts. After meeting up with the short-loop crossover trail, the main white-diamond-blazed trail turns northwest and begins its descent to the floodplain below the dam. The trail's gradient is about as steep as you can comfortably walk on. Now back in boneset, ironweed, and wing-stem country, the trail emerges from weeds and woods at the east end of the dam. As you walk along the dam toward the picnic area, watch for the path that leads to the left up-hill to the Lamping Cemetery. Inside a van-dalized iron fence are the badly weathered, moss-covered tombstones of the Lamping children, who did not survive the harsh real-ity of the Ohio frontier. It is a short walk from there back to the parking area. Before you depart from this early homestead site, try to imagine the hardships suffered by those who came into this country nearly 200 years ago to carve from the wilderness the civi-lization we are enjoying in this new century. We owe a great debt to all those who lie be-neath the decayed wooden crosses in the unknown family burying grounds of Ohio's hill country.

29

Wayne National Forest (Morgan Sisters Trail)

Total distance: 2, 4, or 8 miles (3.2, 6.4, or 12.8 km)

Hiking time: 1.5, 3, or 6 hours

Maximum elevation: 934 feet

Vertical rise: 294 feet

Maps: USGS 7½' Patriot; USFS Wayne National Forest hiking and backpacking trails map

The Morgan Sisters Trails are a real joy to walk. They pass pine plantings, spectacular tall native hardwoods, floodplain forests, and open fields. It is a challenge to read the landscape to determine what occurred on the land before it became national forest. You can take a short, medium, or long loop hike to end back at your vehicle. Best of all, this is a remote wilderness area with no airport flight patterns overhead or interstate highways within earshot. You can lay out your bivy sack or pitch your tent wherever you wish, as long as you leave no imprint upon the land. Where can you go wrong?

The trail for this hike is, as you might speculate, named for a pair of spinsters named Morgan who lived for many years near the end of Morgan Sisters Road, close to the center of the trail.

How to Get There

Located near the northern boundary of Gallia County, the Morgan Sisters trailhead can be reached by taking US 35 east from Chillicothe past Jackson to the Rio Grande exit. Continue south on OH 325 to OH 141, then west to OH 233. About 3 miles past that last intersection, where OH 233 makes a hard left turn, Pumpkintown Road (County Road 25) goes to the right (north). One mile up this road, a drive leaving to the right leads to Kenton Lake and a parking area for the Morgan Sisters Trail System. The distance from Columbus is about 120 miles.

This is the place to park if you plan to walk the Coal Branch Loop, that loop plus

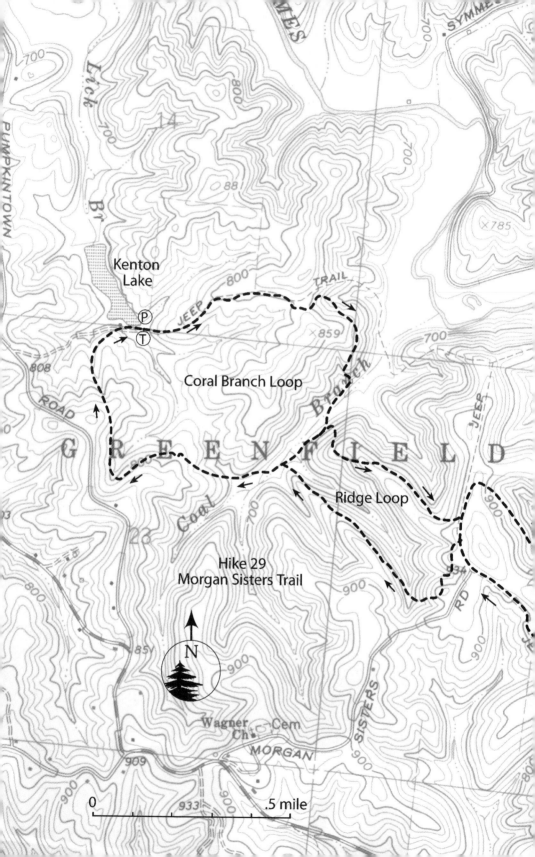

Kenton
Lake

P
T

JEEP

TRAIL

×859

Coral Branch Loop

Coral Branch

G R E E N F I E L D

Coal Branch

Ridge Loop

JEEP

×834

RD

Hike 29
Morgan Sisters Trail

N

Wagner
Ch
Cem

MORGAN

SISTERS

0   .5 mile

Hike 30
Symmes Creek Trail

Connector

Schoolhouse Loop

the Ridge Loop, or the entire trail including the Schoolhouse Loop. There is another spot where I have parked a number of times to access the Schoolhouse and Ridge Loops. This is at the end of Morgan Sisters Road, which runs north from OH 233, not quite 1 mile east of Pumpkintown Road. These are remote parking areas so drive your oldest vehicle and don't leave anything of value in it.

The Trail

The driveway to the Kenton Lake trailhead is fairly steep; it can be muddy, deeply rutted, and somewhat treacherous to drive during and after prolonged bad weather. Take it easy as you enter. Park at the far end of the drive to the left of the old road (to the right of the parking area), where the trail begins. The trailhead is clearly marked. The blazing for this trail is the forest service's white diamond with a yellow disk attached, but many of the yellow disks have fallen off. Whoever nailed them up drove the nails all the way in and as the trees grew, the disks, and in some cases the diamonds, popped off.

From the trailhead it is a steady but reasonable climb up what the topo map calls a jeep trail. As the trail reaches the ridge, it swings to the left and a blaze warns of a turn ahead. Do not turn too soon. After a hard right leaving the jeep trail, it is easy to be fooled into believing that the trail climbs uphill through the grass and among the pines. It does not. One diamond is visible from the turn. Go to it, then look beyond and to the left for a hole in the edge of the woods where the trail enters. Once inside the young forest, look down the trail to find the next blaze. If you see one nailed to a tree, you are on the trail. There are lots of brambles and greenbriers along your way in this Appalachian oak forest. The trail follows around the side of the hill at about the same

elevation for a few hundred yards; then, as it passes some exposed sandstone, it drops to Coal Branch. The slope is gentle at first but steep toward the bottom. Along much of this hillside trail the route is not well defined; it is a good idea to spot the next blaze each time one is passed.

On the floodplain of Coal Branch, the herbaceous growth sometimes falls over the trail by the end of the summer, again requiring careful sighting of the next blaze. Eventually the trail works its way to the bank of Coal Branch, where it is necessary to wade or step across the water. Once across the stream, the trail turns to the right (southwest) and moves along the creek for several hundred yards. Very shortly you will pass the junction with the Ridge Loop. It goes to the left straight up the end of a hill. The option to take it is yours; the Ridge Loop will add less than 2 miles to your hike.

There is a nearly pure stand of tuliptrees along the Coal Branch Loop here. If you continue on that loop, the trail will pass the open end of a valley and cross a very small side stream and the end of the ridge before reaching the other side of the Ridge Loop. It goes to the left up an old township or logging road. Again, the option is yours. On the Coal Branch Loop, the trail crosses another small creek and then passes a nice stand of treelike club moss, the second species of club moss seen along this trail. Blazes are a bit scarce or hard to see here, but after a short distance the trail crosses Coal Branch at a sandbar, making the crossing easier. On the other side of the stream the trail goes to the left, where it begins climbing along an old logging skid, but soon it gets out of the gully and goes right up the spine of the ridge for a ways before returning to a shallower skid.

Where the logging trail appears to head toward Pumpkintown Road, the trail leaves

Kenton Lake

it to the right to hang on the hillside, passing groves of white pines. It crosses the head of a small gully and soon passes a diamond with an arrow pointing to the right, indicating a sharp right turn ahead. Beyond the turn, the road arcs to the left and soon goes down the hillside through a beautiful stand of white pine trees. This would be my choice of locations to camp along this trail. Remember to follow the blazes carefully so you don't miss the trail's drop to a streambed to the right. It will be but a minute before the trail reaches the driveway to Kenton Lake and the short walk to the parking lot.

The forest in the valley between the two arms of the Ridge Loop is among the nicest in southeastern Ohio. It is a Forest Service Special Interest Area and a candidate for recognition as an outstanding old-growth forest. The trail along the northeast side runs right up the hill from Coal Branch, sometimes hanging onto the hillside, but usually staying right along the ridge. Eventually it intersects with an old road or jeep trail that carries on toward the Schoolhouse Loop, the longest of the three loops. To include the Schoolhouse Loop in a hike, turn left. To complete the Ridge Loop, turn right and travel the combined trails for a very short distance, watching for an exit to the right. It is marked with a white diamond (the yellow disk has disappeared). The trail begins to go downhill as soon as it leaves the road. It then skirts around the upper end of a hollow, working its way to the ridge on the southwestern side. The blazes are difficult to find, but if you head for the ridge and then follow it downhill you should be on the trail. Part of the way it utilizes an old logging skid as it travels in a nearly straight line to its intersection with the Ridge Loop. Once at the bottom, turn left to head to the white pine woods and Kenton Lake, or right to complete the Ridge Loop or to go to Kenton Lake via the other side of the Coal Branch Loop.

The Schoolhouse Loop can be accessed by foot from Lake Kenton via the Coal Branch and Ridge Loops, by vehicle from a parking lot at the end of Morgan Sisters Road (it crosses the end of the road), or by foot on a connecting trail from the Symmes Creek Trail.

From the end of Morgan Sisters Road, or from either intersection of the Ridge Trail with the Schoolhouse Loop, head north on the old township road, following the white diamonds (often without yellow disks) until you see an arrow pointing to the right. The trail heads uphill at an angle to the left, reaching the top of the ridge after a couple of hundred feet. It then starts its downhill trend through a valley filled with hardwood forest. The blazes are far apart, but the last time I hiked it pieces of red engineering tape that were tied to trees when the trail was laid out were still visible, helping you follow the intended route. It will be almost a mile of hiking—over several ravines and creeks, over one ridge, and around a knob—before the trail reaches the floodplain and an intersection with the connector to the Symmes Creek Trail. Sometimes the trail uses what looks like the logging skids of the last timber harvest; other times it uses new trail whose tread is not too obvious. The connector trail—identified as such on a Carsonite post—goes straight ahead toward Symmes Creek Road, a distance of about .3 mile.

To connect with the 6-mile Symmes Creek Trail (another loop), turn right on the road; soon after crossing the creek on a bridge, follow the connector trail that exits the road on the left (north) and climbs to a trail junction. The Symmes Creek Trail is blazed with white diamonds with red dots, but many of the latter are missing as well. If you choose to add the Symmes Creek Trail to the Morgan Sisters Trail hike, you will walk 14 miles (22.4 km).

At the junction with the connector, the Schoolhouse Loop Trail turns right to cross two bridges; then it turns left across another short bridge and begins climbing on a narrow "goat trail" that hugs the hillside above a sandstone cliff. Mosses, lichens, club mosses, mountain laurel, and rattlesnake plantain are but a few of the plants that greet you on this sandstone-boulder-strewn hillside. The trail soon returns to the floodplain at a location where early maps show a road once forded Symmes Creek. In late winter, this broad floodplain is a breeding spot for hundreds of spring peepers and mountain chorus frogs. The trail turns left on the old roadbed, now carpeted with moss. After a rise of 160 feet, it reaches a grassy area about an acre in size in a col. To the left are the ruins of a building, its stone fireplace and chimney still standing. It is difficult to tell what the structure was built of, but brick was used in what looks like a wall around the building. Perhaps this is the schoolhouse of Schoolhouse Ridge, but I could find no symbol for a flag-bearing structure on this ridge on either the 7.5' or 15' quadrangle map of the area.

It is difficult to find any blazes or a well-defined pathway in this opening, but the trail goes to the right past the ruins of another building and onto another old road at the base of the hillside. Just beyond the building, the trail turns up the hill to the right from the road to pass through an opening in the thicket and reach another roadbed. This would be an easy turn to miss. From here, the trail follows the old track around the hillside for perhaps .5 mile, at first with the hill on the right. After the trail passes through a

➤ The Land Speaks

Reading the landscape along the trail becomes a game, in a way (and it's much more exciting than reading license plates along the highway!). You assemble various clues in your mind on the basis of what intuitive knowledge you possess or what you have learned from printed material or other sources. Then, as you walk along the trail, you try to unravel the mystery of what took place on the land in years gone by. It may be the natural history or the cultural history that you are trying to understand, or both. The process is essentially the same for either.

For example, from its size or shape, you can usually identify a crumbling structure that was once a one-room schoolhouse. If there is no building, but an old map indicates that a schoolhouse once stood in the vicinity, you may identify the site by finding a rusty pump, the remains of privies, non-native plants such as jonquils growing in the woods, or old trees that look as if they once stood in the open. You can

bet that a homestead once stood along a long-abandoned road where lilacs, daffodils, and daylilies still persist.

Roads that 100 years ago were the routes of shortline railroads are easily detected by their gentle grades and sweeping curves (and sometimes their names— Wally Road, for instance, which was once the route of the Walhonding Railroad southeast of Loudonville). In southeastern Ohio, the presence of a foundation made of hand-cut sandstone blocks (limestone in the western half of the state) under a steel bridge often means that a covered wooden span once stood there. Tall red-cedar trees with dying crowns growing just below the canopy in a hardwood forest are a good indicator that the area was once a field or pasture, and that limestone or dolomite bedrock is close to the surface. After being abandoned, old fields progress to cedar thickets before serving as nurseries for hardwood species that eventually overtop the cedars. See how many stories you can read in the land around you.

---

saddle, the higher elevation—an 800-foot knob—is to the left.

Until World War II, there were lots of cabins, shacks, and shanties up these valleys and on the ridges, but they are nearly all gone now. When young soldiers and sailors came home from the war, most were not content to return to this land. They moved to the cities to work in factories, drive trucks, and, in some cases, use the GI Bill for a college education. When they could, they moved the old folks left behind to better homes. The houses fell in, the roads were closed, and nature reclaimed the small pastures, corn and potato fields,

and gardens. In the last 15 years, the forest service has been aggressively acquiring land to consolidate its holdings into large blocks of solid ownership. From this point on the trail, only one farmhouse is visible, far in the distance.

There are a few pines and an occasional red-cedar along this ridge, and at one point there is a great bed of myrtle on the forest floor indicating that there probably was once a dwelling, church, or cemetery nearby. The hardwoods are mixed, with some nice tall tuliptrees among the oaks; in places, there are stands of scrub pine. At a white triangle with an arrow pointing right,

---

the trail turns right onto the abandoned Bethel Road. One-half mile to the left the road is still open to the Bethel Cemetery and the abandoned Bethel Church.

Along the trail there is an open area of grass under large trees where daffodils bloom in the spring. This area seems likely to be the site of the schoolhouse that gives the loop trail its name. Can you imagine trudging along this road on foot or in a horse-drawn sleigh headed for school on a dark, cold winter morning?

Beyond here the old road appears to hook left off the hill, with jeep trails going straight ahead and slightly to the right. The trail follows the right fork. Along here, the forest is of very poor quality, with lots of greenbrier beneath it. The trail emerges from the woods to pass a meadow on the left and then reach the end of Morgan Sisters Road. If your vehicle is at Kenton Lake, head right on the abandoned road to take either leg of the Ridge Loop and the Coal Branch Loop.

30

Wayne National Forest (Symmes Creek Trail)

Total distance: 6 miles (10 km)

Hiking time: 4.5 hours

Maximum elevation: 883 feet

Vertical rise: 247 feet

Maps: USGS 7½' Patriot; USFS Wayne National Forest hiking and backpacking trails map

The narrow, 356-square-mile Symmes Creek watershed includes parts of Lawrence, Gallia, and Jackson Counties. The stream originates near Oak Hill and flows south, emptying into the Ohio River at Chesapeake. It was not always this way. Though deep in the heart of southern Ohio's unglaciated plateau, this stream was affected by the coming of the ice age to Ohio. Prior to the advance of glacial ice across the state, the stream that occupies the northern two-thirds of the Symmes Creek watershed was a north-flowing tributary of the Teayes River. Ice advancing from the north overran the Teayes River System and blocked movement of water to the north. The river valley became a lake, and when it rose high enough it flowed through a col in the hills to the south and made a new outlet to the developing Ohio River System. Today, in the southern part of its watershed, you can see where Symmes Creek flows through a "narrows," marking the point where the stream made the cut that reversed its direction of flow. In the northern parts of the watershed, the valley is wider and the pattern of tributaries clearly indicates that at one time it drained to the north.

Though many miles north of the narrows of Symmes Creek, the area where the Symmes Creek Trail is located is also narrow. Here, eons ago, the stream had to cut its way through massive sandstone that at this point was at the earth's surface. Upstream and downstream from the area of the trail, the wide valley of the preglacial

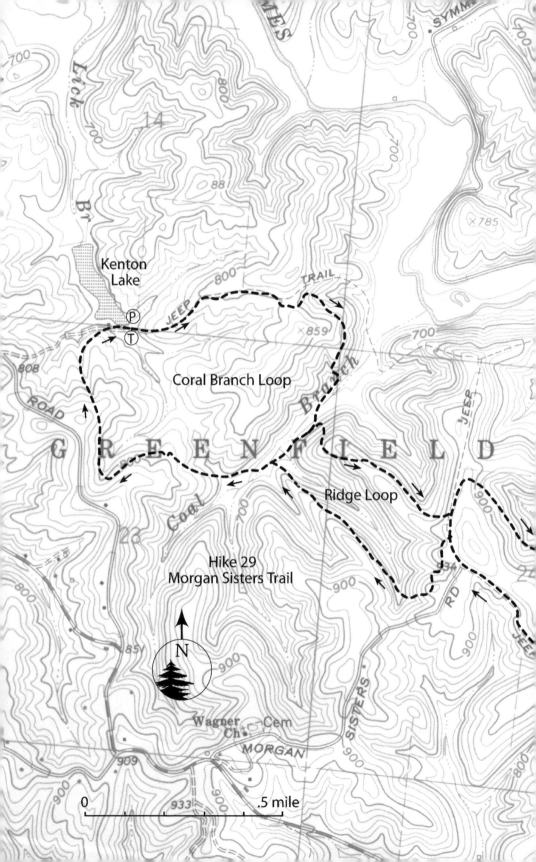

Kenton
Lake

Coral Branch Loop

GREENFIELD

Ridge Loop

Hike 29
Morgan Sisters Trail

N

Wagner Cem
Ch

MORGAN

SISTERS RD

JEEP

TRAIL

0   .5 mile

Hike 30
Symmes Creek Trail

Connector

Schoolhouse Loop

stream is clearly seen. When you hike the Symmes Creek Trail, you walk along the now south-flowing stream below huge sandstone cliffs in a cut made millennia ago by a stream that was flowing to the north.

How to Get There

To explore this bit of geological history, travel east from Chillicothe on US 35 past Jackson to the Rio Grande exit, OH 325. Turn right and travel about 4.25 miles south of US 35, then turn right onto Roush Road and follow it slightly less than 3 miles to where it makes a T with Symmes Creek Road. Turn to the right and drive a little over 0.5 mile to where a gravel drive on the right leads to a parking area. (There is a second parking area about 1.75 miles farther west, but it is only a small grassy area along the road.)

The Trail

At the back edge of the parking lot, a single trail enters the woods, crosses a creek on a bridge, and goes up the hill on an old road to take you to the Symmes Creek Loop Trail. Vehicle entrance to this road has been blocked at a number of places by strategically placed piles of dirt that you must walk around. The Symmes Creek Loop begins where the white-diamond-with-red-disk blazes indicate a trail going left and a trail going straight up the hill on the old road. The trail to the left is the return route. It has not been many years since the road was abandoned, so the trail straight ahead is easy to follow. I suggest going that way, making the loop counterclockwise.

After hanging onto the left side of one hill, the trail climbs up a ridge and passes to the right of the summit on the next hill. It then goes up and over the top of an 883-foot crest. Turning west now along this brushy ridge, the trail rises and dips for about .5 mile before it exits left in a saddle to follow a foot trail at a fairly level elevation around the hillside, thus avoiding a climb over the 900-foot knob. A half mile later the trail returns to the abandoned road, turns left, and heads west again. Very soon it passes a gravel road to the right that leads to a grassy area. This road from the north appears to be open to this point, meaning that the area is probably reachable by car. It does not look to be a good place to leave a car, though. There was freshly dumped trash on the day I visited the area, and it is a remote place where an unoccupied vehicle might easily be vandalized. The forest service recommends against parking here.

The trail, still on the old road, soon begins to swing left, dropping gently off the hill and traveling in a great circle to the left. It hugs the hillside with older trees uphill to the right. Fifty or 60 feet above the Symmes Creek floodplain that lies out in front of it, the old road makes a hard right turn. With sandstone cliffs above and scattered slump blocks nearby, the trail moves downhill heading southeast. At a point just before reaching the floodplain, where the trail turns west toward a gate about 100 yards away on Symmes Creek Road, it meets the other leg of the Symmes Creek Trail coming in from the east. Unless you have a need to go to the road, turn left at this trail junction to begin the return to your car. The trail is well marked, with diamonds and arrows pointing out each leg. Follow the white-diamond-with-red-disk blazes north from the intersection on yet another old road, paralleling what was probably an old boundary fence as it drops to the floodplain. There, box elders replace the sugar maples that were on the hillsides. By late summer, wing-stem, nettles, spotted jewelweed, multiflora rose, tickseed, asters, and other tall herbaceous plants often overhang the trail.

Symmes Creek Trail

A hundred feet of boardwalk right down near stream level carries the trail to a white pine plantation. The water may have risen high enough in this valley to float that boardwalk away in the storm of early March 1997. In any case, the trail should be passable. The floodplain trail goes right, with the turn of the meandering creek, then heads uphill among the pines for a short way before returning to the low ground. It next bobs and weaves among box elders and planted pines along the base of the hill, but it soon is traveling with sandstone cliffs close by on the left and slump blocks with their feet in the creek to the right. There are hemlock trees here, and rock polypody, or rockcap fern, covers the slump blocks. The beautiful, short, sky-blue relative of joe-pye weed known as mist flower blooms along the trail here in late August and September. Like all of its relatives (the Eupatoriums), it attracts butterflies; a pearl crescent was nectaring

on a blossom when I passed by. The gorgeous red lobelia commonly called cardinal flower also blooms here. It is one of only five species of native Ohio wildflowers with bright red blossoms.

For the next .25 mile the trail travels on the floodplain below spectacular sandstone cliffs with rock shelters varying from close to the creek to 10 or 15 feet up the hillside. The lovely tree-lined stream meanders back and forth between hillside and road. Pileated woodpeckers were calling back and forth when I explored this spectacular area. Eventually the trail leaves the valley floor to rise above the sandstone and return to the oak woods. There are more moss- and fern-covered slump blocks where the trail crosses the mouth of a side ravine. Now more than 100 feet above the floodplain, the trail reaches a point where it makes a sharp turn to the left with the blazes clearly indicating that it goes uphill.

At this point there is also a diamond with an arrow pointing straight ahead. This is the connector trail to the Morgan Sisters Trail. No flat Carsonite post here. How would you pound it into the ground when all beneath your feet is solid sandstone?

Make a left turn at that junction to stay on the red-dot-blazed Symmes Creek Trail as it rises up the hillside. Once on the upland, the trail turns to the right and begins winding through woods and brambles. There are some massive white oaks and maples in these woods. The only way to follow the trail is to find the blazes. The map would lead you to believe that the only reason for these perambulations would be to lengthen the trail, but if you follow it you will understand that its bends and turns allow views of some of the real monarchs of the forest. After twisting and turning and rising 800 feet, the trail descends toward the north then makes a right angle to meet with the road that carries the outgoing trail. At that intersection, diamonds with arrows point both right and left. A right turn will lead you to your car. As I walked there a number of years ago, along the trail there was a large still-living post oak tree with a carpenter ant-eaten bole. (The leaves of post oak are similar to those of a white oak, except that the lobes are in the shape of a cross.) No wonder that I had been hearing the calls of pileated woodpeckers. There are few foods they relish more than carpenter ants. The trail soon crosses the creek and ends where it began at the parking lot. Hikers who do not want to carry their camping gear with them might opt to camp here. Like other parking lots in the national forest, this one is used by hunters during turkey and deer seasons.

31

Wayne National Forest (Vesuvius Recreation Area, Lakeshore Trail)

Total distance: 8 miles (12.8 km)

Hiking time: 6 hours

Maximum elevation: 710 feet

Vertical rise: 104 feet

Maps: USGS 7½' Kitts Hill; USGS 7½' Sherrits; USGS 7½' Ironton; USGS 7½' Pedro; USGS 15' Ironton (OH and KY); USFS Wayne National Forest Lake Vesuvius Trail guide, Wayne National Forest hiking and backpacking trails map guide

The production of iron in the area that became known as the Hanging Rock Iron Region began with the construction of the Union Furnace in western Lawrence County by John Means in 1826. Before the whistle signaling the last cast of charcoal iron sounded at the Jefferson Furnace near Oak Hill in December 1916, a total of 46 furnaces had been built in this area of Ohio, 24 on the Kentucky side of the river. Each furnace was capable of producing 2,000 to 3,000 tons of iron per year. They helped arm the Union forces during the Civil War and were an important segment of the early years of America's industrial revolution. Now, a century after their heyday, only 17 of the old furnaces still stand in the region, surrounded by the crumbling ghosts of what were once thriving communities with the houses, stores, rail spurs, schools, churches, and cemeteries needed to keep the enterprises going. A map detailing the locations of the Ohio furnaces is available from the Ohio Historical Society in Columbus, and the same agency maintains the restored Buckeye Furnace in Jackson County, well worth a visit.

Vesuvius Furnace, at the heart of the Lake Vesuvius Recreation Area within the Wayne National Forest, is one of the best preserved. Though it looks like the other furnaces, it has a special claim to fame: It was supposedly the first hot-blast furnace erected in America. John Campbell, who along with Robert Hamilton built the nearby Mount Vernon Furnace (later known only as Vernon), had experimented with his cold-blast operation by placing the boilers and blast over the tunnel head to provide a hot blast. In 1837 Campbell and three other ironmasters agreed to cover any loss incurred if William Firmstone would test the hot-blast principle on his new Vesuvius Furnace. This hot-blast furnace continued in operation until 1906, but iron production inflicted a heavy toll on the land. Not only were the hillsides carved up to extract iron ore, but also between 300 and 350 acres of timber were cut and converted to charcoal each year for each furnace, thereby effectively denuding the land. By the time the furnaces were finally silenced by competition from richer ores and more productive furnaces in other parts of the country, the land had been cut over many times.

The trails of the Lake Vesuvius Recreation Area take you through beautiful countryside. The mixed hardwood forests of the east-facing slopes, the oaks of the ridgetops and southern exposures, and the hemlock of the sandstone-lined ravines give variety to the landscape. Ruins of old roads, homes, industries, and early park development turn back the pages of time for the visitor. With trails that are well designed without severe climbs, the area is especially good for beginning backpackers. Options that allow for one to several days on the trail make it one of Ohio's choice hiking areas.

The 8-mile Lakeshore Trail is perfect for a day hike. The Vesuvius Recreation Area—no camping allowed—has been expanded to include the entire area surrounding the Lakeshore Trail. So if you want to do a backpack trip, you must use the 16-mile designated Backpack Trail. It begins and ends at the same trailhead as the Lakeshore Trail and is one of Ohio's best trails for a one- or two-night trek. Both are laid out using gentle gradients, with no really hard climbs. Like the other units within the Wayne Forest complex, camping is allowed anywhere along the trail. There are no convenient sources of drinking water, so you need to carry water or cache your supply at a road crossing. Open fires are discouraged, and prohibited at times of high fire danger, so be prepared to use stoves for cooking. Human waste must be buried properly, and all trash must be carried out. Lake Vesuvius and the shoreline facilities underwent a multimillion-dollar renovation in the opening years of the century. The lake was drained and dredged, the dam and spillway rebuilt, and a new shoreline walkway constructed. It was reopened with a gala celebration on President's Day weekend, February 15-16, 2003. There are two forest service public campgrounds close by. I generally use the Iron Ridge Campground when I visit the area.

How to Get There

To reach the Vesuvius Recreation Area, travel US 23 from Columbus, or OH 32 and US 23 from Cincinnati, to Portsmouth. Take US 52 east to OH 93 in Ironton—about 120 miles from Columbus and 130 from Cincinnati. At Ironton, travel just over 6 miles north on OH 93 to where highway and forest service signs direct you right onto County Road 29. (Note that the U.S. Forest Service Ironton Ranger District office is located just north of this intersection on the right, or east, side of the highway, so stop there before going to the trailhead if you need information, maps, or other literature.) After about 1 mile on County Road 29, turn left on a forest service road just before reaching the dam and furnace. Travel this road not quite 0.5 mile to the dock area and trailhead parking lot on the right. Park here and lock your car.

Backpack Trail

Lakeshore Trail

Backpack Trail

Backpack Trail

Big Bend Beach

Oak Hill
Campground

Iron Ridge
Campground

Whiskey Run
Trail

0   1.0 mile

N

LAKE
VESUVIUS

LAKE VESUVIUS

VESUVIUS RECREATION AREA

VESUVIUS
RECREATION AREA

E L I Z A B E T H

Sand Hill

Hungry Hollow

Storms Cr.

Elizabeth

R
W
1
2
3
4
5
6
7
T
P
P
P

The Trail

The trail begins from a trailhead kiosk at the lake end of the parking lot. The Lakeshore Trail is marked with white-diamond blazes with a blue dot, the Backpack Trail with the diamonds and a yellow dot. Mileage is marked on both trails. The combined trail leaves the boathouse to climb a short distance into the woods and into what is the first of many pine plantings encountered along the way. The views along the first mile of this trail are extraordinary, especially in autumn. A large sandstone promontory across the lake creates a picture-postcard scene.

Following the shore of the lake, the trail passes a now-abandoned beach left from Civilian Conservation Corps days, and then goes by a building and intake structure from a water system abandoned in 1980. Moving slightly away from the shore, the trail follows an old road for a short way before crossing a side stream. About 100 feet beyond this crossing the trail splits, with the yellow-dotted Backpack Trail leaving to the left. There should be a sign pointing out the trails, but if it has been vandalized, be alert for the fork in the trail as it is easy to miss.

Continuing straight ahead, the Lakeshore Trail soon passes mile marker 1. It continues along the shore until just before the Big Bend Beach area, where it cuts left. Next it crosses a wooden bridge and follows the fence around the bathhouse. Rest rooms and water are available here during the warm part of the year. The trail soon passes a 50-foot-long sandstone outcrop before climbing the side of the ridge at a moderate angle. At one point along this section of trail it is possible to see the lake on both sides of the peninsula. Past mile marker 2, the trail doubles back to drop toward the shoreline. It then passes a wetland

area between it and the lake and turns left up a small hollow. After crossing a creek, the trail turns right to travel again near the shoreline. A small pond lies between trail and the lake. Climbing away from the lake on the slope, the trail passes through more stands of planted pines and then above a rock exposure with a 25-foot cliff below. Just beyond is mile marker 3. The trail next turns right as it climbs a ridge that goes toward the lake. There is a footpath out to the point overlooking the lake, but the trail turns left to drop down to the shoreline. From here, it stays at lake level until it begins its return route on the opposite shore. The lake is quite narrow at this point. The trail uses a service road to continue upstream. Just after crossing a small side stream, signs identify the junction with the Backpack Trail ahead and the trails join together to cross Storms Creek.

This crossing is usually no problem, but in periods of high water it can be difficult. Beyond the crossing, the trail turns right through an old field and reenters the woods. At a fork in the trail, the combined Lakeshore/Backpack Trail stays along the forest edge, soon passing mile marker 4. It then leaves the lakeshore to travel up the left side of a side ravine. The two trails split, with the Lakeshore Trail making a right turn across the creek bed before climbing the hillside. The Lakeshore Trail next descends to cross another stream before making a fairly steep climb to once again overlook the lake. Past mile marker 5, it turns left to go around yet another inlet. After dropping once more to near lake level to cross two streambeds, the trail takes you to one of the nicest viewpoints of the hike.

Following a clockwise swing around a much longer inlet, there is an intersection with the .5-mile Whiskey Run Trail. It goes past abandoned charcoal pits and at one

A comfortable camp on Iron Ridge

time you could see remnants of a whiskey still and barrels, which gave the trail its name. It makes a loop that begins at the Iron Ridge Campground. A short, steep climb up the Whiskey Run Trail will lead you to a rock shelter where that moonshine is said to have been made. Beyond and on uphill is the campground.

The combined Lakeshore/Whiskey Run Trail travels north to round a point nearly opposite the Big Bend Beach before heading due south for the next .6 mile. After it enters another pine stand, the trail splits as the Whiskey Run Trail departs to the left. The old beach and water intake become visible across the lake on the right, and there are sandstone outcroppings on the hill above the trail on the left. After passing mile marker 7, the trail comes to another rock shelter, this one vandalized with spray-paint graffiti. The trail then drops closer to the lake and rounds the sandstone cliff

face that was visible in the early part of the hike.

Now rounding the last inlet before the dam, the trail stays close to the lake and crosses two small streambeds. After rising slightly, it returns to near lake level and passes below a rock cliff with nearly square slump blocks on the hillside below. One cannot help but wonder if the sandstone used to build the Vesuvius Furnace was quarried here. The trail follows the lake edge and arrives shortly at the dam spillway. There it makes a left turn, to be joined by the Backpack Trail. You descend concrete steps along a chain-link fence to arrive at the lawn and road within sight of the Vesuvius Furnace.

The trail follows Storms Creek through pine plantings to the County Road 29 bridge, which it crosses. Turning right beyond the bridge, it climbs to the top of the dam and then heads toward the shoreline boardwalk, which it uses to return to the trailhead. My father grew up in Lawrence County not far from this area. There is no place nicer to be on an Ohio autumn afternoon than on the Shoreline Trail at Lake Vesuvius.

Note: The Wayne National Forest earnestly solicits volunteers to assist in trail maintenance. If you or your group would like to help, please contact the Ironton Ranger District office at 704-534-6500.

32

Wayne National Forest (Wildcat Hollow Trail)

Total distance: 5 or 15 miles (7.25 or 21 km)

Hiking time: 4 hours or 12 hours to 2 days

Maximum elevation: 1,080 feet

Vertical rise: 350 feet

Maps: USGS 7½' Corning; USGS 7½' Beavertown; USFS Wildcat Hollow brochure, WNF hiking and backpacking trail map

In recent years sightings of wildcat are once again being reported from around Ohio. At one time these secretive felines were found in most of the state, especially in the rocky hollows of the southeast. History does not record how Wildcat Hollow on the Morgan/Perry county line got its name, but it would probably be safe to guess that a den of the elusive cats was thought to have been in the area.

Located in what is now the Wayne National Forest, Wildcat Hollow is the site of one of Ohio's best hiking trails. The 15-mile route is laid out entirely on national forest land, mostly on high ground between drainage systems. The trail is typical of those developed by the forest service. It is well designed, with gentle grades and switchbacks as needed. It is also well marked with square Carsonite posts and white-diamond blazes nailed to trees. The miles are marked most of the way, and the standard federal agency BACKPACKER signs are used in many places. A connecting trail of just over .25 mile allows the trail to be shortened to 5 miles for a nice day hike. There are no designated campsites along the trail, but you may camp anywhere. There are neither fire rings nor latrines. The only rest rooms are at the trailhead parking area. Portable stoves are suggested as an alternative to open fires. Because there are no water sources along the trail, water must be carried in. Human waste must be buried, and trash carried out. No permit is required. A map that includes rules for use can be obtained from Wayne National Forest (see the

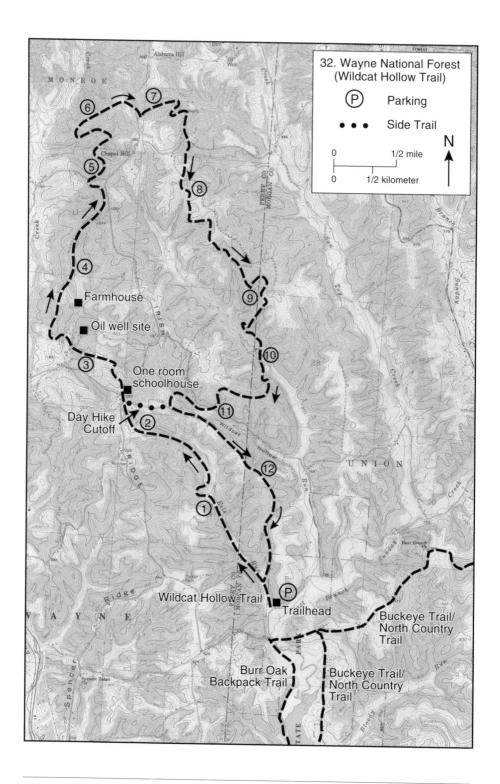

32. Wayne National Forest
(Wildcat Hollow Trail)

Ⓟ   Parking

•••   Side Trail

N

0   1/2 mile
0   1/2 kilometer

introduction for the complete address).

Since Wildcat Hollow Trail is located adjacent to Burr Oak State Park, this hike can be combined with the Burr Oak Backpack Trail for a trek of about 34 miles. Such a hike would form an hourglass route: The Wildcat Hollow parking lot would be at the pinch of the hourglass, and parking here would allow you to stash your trash in your car and pick up additional supplies and water midway through your hike. The Burr Oak Trail is laid out differently than the Wildcat Hollow Trail, so extra planning considerations are necessary. Much of the Burr Oak Trail is close to the water's edge and lake conditions must be taken into account. The connecting trail to the Burr Oak Backpack is located about .125 mile west of the Wildcat Hollow trailhead, on the south side of the road. There are also steeper climbs on the state park trail. Contact the Burr Oak park office for a map of their Backpack Trail.

This Wildcat Hollow Trail is an excellent choice for the fledgling backpacker or for a weekend trek. It is not heavily used, so crowding is not a problem. It is, however, within an area designated for hunting with primitive weapons, so it is probably best to avoid the trail in deer and turkey season. During small-game season, some hunter-orange apparel would seem appropriate.

How to Get There

To reach Wildcat Hollow from the central Ohio area, travel US 33 southeast to Nelsonville. Take OH 78 east to Glouster, and then turn left (north) onto OH 13 and travel 5 miles to Township Road 289. Turn right (east) there and follow the forest service signs for 3 miles to the trailhead, using Irish Ridge and Dew Roads. The drive takes about 2 hours from Columbus.

From Cleveland, travel I-77 south to I-70.

Take I-70 west to Exit 154 in Zanesville. Turn south on OH 60, then turn south onto OH 93 in Zanesville. When OH 93 intersects OH 13, 21 miles south of Zanesville, turn left (south) on OH 13. Take it 13.5 miles to Township Road 289, turn left, and follow the signs noted above for drivers coming from Columbus. The distance from Cleveland is about 180 miles.

From Cincinnati, travel OH 32 east to Athens. Take US 33 north to Nelsonville, OH 78 east to Glouster, and OH 13 north to Township Road 289, also a trip distance of about 180 miles.

The Trail

Departing the open area around the parking lot from the left rear corner, the trail immediately enters a lovely pine grove, crosses a short bridge, and then heads up the Eels Run valley. Remember to carry ample water; none is available on the trail. For the next mile, the trail goes in and out of these pines and back and forth across the stream several times. Just beyond the first creek crossing, a sign points both ahead and to the left. This is where the return trail completes the loop. The trail seems to be designed for a clockwise route, with the outbound trail going left at this juncture.

When Eels Run splits, the trail follows the left branch. Mile marker 1 is just beyond this point. A few yards after the mile marker, the trail heads up the right slope to move counterclockwise around the end of the ridge. It hangs on the left slope of the valley, gently climbing toward Irish Ridge. Beech/maple and mixed mesophytic forest cover these hillsides, along with a healthy shrub layer of bush honeysuckle, evidence of a former homestead. Apple trees not surrounded by the secondary succession forest give further evidence of human activity in the area. As the trail moves higher up the hillside heading toward the ridge, it enters an open area where it passes mile marker 2. There, at an elevation of 1,000 feet, the trail has risen almost exactly 200 feet in 2 miles—a nice, gentle gradient for backpacking.

As the trail swings to the right toward its intersection with Irish Ridge Road, it passes more tall white pines, here with ground cedar covering the forest floor. Just after the trail joins Irish Ridge Road, a dirt road enters from the right. Obviously built for some other purpose, the .25-mile track is the connector to the returning trail, creating a short loop of about 5 miles. The connector needs no description since it is an almost straight, level trail through brush and successional forest.

The main trail continues on Irish Ridge Road to its intersection with County Road 70, or Waterworks Road. Watch for an old wooden schoolhouse that sits near here, almost hidden from view by the encroaching forest. The trail turns left to travel very briefly on Waterworks Road, shortly to drop off the right side into white pines and young successional hardwood. The trail turns left to parallel the road for a short distance. It then turns right, passes directly under a power line, and uses switchbacks to drop into the head of a ravine, which it follows downstream. As you pass mile marker 3, more whispery white pines appear alongside the trail. When I backpacked this trail a number of years ago carrying only a bivy sack for a night's rest, I sought out the white pine stands for my overnight stops.

Where the ravine widens and becomes a hollow, a large number of old oil-well shacks and collection pipes can be seen. The trail is not easy to follow as it turns to the right up the hollow. It ducks under a cable, and then joins an oil-well service road to cross the creek. Then it passes under an overhead collection pipe before turning left to reenter the forest. A sign for the Wildcat Hollow Backpack Trail reassures you that you're on the correct route. The trail next curves to the left on the hillside as it climbs, using switchbacks, to reach the ridge. Passing through more pines as it swings right, the trail eventually hits an old dirt road that it follows to the right. Still climbing, the trail ignores another dirt road leaving to the left and continues to the top, where it turns left to follow the ridge. Less than 1 mile beyond, you pass mile marker 4.

The trail continues on this narrow ridge for another .5 mile, passing an area on the left that had at one time been clear-cut. At this point the trail becomes a haul road, providing access to Irish Ridge Road. The trail makes an easily-missed left turn several hundred yards before this sometimes muddy road reaches the gravel road. After leaving the haul road, the path circles to the left above a hollow, passes an oil well, and then climbs to Chapel Hill Road. There it turns right, going up the road about 100 feet to where, just before the road curves left, it exits left into the woods. Mile marker 5 is but a short way beyond.

Following the hillside to the right, the trail crosses several washes and then turns left on an old track. As you head downslope, there is a good view of the Perry County countryside. Leaving the old road, the trail winds past a series of white pipes that denote the presence of a gas transmission line. Using switchbacks, it drops to the valley floor and heads downstream. Still within sight of gas-line markers, the path curves right to begin climbing the hillside beside more pipeline markers. After it passes mile marker 6, it makes a single curving switchback to the right before gaining the ridgetop. Eventually the trail reaches 1,060 feet and curves right to meet Irish Ridge Road for the last time. This is another cross-

A marker on the Wildcat Hollow Trail

ing where there is an offset to the continuation of the trail. Turn right onto the road and walk about 100 feet to where a BACKPACKER sign indicates that the trail exits the road to the left. Still following the ridgetop, it passes the 7-mile marker about 250 feet after leaving Irish Ridge Road.

The trail next leaves the ridge, swinging right as it drops into a hollow. At a split, the blazed Wildcat Hollow Trail takes the right fork. It then goes in and out of a side hollow before turning right and starting to climb again to higher ground. The ascent begins with a short, fairly steep climb, and then continues at a gentler grade, passing through another white pine planting and close to a wildlife watering hole. Where the trail reaches Township Road 13, the trail cuts diagonally to the right to climb some log steps. Soon it crosses a gas-line right-of-way before emerging onto another gravel road. This road—Township Road 297 in

Perry County and Township Road 113 in Morgan County—that follows the ridges southeast through national forest land, is closed less than 1 mile to the left of this crossing. It is now used as a bridle trail and footpath.

Across the road from where the trail emerges, a dirt track enters. The Wildcat Hollow Trail does not take this track, but instead exits the road just to its left. Shortly, it passes another wildlife watering hole. For the next 1.5 miles, the trail stays high on the hillside east of Cedar Run, passing by or through four areas where timber was clearcut. Because regrowth from live tree stumps is rapid during the growing season, many blazes are obscured by vegetation and difficult to find. Keep a constant watch for markings. At one point the trail uses another old roadbed for a short distance but soon leaves it, turning to the left. Not all the woods along this ridge have been logged, and in the area of mile marker 9 there is a very nice stand of mature mixed oak forest. Here the trail swings around the heads of ravines as it approaches another area that was clear-cut recently. With the timber-harvest area on the right, the trail descends to Cedar Run Hollow using a single switchback. Once in the valley, the trail crosses the main stem and then a small side stream of Cedar Run on log bridges. The last crossing is close to the 10-mile mark.

The trail turns downstream on the low hillside, but after crossing a dry wash in a side ravine, it makes a sharp right turn to begin ascending the ridge. Using only one switchback, the path swings gently to the right as it climbs. As it approaches a fence between national forest land and an inholding still being farmed, the trail turns left and begins descending into a small side ravine of Wildcat Hollow. As it leaves the forest it crosses Township Road 300, then turns right to move upstream parallel to the road. The path next passes a swampy area and another old oil collection area. After crossing the creek, the trail rises up the side of the valley wall, still headed upstream. It then makes a left turn to climb 100 feet to the ridge in less than 1,000 feet. The trail has come over 11 miles and now meets the connecting track for the shorter day hike. There

are blazes on the trails going left and right.

To complete the 15-mile loop trail, turn left at this intersection. The dirt road soon divides, with the Wildcat Hollow Trail taking the left fork. A fairly open area on the right affords a view back into Wildcat Hollow. The trail continues along the left side of the ridge, eventually reaching a brushy area where it crosses an old cement floor. This spot is near the 12-mile point of the trail. For a brief time the trail returns to the woodlands, but it soon enters another open area. Once again the trail uses the tracks of an early road as it traverses the left side of the ridgetop for just under .5 mile. After turning right off the old road, the trail passes through the middle of another formerly open area now closing in. Then it reenters the woodlands as it drops gently off the right side of the ridge to the valley floor. Following a dry wash downstream for a few hundred feet, it meets the outbound trail about 500 feet up Eels Run from the trailhead parking lot. There could hardly be a more fitting finish to a hike on the Wildcat Hollow Trail than the grove of pines through which the trail passes as it comes to an end. Check out the boot-cleaning station and learn why thoroughly cleaning your footwear after every hike is important in the fight against the spread of invasive alien plants.

33

Zaleski State Forest

*Total distance: 9.9 to 23.5 miles
(15.8 to 37.6 km)*

*Hiking time: 8 hours (day hike) to
3 days (backpack)*

Maximum elevation: 1,030 feet

Vertical rise: 307 feet

*Maps: USGS 7½' Mineral; USGS 7½'
Union Furnace; ODNR Zaleski State
Forest and Backpack Trail map*

Count Peter Zaleski never saw the land in southeastern Ohio that bears his name. An exile from Poland, Zaleski was active in the Paris banking scene. Using investment monies largely received from Polish émigrés, he formed the Zaleski Mining Company to exploit the resources of Vinton County, Ohio. In 1856, the town of Zaleski was laid out, and two years later a charcoal-fired iron furnace known as the Zaleski Furnace was constructed just north of the settlement.

It was not the first furnace in the area. Hope Furnace on Sandy Run a few miles to the north had been in blast for two years, producing high-quality iron from the local ore and limestone and burning charcoal made from the abundant timber of the area. Elsewhere in the county the Eagle Furnace and the Hamden Furnace were already producing iron. Nor was Zaleski's industrial enterprise the first to come to Vinton County since settlement by European whites. In the first half of the century, millstones had been produced from native rock at a site now under the waters of Lake Hope. By 1880 Madison Township, in which Zaleski was the only sizable community, had 2,217 residents, by far the most of any township in Vinton County.

Zaleski's town is still here but the furnace is gone, as are most of the people. Like most of the furnaces of the area, it survived long enough to flourish during the Civil War but was shut down within 10 years of the end of that bitter conflict. The operations had denuded the hills of timber for miles around, and the remains of the already thin iron-bearing veins were now so far under the hills that it was unprofitable to mine them. New sources of high-grade ore and better smelting processes doomed the furnaces. The only remaining evidence of the iron industry here are Hope Furnace, preserved at Lake Hope State Park, and traces of haul roads along which ore, limestone, and wood were carted to the furnace.

Prosperity never really returned to Vinton County. In the mid-20th century the thin veins of high-sulfur coal were exploited, mostly by drift mining. Unfortunately, that left many of the small valleys of the area awash with "yellow boy," a yellowish deposit leached from mines, and the streams and rivers were unable to sustain life because of high acidity. Where there is yellow boy, the pH of the water is very low from sulfuric acid pollution, and that spells death to all creatures great and small. Today, strip-mining for coal, logging of secondary forests, blasting powder production, and tourism are the main industries of the area.

Established during the early 1930s, 26,867-acre Zaleski State Forest was the site of a Civilian Conservation Corps camp during the Depression. It also holds Ohio's first resort-type park development, the Lake Hope Lodge and Cabins. (The lodge was destroyed by fire during the winter of 2005–2006.) Lake Hope State Park, now 3,223 acres, was carved from the state forest in 1949 when the Department of Natural Resources came into being. It includes all the recreational facilities of the state-owned land except the Backpack and bridle trails.

The Zaleski Backpack Trail was established in the mid-1970s. It is laid out in a long loop (a connecting side trail at its "waist"), with a smaller loop attached by a two-way trail at its north end. This layout allows the trail to be walked in several combinations. A hike on just the southern part of the large loop covers 9.9 miles and can be walked as a day hike or an overnight, since there are two designated campgrounds along the way. Adding the rest of the central loop brings the hike to 17.8 miles—or 19.8 miles if a third campsite a mile beyond is used. The northern loop, which isn't described here, could be added to bring the total to 23.5 miles, with three campsites, although it can be hiked using only two overnights. It is signed so that it can be easily hiked in either direction.

Camping is permitted at designated sites only. Each of these has a privy and a fire ring, with fresh water close by. There is no fee for hiking, and for safety reasons hikers are required to register at the trailhead kiosk before starting. This backpack trail is the only one in Ohio with self-guided interpretive information on the map. The "Zaleski State Forest and Backpack Trail" map is available from the ODNR publications office, and it can also usually be found at the trailhead. The interpretive information is keyed to information on brown Carsonite posts along the trail, which is divided into short sections between points designated by letters. The main trail is blazed with orange paint, usually on trees; the side trails with white paint. The trail has been "ground truthed" with GPS instruments so the map available from the Division of Forestry is quite accurate.

Whether done in its entirety over several days or in pieces as day walks, hiking the Zaleski Trail is an exhilarating experience. The wildflowers of both woods and open areas are lovely during the growing season, and wildlife is common throughout the year. Because of the vast expanse of woodland, Zaleski is good breeding country for the woodland birds that make their way to Ohio each spring. Amphibians and reptiles, in-

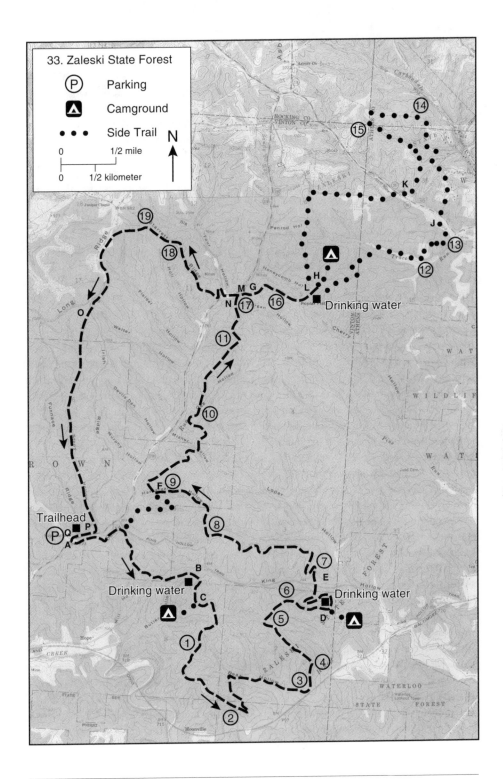

cluding copperheads and timber rattlesnakes, are also found in this wild area. The Zaleski Backpack Trail is an ideal trail for the naturalist-hiker at any time of year. I recall being alone at a campsite on the morning after Easter Sunday of 1989, awakened shortly after sunrise by the calling of a barred owl, whippoorwills, and the drumming of ruffed grouse. What a wake-up call. (That, incidentally, was the weekend of the oil spill of the Exxon Valdez on Bligh Reef in Prince William Sound, Alaska. I was scheduled to be in Valdez three months later leading an ecotourism tour, a trip that I will never forget.)

How to Get There

The trailhead can be reached from the Columbus area by traveling southeast on US 33 past Logan. Turn right (south) on OH 328, then left (east) on US 56. At OH 278, turn right (south) and travel 4 miles to the upper end of Lake Hope. The trailhead is located at a parking lot on the east side of OH 278 opposite the Hope Furnace parking lot. An information kiosk at the trailhead has registration forms that must be completed. An alternative from Columbus is to take US 23 south to Circleville and then OH 56 east to OH 278, where you turn right. The trip takes two hours either way.

From western and southwestern Ohio, take US 35 east to Chillicothe from I-71. From Chillicothe, travel US 50 east through McArthur to OH 677. Turn left (north), and at OH 278 turn left (north) and drive to the parking lot about 1 mile north of the Lake Hope dam (a three hour trip).

From Cleveland, the trip takes about 4.5 hours via the Columbus route.

The Trail

Registration information and maps are provided at a kiosk beside a parking lot located on the east side of OH 278. Carsonite posts at two corners of that lot point out where to begin for either direction of travel. Begin hiking by walking southwest on the left side of the highway. Just after crossing the bridge over Sandy Run, a sign identifies the shared entrance to the Zaleski Backpack Trail and the 2-mile Olds Hollow Trail. The combined trails cross a metal bridge built by students from nearby Hocking Technical College. Then a series of wooden block steps carry the trail above the floodplain. Shortly, the trails go their separate ways. This is Point A on the Backpack Trail, and the direction of travel is shown as "A–B," with an arrow on a Carsonite post. This method is used to give directions along the entire Backpack Trail; letters designate the trail segment and arrows point the direction of travel. At campsites, a tent symbol and an arrow point to the camp's location and a water tap symbol and arrow give the location of the drinking water supply. The trail route is also delineated by frequent orange paint blazes on trees.

At Point A, either trail can be taken to begin hiking the Backpack Trail, since both come back together about a mile down the trail. Although the Olds Hollow Trail is a bit more rigorous and just a tiny bit longer, it is an interesting alternate route. It passes by the cemetery that once served the community of Hope, the town now covered by the lake of that name, and by a small but interesting rock shelter. The Olds Hollow Trail goes right at the juncture, and the Backpack Trail goes left.

The Backpack Trail immediately enters a lovely pine grove that has a cathedral-like quality. It then drops back to the swampy land along Sandy Run and crosses a wooden footbridge. Climbing to a fork, an arrow indicates that the left branch is the route to follow. After passing through another stand of pine, the trail drops to another footbridge and to the junction with the returning Olds Hollow Trail. The rock shelter on the Olds Hollow Trail is just a few yards straight ahead.

The Backpack Trail turns left and begins to climb the hillside. It then swings down and back up before dropping to King Hollow. To the left is a bridge for the side trail that returns from Point F, creating the 9.9-mile loop. The main trail turns right and almost immediately begins climbing the ridge, gaining 840 feet in a little over .3 mile. As it reaches the ridge, the trail joins an old road to travel the high ground through a wonderful mixed oak forest. The trail stays on or just off the ridge, curving gently to the left. A sign announces Point B and the first drinking water source, located downhill to the right. You have come 1.5 miles.

The trail continues on the old ridge road as it swings south. After less than .25 mile it reaches Point C, where a white-blazed side trail leads out a side ridge to the first campground. Since the next campsite is only 4.3 miles down the trail, this one is usually used only by hikers who got a late start.

Still following the ridgetop road, the trail turns east from Point C and then curves to the right and heads south once again. About .5 mile after Point C you reach the first sign keyed to the interpretive material on the ODNR map. The text indicates that the trail runs on the old Marietta-to-Chillicothe road that passed through Athens. The route was used by prehistoric Native Americans of the Fort Ancient culture, as well as by settlers, and was abandoned in 1870. A half mile beyond this sign, the old road leaves the ridge to the right as the trail continues straight ahead. After another .5 mile, the trail descends over rocky

outcrops to arrive at interpretive Stop 2, the Moonville overlook.

According to legend, the portion of the B&O Railroad track in the valley below is haunted by the ghost of Moonville. As the story goes, at the turn of the last century a brakeman was killed near the Moonville tunnel as he waved his lantern to stop a train. Being exceedingly drunk, he apparently swayed into the path of the oncoming locomotive. He is reportedly buried in the Moonville graveyard, and on some nights his lantern can be seen "a-glimmerin' and a-wavin'," still trying to stop that train. Unfortunately, it is difficult to see Moonville, or even the railroad track, when the trees are in leaf, so I did not attempt to verify the presence of the ghost at night.

After leaving Stop 2, the trail turns left over the ridge, drops slightly, and crosses another ridge before descending a ravine into Bear Hollow. At an intersection with another old road, the trail turns right to head down the hollow. Following the old road, the trail makes a couple of stream crossings and passes a beaver pond full of standing dead trees. After climbing the hillside a bit it arrives at Stop 3, the main street of an early mining town known as Ingham Station. Though it takes a sharp eye to see any evidence of the town that existed here over 100 years ago, the settlement supported a store, a train depot, and several families in the 1870s. An old cellar hole is visible along the trail. Ancient apple trees and ornamental shrubs betray the past human occupation. Closed off and difficult to locate, the entrance to the old Ingham coal mine is farther up the trail on the left.

Leaving Ingham Station, do not follow the old road up the ridge, although it appears as if most hikers go this way. The trail actually turns right, off the road it was following. It passes through heavy herbaceous vegetation, and then hits another old road, which it soon leaves to the left to pass a closed drift mine. Next it makes a very steep climb. As it begins to level off, the trail takes a switchback to pass a sandstone outcrop, and then turns right to reach and climb steps that lead to a juncture with the old road up the ridge. Stop 4 on the interpretive trail is at the overlook at the top of the hill. It describes yet another old town, this one called King Station. According to the guide, the stretch of railroad track from Moonville through Ingham to Mineral is considered by many to be "the loneliest in the state of Ohio."

From Stop 4, the trail follows another old road along the ridge. About .5 mile beyond Stop 4 it arrives at Stop 5, an archaeological site. To the right of the trail is a small, doughnut-shaped ceremonial ring built and used by Native Americans of the Adena culture, who were active in southern Ohio between 800 B.C. and A.D. 700. Underfoot on the trail, you can see chips of the dark Zaleski flint they worked into arrow points. Native to Vinton County, this type of flint was the third most important flint to early inhabitants in Ohio.

Swinging right but still following the ridge, in about .5 mile the trail comes to Stop 6, where it once again travels the old Marietta-to-Chillicothe road, this time going east. Another .5 mile along the ridge brings you to Point D, where a CAMPSITE sign points right to a white-blazed trail down the old road. A water hydrant is off the trail to the left.

The main trail now makes two quick left turns and then begins descending into King Hollow. Using the water haul road part of the way, it drops into a ravine and then climbs to the King Hollow Trail. It shortly arrives at Point E, about 6.4 miles from the start. Leaving the King Hollow Trail to reenter the woods at Point E, the trail begins a .5-mile, 221-foot climb, using one switchback to

reach a ridge spur that it follows for only a short distance. Stop 7 is the site of a wildfire that occurred on February 14, 2000. It burned 10 acres and was started from an unattended campfire. You can still see black scorches on some trees as well as dead trees that succumbed to the flames. At the main ridge, the trail turns left on a logging haul road, which it follows until it runs into a dirt road at Stop 8. A sign along the road identifies this part of the state forest as the Zaleski Turkey Management Area. This venture is a cooperative effort of the Divisions of Forestry and Wildlife to provide suitable habitat for the propagation of wild turkeys. It apparently has been successful, for when I stayed at the campsite at Point H I was awakened in the morning by the gobbling of turkeys close by.

After crossing the dirt road the trail soon intersects a gas-well service road, and then turns left to drop into Harbargar Hollow. Next it passes a sandstone cliff with a small recess cave on the left. Not far beyond, a sign along the right side of the trail indicates that Points G and H are ahead. This is Point F. At the Stop 9 sign, look at the rock outcropping on the south side of the trail. The vertical grooves visible in the face of the sandstone are actually drilling marks left when this site was a quarry. A line of holes was drilled into the rock and then explosive charges were placed in the holes. When detonated, they separated large sections of rock from the cliff. The shallow pocket that can be seen at the bottom of the drill marks is where the explosion took place. Sandstone from this site could have been used to build local iron furnaces, railroad bridge abutments, or local structures. The main Backpack Trail turns right just beyond this sign. Another sign dead ahead reads DAY LOOP RETURN TO POINT A. If you plan to return to Point A to complete the 9.9-mile

A beaver pond along the Zaleski Backpack Trail

loop, take this side trail straight ahead.

The side trail returning to Point A soon turns left around the end of a ridge, then goes in and out of a small hollow that has sandstone outcrops and several recess caves. Approaching Sandy Run, it swings left to parallel the stream and OH 278. Once more it turns in and out of a short hollow, passing over the top of another rock shelter. As the trail leaves the woodland, it passes through tall bottomland weeds to reach the King Hollow Trail. A short distance beyond the road, the trail crosses a wooden footbridge, and then climbs to a junction with the outgoing trail. Turning right, it returns to the trailhead after about another .75 mile through pine groves.

For those continuing on the longer trails from Point F, the trail heads up the east side of the Sandy Run valley. Then it crosses dry washes in the heads of several ravines before climbing to a ridge. Timber was harvested in this area in 2005. Next, the trail drops into Mizner Hollow. From there, it angles left up the hillside and turns right, up the ridge. The footpath then turns left, going counterclockwise around the hillside before turning right to angle down the slope into Ogg Hollow. At Stop 10 there is a test of how well you know your trees. There are 14 numbered trees in the immediate vicinity of this post. Can you identify them all? The answers are on the Division of Forestry's Backpack Trail map. Here the trail turns upstream. Leaving the creek, it travels to the left and heads up the hillside. Gaining 250 feet in less than .25 mile, the climb toward the ridge is one of the more strenuous on the trail. Follow the slight rises and falls along the ridge for not quite .5 mile, until you reach a knob with a panoramic view. This is Stop 11, where managers have enhanced the natural cycle of the forest by creating an opening in the canopy to allow sunlight to reach the forest floor. This practice encourages certain tree species, such as oaks and hickories, to thrive naturally. Wildlife like ruffed grouse also benefit from the variation in cover height resulting from this practice. Similar areas are found throughout the forest. In 2002, a prescribed burn was conducted on this site. The objective was to reduce the probability of future uncontrolled forest fires and to encourage the regeneration of oaks.

From Stop 11, the trail turns sharply left, still on the ridge. A short distance after it makes a curve to the right, you begin the descent into Morgan Hollow. The trail drops to the creek using only one switchback. There is a short, rather steep section near the bottom. Point G is just a few steps beyond the creek. Here the southern loop goes to the left and the connector to the campground at Point H, and the northern loop goes right. OH 278 is a few hundred feet down the valley to the left.

From the Point G intersection to the campground at Point H, the trail covers 1 mile. This section is the only part of the main Zaleski Backpack Trail that must be hiked in both directions. The connecting trail heads to the right and upstream for several hundred feet, then turns left to climb the ridge. There, turning right, it begins following another old road. Stop 16 tells the story of this road, which was used during the 1860s to haul charcoal to Hope Furnace. The charcoal used to fire the iron furnace was made by piling wood in large stacks, lighting it, covering it with wet earth and leaves, and leaving it to burn for 10 to 12 days. Stop 16 seems out of sequence but it actually follows Stop 15 on the northern loop.

Just beyond the interpretive stop, the trail turns left. A path entering from the right is an earlier route of this trail. A few hundred yards of nearly level ridgetop trail leads to the gravel road used to supply water to the tank just ahead. The trail follows the gravel road, soon reaching the sign for Point L. Across the road on the right is the drinking water hydrant, and the campsite is only moments away. Less than 100 feet ahead on the road is Point H, where the nice, wooded campsite is within view. The privy is several hundred feet beyond the campfire area.

After camping, if you are not going to hike the northern loop, you must hike back to Point G to begin your return to the trailhead. Shortly after again passing Stop 16, the old road leaves the ridge, going down the slope to the right. The Backpack Trail continues ahead to drop off the left side of the ridge into Morgan Hollow. Follow the stream out of the hollow, arriving at Point G. To continue your return to the trailhead, turn right on the segment labeled G–M. The trail reaches Sandy Run and Point M in 0.1 mile.

If you plan to hike the 5.7-mile northern loop, when you return to the main trail, turn left onto the H–J section as it climbs a hillside heading east-southeast before turning northeast along the ridgetops, in places above 1,000 feet. Here the trail crosses into Athens County. Still heading northeast, the trail next descends into the valley of Trace Run, where it turns east for about .3 mile. Stop 12 is in an old auger mine area. As implied by the name, a large auger was used to drill and extract coal from the vein. If you look southwest you can still see remnants of the trolley car railroad used to haul coal from the site.

The trail then makes an abrupt left turn and climbs about 80 feet up the hillside, where it turns right and goes in and out of the heads of two ravines at a consistent elevation. From Site 13 the trail passes through part of a 59-acre selective timber harvest completed in 1993. Foresters implemented this type of harvest to improve the health and vigor of the remaining trees and also to salvage deteriorating trees in the area. Very little evidence remains of the logging activity, but if you look closely you can still see some of the stumps and tree-tops from harvested trees. You will also notice an abundance of young trees growing under the canopy.

The trail swings north-northeast to drop to Point J, a stream crossing, and OH 56. Beyond the highway crossing, the Backpack Trail utilizes another old township road to climb the next ridge to the north, and then travels northwest for .25 mile before leaving the ridge to turn due north and drop 100 feet to a small stream crossing just below an impoundment. Next the trail heads west, skirting the north shore of a pond, beyond which it heads north up a ravine to join another old track on the ridge. There, at Point 14, you are as far away from the trailhead as you are going to get—about 4.5 miles "as the crow flies."

At this point, the trail enters a mixed pine stand known as the Doolittle, Enderline, York, or Carbondale Forest. Botanists have been interested in this area because it is one of the oldest unmanaged plantations in southeastern Ohio. It is composed of conifer plantings with an understory of woody and herbaceous plants. A total of 197 species of vascular plants were collected, identified, and deposited in the Bartley Herbarium at Ohio University during a 1964–65 ecological study of the forest. The planting started in 1906 and continued for nearly 30 years. Over 200 acres were planted, of which about 60 remain. The Backpack Trail uses the old track along the ridge to travel .5 mile west to the county line.

Now the trail turns south down a slope and across a footbridge to the valley upstream from the pond passed earlier. It travels about .5 mile down that valley and past

➤ Return of the Turkey

The wild turkey (Meleagris gallopavo) *is said to have been abundant in Ohio at the time of European settlement. Throughout the state, flocks of 30 to 50 were regularly encountered during the winter, and they were seen as scattered individuals the rest of the year. But unregulated hunting and changes in habitat sent the population into a downward spiral. Wild turkeys were extirpated from Ohio by the end of the 19th century. After a short, unsuccessful attempt at pen-rearing wild turkeys for release into the wild, in the mid-1950s the Division of Wildlife obtained some trapped wild birds from a game agency in another state. In February 1956, 10 were released in Vinton County. Between 1956 and 1971, another 397 turkeys were released in southeastern Ohio. By 1983, wild turkeys were known to be in 32 counties, and there were estimated to be 7,677 individuals.*

With the Division of Wildlife continuing its trap-and-release program, wild turkeys are now found in most areas of the state where suitable habitat exists. There are hunting seasons in fall and spring, with various restrictions to allow the population to continue to expand. I see turkeys often as I hike the trails around the state—sizable flocks in the forest in the winter and females with their broods in fields near the edge of the woods in late spring or early summer. It's a thrill to see them at any time of year.

a beaver pond, then zigzags up the hill and over to Point K and OH 56. From Points J to K, the trail covers 2.2 miles. The 1.6-mile K–L section begins as the trail turns west to cross the highway. It then follows another old road up a ravine to the ridgetops to the west.

Almost 1 mile from Point K, and after crossing back into Vinton County, the old road turns right (north) and the Backpack Trail turns south. It then dips and rises along the ridges as it passes over a 1,040-foot knob to close the loop at Point I. After a good night's rest and a hearty breakfast at the campsite down the white-blazed trail from this intersection, it's time to fill your water containers—the last drinking water source on the trail is at Point L—and begin the 5.3-mile trek on the north side of the loop.

Less than a mile in length, the two-way L-to-G trail travels the high ground between Honeycomb Hollow to the north and Morgan Hollow to the south, eventually dropping into the latter. Turning right, it follows the stream to the mouth of the hollow at Sandy Run and OH 278.

After crossing OH 278, turn left to follow the highway for 0.1 mile. A corrugated steel building on the left side of the road is Stop 171, a metering station utilized in the Lake Hope mine-sealing demonstration project. It contains instruments that monitor water quality and flow. The objective of the project is to prevent acid mine drainage from old drift mines upstream from entering the Lake Hope area.

Point N, where the trail leaves the highway to the west, is at the end of the guardrail on the right side of the road. From the road, the trail climbs steeply, gaining 200 feet in a very short distance. As you continue up Starrett Ridge, it becomes obvious that the trail is following an old road. Stop 18 is a reminder that this was once a township road, used until about 1920. It was about that time when the last few farms in what is now Zaleski State Forest were abandoned. The road and trail follow the ridge for about .5 mile, rising gently. The trail turns left to climb to an area now overgrown with shrubs, which Stop 19 identifies as the

site of a former farm. The foundation stones, old wells, and cellars have all but disappeared, but fencerows and ornamental, shade, and fruit trees reveal its past use. From the homestead site, the trail follows old roads south on Long Ridge. It makes a left turn, and then almost immediately a right. After paralleling Road 11B on Long Ridge for about .75 mile, the trail meets Irish Ridge Road at Point O.

The next section of trail goes through what is perhaps the longest, loveliest hollow in the area. After crossing Irish Ridge Road (Point O), the trail goes out a lightly wooded side ridge, then drops into the upper end of Stony Hollow. The hollow hosts one of the better displays of wildflowers in April and May. Reaching the bottom first in a side ravine, the trail turns right to enter the main hollow and turn left downstream. For the next 1.75 miles, the trail follows the stream toward Sandy Run. For the most part it stays on the left side of the hollow, at three points climbing partway up the hillside, only to return to the valley. It crosses the stream eight or nine times, but the crossings are easy except in bad weather. It also passes by a rock shelter big enough to walk into. For many years an old slab pile marked where a portable sawmill operated during the early 1950s. Mother Nature seems to have claimed it, though, because the last time I walked here I could see no trace of it. After several more stream crossings, the trail again climbs the hillside, traveling between a sandstone cliff and a slump block. After climbing above a wide curve in the creek below, the trail drops to meet the campground entry road at Point P.

Following the hard-surfaced road to the left, the trail quickly reaches OH 278, where it turns right. After just over .25 mile, you pass Hope Furnace on the right and arrive at the trailhead parking lot.

34

Caesar Creek Gorge State Nature Preserve

Total distance: 2 miles (4 km)

Hiking time: 1.5 hours

Maximum elevation: 900 feet

Vertical rise: 200 feet

Maps: USGS 7½' Oregonia; ODNR/DNAP Caesar Creek Gorge State Nature Preserve brochure; Friends of Caesar Creek, Caesar Creek Lake Map and Guide to Trails, Plants, and Fossils

Caesar Creek is flanked by 180-foot cliffs of fossil-rich Ordovician limestone and shales where it flows through this 463-acre state nature preserve. Great volumes of glacial meltwater cut through the Cuba Moraine east of the preserve, then through the exposed, relatively soft Ordovician bedrock in the preserve, on its way south to the Ohio and Mississippi watersheds, and ultimately to the Gulf of Mexico and the Atlantic Ocean.

Though dammed to create Caesar Creek Lake—an Army Corps of Engineers impoundment just east of the preserve—the creek supports rich aquatic animal life, and its banks a wide variety of plants. The slopes to the creek are forested with mature hardwoods such as beech, oaks, and maples. The uplands show evidence of pasturing and some row-crop farming, but the state acquired the property more than 30 years ago and those fields are fast turning into young forest. Several state-listed plant species are found in the preserve. Interestingly, prairie dock and shooting star, both with high affinity to native prairies, are present here.

Old roads, foundation stones, fruit trees, and non-native plants often associated with pioneer homesites betray the former presence of white settlers. Earlier occupancy by successive cultures of Native Americans is well documented. Many earthworks thought to be of Hopewell origins are found within a few miles of the Caesar Creek Preserve.

The preserve extends to the east bank of the nearby Little Miami State and National Scenic River, protecting the floodplain and

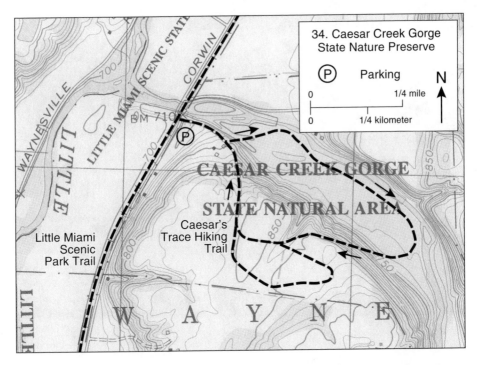

The map shows:

34. Caesar Creek Gorge State Nature Preserve

(P) Parking N

0 — 1/4 mile
0 — 1/4 kilometer

CAESAR CREEK GORGE STATE NATURAL AREA

Little Miami Scenic Park Trail

Caesar's Trace Hiking Trail

W A Y N E

helping to stabilize the riverbanks. Even the shared name of the creek and preserve relates to the Indians. In 1776, a Shawnee party attacked a flatboat on the Ohio River and took captive a black slave called Cizar. He was adopted into the tribe and spent much of his time hunting near a stream he liked so well he named it after himself. When Simon Kenton planned his escape from Oldtown, it was Cizar who advised him to follow Caesar Creek down to the east bank of the Little Miami to avoid the west-bank Indian trail.

The spring flora of the sweet soil of the forested hillsides on both sides of the creek is especially luxuriant. It's a good place to photograph native wildflowers, protected from the annoying breezes by the steep-walled valley. Unfortunately, like so much of this part of Ohio, invasion by bush honeysuckle, garlic mustard, and other alien plants is a problem.

The Little Miami Scenic Park bike trail, which extends from Springfield to Cincinnati, passes through the preserve along Corwin Road. As with most state nature preserves, there are minimal facilities. But Caesar Creek State Park, located just a few miles east of the preserve, offers a great variety of outdoor recreation opportunities and facilities. There are a number of privately operated canoe/kayak/raft rental operations up and down the Little Miami River.

How to Get There
Caesar Creek Nature Preserve is located in Wayne Township in northeastern Warren County. The trail parking lot is located 3 miles north of the village of Oregonia and 2 miles south of the village of Corwin, on the east side of Corwin Road. To reach it, take US 42 to OH 73 at Waynesville. Then turn east 1 mile to Clarksville Road and travel 1.25 miles south to Middletown. Turn left (west) and go

Caesar Creek

2 miles to Corwin Road. Then turn left and travel 0.5 mile to the preserve parking lot on the east (left) side of Corwin Road.

The Trail

The 2-mile long Caesar's Trace Hiking Trail begins from the northeast corner of the parking lot. It curves to the right and climbs to join an old gravel road coming up from Corwin Road. There you will find a bulletin board with information about this preserve and other preserves and events of the Division of Natural Areas and Preserves. Turn and follow the wide trail uphill to where an arrow on a post on the left side of the road points to the left. Here a natural-surface trail, dressed for a few yards with wood chips, heads at an angle downhill toward Caesar Creek. The forest changes from the mixed mesophytic association of the north-facing hillside to floodplain forest. There are lots of large cottonwoods, sycamores, box elders, black walnuts, and, in the understory, pawpaw. Visible on the hot day in August when I scouted the trail were many of the wildflower species that still have foliage in midsummer. The mayapples had nearly ripe fruit, awaiting consumption for a wandering box turtle. White snakeroot, the plant associated with milk sickness, was in bloom where sunlight reached the floor of the woodland. A number of "wild" trails lead to the bank of the creek, likely made by fishermen. Some sandy areas are covered with scouring rush. Here and there stand young red-cedar trees, pioneers in the abandoned field of 25 years ago but now being crowded out by the floodplain hardwoods.

The silence of my hike was soon broken by the sound of rippling water, a shallow rapid in the creek. I followed a side trail to the bank and was rewarded with a wonderful view of the 180-foot calcareous shale cliff on the opposite side of the stream.

50 Hikes in Ohio

Large granite glacial erratics stood out in the stream, carried here by ice and water during one of the periods of glaciation.

Moving away from the creek, the trail utilizes a set of eight steps as it makes a turnabout to angle up the hillside to the high ground. The steps, a bridge, water bars, and other trail improvements were built in May 1998, by Boy Scouts from Troop 85 of Beavercreek under the supervision of Eagle Scout candidate Mike McClurg. The trail appears to be an early road or farm lane. In some places crushed limestone or wood chips have been applied to the trail to reduce erosion and improve the walking surface.

On the high ground at last, arrows on posts point to the left and right. The left trail goes east then circles back around toward the trailhead, passing through former farm fields rapidly being overgrown with red-cedars and young hardwoods. The trail to the right heads west, back away from edge of the hill, winding among weed trees such as red-cedars, black locust, and hackberry. Soon the other trail that circled through the old fields comes in from the right rear. Caesar's Trace winds its way down the long gentle slope to the trailhead bulletin board and the grass path to the left that leads to the parking lot.

35

Chaparral Prairie State Nature Preserve

Total distance: 1.5 miles (2.4 km)

Hiking time: 1 hour

Maximum elevation: 960 feet

Vertical rise: 63 feet

Maps: USGS 7½' West Union; ODNR/DNAP Chaparral Prairie State Nature Preserve brochure

The articles of dedication that created this preserve call for its preservation as a "black-jack–post oak prairie opening." That description does not do justice to this very special 67-acre Adams County preserve. Even though it was farmed for many years, ending only in 1984, it isn't nearly as eroded as other prairie preserves in the West Union area. It has a well-defined trail that goes through a variety of interesting habitats. There is a man-made pond near the entrance that can be alive with amorous singing male frogs of several species in the spring and nearly a dozen state-listed plant species are found on the preserve. In July, when the prairie plants are in full bloom, it is a place of rare beauty. Just inside of the preserve, the lay of the land allows a sweeping vista of a hillside that will be covered with rattlesnake master, prairie dock, tall coreopsis, prairie false-indigo, and tall blazing star in a good water year. (In the southwestern corner of the preserve, some of tall blazing star plants along the trail bloom white instead of their usual lavender.) Amid this spectacular display of prairie forbs, the blackjack and post oaks are so close to the trail that you can't miss seeing them.

Because of the area's past agricultural use, management efforts are largely aimed at eliminating alien plants that remain from that period. Restoration of additional prairie using seed harvested in the area is also a part of the program. Lastly, but of great importance, is the continuous task of monitoring the health of the populations of rare plants that grow in the preserve.

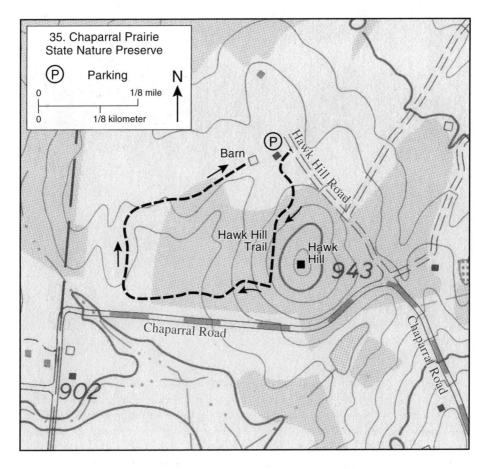

Management techniques include prescribed burning of selected areas, occasional use of a selective herbicide to eliminate nuisance species, and hand removal followed by stump spray of an herbicide of some woody species such as the invasive red-cedar. The forage legumes, white and yellow sweet clover, that remain from the farming operation are especially difficult to remove. Along with the statewide nuisance garlic mustard, they succumb best to persistence hand removal over many seasons.

Purple milkweed (*Asclepias purpurascens*), a plant that I'm very fond of, grows here in the old farm fields instead of the prairie patches. Along with the common milkweed (*A. syriaca*), also in the old fields, and the rarer whorled milkweed (*A. verticillata*), it can be relied on to draw monarch butterflies to the area in midsummer.

How to Get There

Chaparral Prairie Preserve is located in Tiffin Township (named for one of Ohio's founding fathers, patriot, politician, physician, and Methodist preacher, Edwin Tiffen) in rural Adams County. To reach it from West Union, the county seat (located on OH 125), travel north 0.7 mile on OH 247, then turn left on Chaparral Road and go 2.7 miles to where the paved road makes a

An area regenerating following a prescribed burn

sharp left turn. Instead of turning, go straight north on graveled Hawk Hill Road (TR 23). The entrance to the preserve is on the left about 0.2 mile from the intersection. There is a DNAP district maintenance facility just inside the gate, but no pubic facilities. If the gate is open, park inside; if not, park outside that gate but do not block entry.

The Trail

Begin your hike by visiting the bulletin board and then heading out on the Hawk Hill Trail. The presence of an apple tree close to the trail gives away the fact that there was once a farmhouse close by. The grass-surfaced trail goes to the left, first downhill, then up-hill to the edge of the forest on Hawk Hill. There are well-written interpretive signs along the trail that tell about the habitat, the plants and animal species, and the management practices that you will encounter.

Take time to read them. The sweep of prairie vista that was described in the introduction to this chapter is the hillside prairie the trail passes through on the way to the oak woods on Hawk Hill. Once inside the woods, the trail turns to the right and moves from one prairie opening to another, crossing an occasional footbridge as it slowly drops to the stream that drains the preserve.

Note the effect of prescribed fire on the oak woods. Look for prairie dock along the hillside trail. The farm pond that is a breeding site for local amphibians is visible from the hillside trail. A power line that crosses the preserve needs no tree removal when it hangs over native prairie. In this country of soils derived from calcareous bedrock, red-cedar is an early invader of abandoned fields, and that was the case on this land. As you hike the trail, you can clearly see them in the prairie opening and underneath the hardwoods in the woodland. The various effects of treatment with fire are visible. If the fire runs by them quickly, they live to see another year. If they get hit with a crown fire, they probably will succumb. You will see both scenarios, plus the effect of hand removal, as you circumnavigate the preserve on the trail. The preserve is small enough that you can't get lost even if you find yourself on a fire break instead of the designated trail. Because of the presence of endangered and threatened plant species, you must stay on the trails or fire breaks that surround the old farm fields. The trail loops around the best of the prairie area, ending up back at the entrance.

This is the best of several small prairie preserves in the area. At Chaparral Prairie you are in between the till plain of the Illinoian glacier just to the west and the Allegheny Escarpment only a few miles to the east in what is called the Outer Bluegrass Region of Ohio. Most of the region is drained by Ohio Brush Creek and its tributaries, but the runoff from Chaparral Prairie flows directly to the Ohio River via Eagle Creek. The presence of limestone and dolomite bedrock near the surface creates near neutral, or even alkaline soil, so-called "sweet soil," good nourishment for plants. It is essential for a subset of plants that do best or will only grow on that kind of soil, plants botanists call "calciphiles." Consequently, the region is home to a high number of state-listed plants; those found in so few places in the state that they are considered rare, threatened, or potentially threatened.

While you are in the area, plan to hike Adams Lake Prairie State Nature Preserve and one or more of the areas of The Edge of Appalachia Preserve System owned by the Cincinnati Museum Center and The Nature Conservancy.

36

Charleston Falls Preserve

Total distance: 2 miles (3.2 km)

Hiking time: 1.5 hours

Maximum elevation: 900 feet

Vertical rise: 65 feet

Maps: USGS 7½' Tipp City; MCPD Charleston Falls Preserve map

Charleston Falls Preserve is a 216-acre sanctuary located north of Dayton, 3 miles south of Tipp City. It is a facility of the Miami County Park District. Charleston Creek and the falls on that stream get their names from the small community of West Charleston, which lies a mile to the east. The creek arises from a spring just east of the park. The central feature of this petite preserve is the beautiful waterfall where Charleston Creek tumbles over a 37-foot limestone escarpment into a cool shaded ravine. Here, rocks of lower Silurian age, formed from material deposited in the bottom of warm, shallow seas perhaps 400 to 440 million years ago, lie at the surface. The small stream is making its way downhill to the Great Miami River, less than a mile to the west.

The rock exposed at Charleston Falls is essentially the same age as that exposed at the escarpment at the eastern end of Lake Erie. The formation near the surface at the top of the falls is Brassfield limestone. It is especially blocky and tough here, referred to as Bioclastic Brassfield, because it is rich in fossils. Below it are limestones of the Belfast Beds, which are layered and crossbedded, allowing water to penetrate easily. Freezing and thawing action breaks this rock apart, leaving the layer above it. The next stratum down in this valley head is Elkhorn shale, an Ordovician-aged (440 to 500 million years since deposition) member of the Cincinnatian shale. Loose, crumbly, and relatively impenetrable to water, the shale forms a slope away from the base of the rocks above. This remarkable little gorge

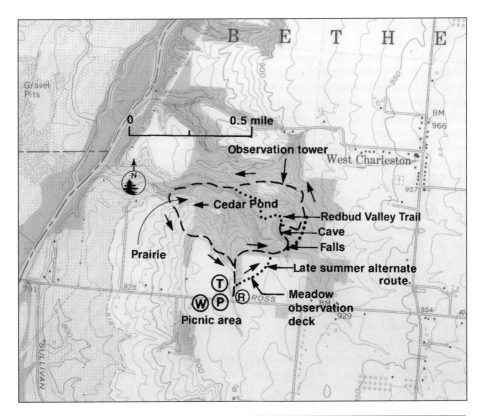

was cut by the massive amounts of glacial meltwater that flowed along this drainage as the last glacier melted, until it was gone from the divide 33 miles to the north.

Managed not as a park for active recreation but as a natural area, Charleston Falls has a trail system that allows visitors to observe its special natural features without damaging them. The only picnic area is close to the road, away from the falls and stream. Rest rooms are located at the rear of the parking lot. Maps at intervals throughout the preserve show where you are.

How to Get There

Take OH 202 north off I-70 (Exit 36). Travel 3 miles to Ross Road and turn left (west); the preserve entrance is on the right. Park at the only lot.

The Trail

Walk east 100 feet, past a bulletin board, to a trail running north and south along a shaded old fenceline. To the right (south) toward the road is the picnic area, and an entrance to another trail to the falls that goes across an open meadow. Choose this trail in late summer, when the goldenrod and New England asters are in bloom and monarchs are nectaring in preparation for their flight toward Mexico. There is an observation deck where you look out over the top of the vegetation. At other times of the year, turn left and follow the .3-mile trail north and then east through the forest to the falls.

In all but the driest of seasons, the falls will be heard before it is seen. Walk to the top of the falls for a careful look from above.

Charleston Falls Preserve

Then backtrack 50 feet to a short trail to the right that leads to wooden and natural stone steps going into the ravine below the falls. Take care, for there are no handrails on the steps or boardwalk below. An observation area allows a closer look at the escarpment. Water comes over the rim in at least two places. In the right light, the falls will produce a beautiful rainbow. Because of the slumping shale at the base of the cliff, no real plunge pool exists. Instead, the water falls onto a rocky talus slope.

Continue across the boardwalk, and then climb more wooden steps to another observation platform for a look at the falls from the left side. From there, scramble up the natural rock "steps" to the base of the dolomite cliff. Follow the trail for about 700 feet below the cliff face, passing a small limestone cave, until it climbs on a few wooden steps to double back on itself. The calcareous soils derived from the limestones of this gorge are especially conducive to the growth of such plants as Virginia bluebell, purple cliffbrake, walking fern, and columbine. Look for them along the way. Turn left at a sign that says RETURN LOOP. Take this trail about 200 feet to where it intersects another trail. Turn left on the trail to the Thorny Badlands.

There is a less rigorous alternative route to continue hiking the Charleston Falls Trail. Instead of taking the steps to the observation area beneath the falls, follow the trail to the east from the overlook area above the falls. Very soon, it curves toward the north and then reaches Charleston Creek where you have the option of crossing on a bridge, fording the creek, or carefully crossing on artificial stepping-stones. Continue directly ahead on the wide path and soon you will be on the trail to the Thorny Badlands. At the top of the first rise, there is a split in the trail. The left fork is the Redbud Valley Trail,

which follows a low route downstream. I suggest opting for the Thorny Badlands Trail, which sticks to the high ground. Here and there to the side of the trail you will see glacial erratics, reminding you of the glacial past of this part of Ohio. At another intersection the Thorny Badlands Trail is joined by the trail connecting to the falls and rim trails. There is nice bench at this juncture, one of many you will find along the trail.

The trail dips to cross a bridge, then rises to an area where white pines were once planted to halt an erosion problem on the abused slope to the left. Here you can see many special year-round residents like barred owls and chickadees and transients like purple finches and pine warblers. You can easily discern when the pines were planted because each whorl of branches represents one year's growth. These trees are lovely now and have served their purpose in controlling erosion. In due time, they will die out as they become overtopped by invading deciduous trees. This is hardwood country.

At the high point on the trail stands a wooden observation tower where you can look over the treetops on the hillside below. When the trail system was designed, this hillside was covered with hawthorn trees. In this part of Ohio, when land is taken out of pasturage, invasion by hawthorns often follows invasion by old field grasses and forbs, ahead of invasion by forest hardwoods. These hawthorns are now being overtopped by tuliptrees, maples, and oaks. Beyond the tower, the land is still recovering from its agricultural past, with sumac trees and old field species along the trail. Soon there is a marked change in environment as the trail enters a forest tunnel. Too dark for many plants, this place is ideal for fungi, the decomposers of the natural world.

At the trail juncture with the Redbud

The sign at Cedar Pond must be read in its reflection

Valley Trail, continue straight ahead. After a short distance, a spur trail to the left leads to a bench overlooking the stream. This is a good place to rest body and soul and to contemplate the words of others, such as Henry David Thoreau, who wrote, "I went to the woods because I wished to live deliberately, to front only the essential facts of life, and see if I could not learn what it had to teach, and not, when I came to die, discover that I had not lived."

Back on the main trail, continue downstream. You soon cross Charleston Creek on man-made stepping stones. The path climbs uphill from the stream, and in about 100 feet comes out into the open at the edge of a small planted prairie. Using seeds gathered from remnant prairies within 50 miles of here, the park staff—under the leadership of the former Miami County Park District director, the late Scott L. Huston—created a prairie where one never before existed. Given its thin soil over limestone, the eroded slope was a good place to plant native prairie grasses and forbs. Small patches of original prairie occur along the Stillwater River not far from here in Miami County, on a variety of mesic and xeric sites. (A good example can be seen in the Miami Park District's Stillwater Prairie Reserve off OH 185, 9 miles west of Piqua.) Leave the main trail and walk the narrow path uphill through the prairie, noting how it looks in this season. Be certain to return to this site during the last week of July or the first week of August for a spectacular show of native prairie flora. For a better understanding of what the pioneers faced when they encountered the prairies of west-central Ohio, turn left and walk through this hilltop prairie.

Returning to the main trail, turn left and walk uphill. Look left at the serene setting of small, man-made Cedar Pond. There is a sign in the pond that reads correctly only in its reflection. Stay long enough to let the green frogs or cricket frogs return to their calling and take time to contemplate how the dragonflies, damselflies, red-winged blackbirds, and swallows fit into the natural world.

Heading due south, follow the main trail to where it turns left (east) along an old fencerow. Ignore the side trail to Locust Grove that leaves the main trail to the right at this corner. After traveling about 600 feet, take the trail to the right as it swings southeast past a small meadow, then heads to the shaded trail leading to the parking lot. Take home some good pictures and lots of good memories; leave only footprints, and return often to walk the trails here at all seasons of the year.

37

East Fork State Park

Total distance: 14 miles (21.2 km)

Hiking time: 8 hours or 2, 3, or 4 days

Maximum elevation: 860 feet

Vertical rise: 125 feet

Maps: USGS 7½' Batavia; USGS 7½' Bethel; USGS 7½' Williamsburg; ODNR East Fork State Park map; USACE William H. Harsha Lake, Ohio, map

William H. Harsha Lake on the East Fork of the Little Miami River was one of the last Army Corps of Engineers flood-control reservoirs built in Ohio. Completed in 1978, the 2,160-acre impoundment locates water-based recreation within 25 miles of Cincinnati. It was named in honor of the former congressman from Portsmouth, whose 21 years in the U.S. House of Representatives included 11 as the ranking Republican on the Public Works and Transportation Committee. The East Fork of the Little Miami River drains 362 square miles of flat, relatively continuous Illinoian ground moraine in the middle of Clermont County. Of the project land area, the corps maintains 660 acres, the Ohio Division of Wildlife manages 2,248 acres for hunting, and the Division of Parks and Recreation manages 5,618 acres as East Fork State Park. State park literature calls the impoundment East Fork Lake, while the Corps of Engineers brochure refers to it as William H. Harsha Lake.

There are two major hiking trails in the park. The one I describe here is the East Fork Backpack Trail, a 14-mile route where 5.5 miles of trail are hiked in two directions and the remaining 3 miles as a loop at the far end. It is located entirely on the south side of Harsha Lake and can be walked as a day hike or as a backpack trip using the two campsites it shares with a longer trail for one, two, or three overnights. The first campsite is just over 3 miles from the trailhead. The second is about 4 miles beyond, at the farthest point on the trail.

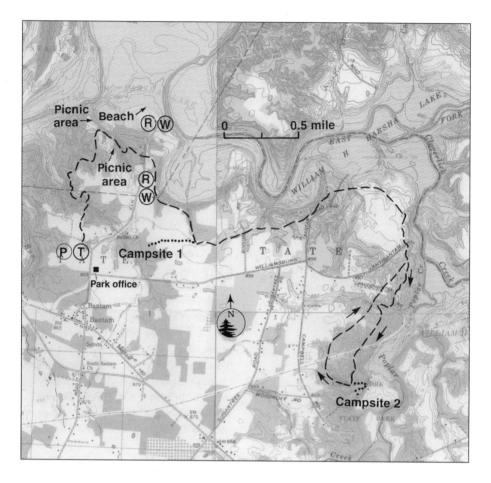

Though admittedly less scenic than some other backpacking trails in Ohio and nearby states, this trail is an excellent introduction to backpacking. The climbs are easy, the distances short and flexible, and the camping facilities good. Even with an "after work on Friday" start, hikers from the Columbus, Dayton, and Cincinnati areas can make the first campsite by dark during the summer months. With a day pack containing lunch and water, you can also make this a day hike. Remember that the area has been in public ownership for just over 30 years. Think what it will be like when it has been protected as long as places like John

Bryan State Park or the parks in Hocking Hills. Enjoy watching it grow.

The state park also maintains a second trail known as the Steve Newman Worldwalker Perimeter Trail in honor of the young man from the area who walked around the globe. This trail is 31.5 miles long, with four overnight sites, and is open to horseback riders as well as hikers. It circumnavigates the lake and requires two unbridged river crossings that are difficult at some times of the year. It is not shown on the map. If you are interested in this hike, a brochure with a map is available from the Department of Natural Resources. In addition, the combined Buckeye Trail, North Country Trail, and American Discovery Trail pass through the park on the north side of East Fork Lake.

How to Get There

The Backpack Trail originates at a parking lot near the park office on the south side of the lake. Take OH 125 east (toward Amelia) from I-275, Exit 65. After about 8 miles, OH 222 enters from the left. One and a half miles beyond, OH 222 turns right. At that intersection, turn left onto Bantam Road. A half mile ahead there is a sign that points left to BACK COUNTRY TRAIL SOUTH ACCESS PARKING. The gravel drive passes between two ponds and ends at the trailhead parking lot. A bulletin board shows the route of both the Backpack and Perimeter Trails. There is no fee for using the trail, but for safety reasons every hiker should self-register.

The Trail

A sign identifies the trail going north from the parking lot as the EAST FORK BACKPACK TRAIL. It is well marked along the entire route with red paint blazes on the main trail and white on side trails. (The Perimeter Trail uses green blazes.)

Leaving the trailhead, the natural-surface path winds its way through an area rapidly succeeding from shrubs to woodland. It soon transitions into older woodlands, heading toward the lake about 1 mile away. At a ravine, it descends downstream to the left on log steps before crossing the stream on stepping-stones. Turning right, it climbs to high ground and then heads left toward the lake. Two smaller streams are spanned by footbridges before the trail makes a sweeping U-turn, staying on the high ground. A bench for the weary or contemplative sits along the trail. After crossing a series of smaller ravines on steps and

bridges, the trail splits. The first mile marker is in this area. Take the left fork along the edge of the woods. Before dropping to the picnic area, the trail crosses an open area where there is a grand view of the lake.

Beyond the road, the trail descends on another set of log steps, then, after about 50 feet, it turns right along an old field before entering the woods. This turn is easy to miss during the growing season. Two wooden bridges span small ravines, and then the trail climbs to an open field. It swings right alongside the woods, enters, and then drops to a deep ravine. Going upstream to cross without a bridge, the trail turns left and climbs to another fork. Now turning right, it travels between forest on the right and brambles on the left. In about 100 feet it enters the woods, turning to the right. The second mile marker is in this vicinity.

When it emerges from the woods, it crosses the beach entrance road. Water is available here during the warmer months, public toilets are present, and there is a picnic area just ahead on the right.

The trail now curves to the right just inside the woods from the picnic area. Pay no attention to the many side trails coming from that area. Staying on the contour around the curve, it intersects another trail, goes left, and proceeds down a set of steps. It turns right to intersect another trail before a bridge, and then turns left to cross the bridge before turning right again. Fortunately, these turns are all well marked with blazes. After crossing a small wash, the trail drops to a bridge. It then climbs back to the edge of the high ground, which it follows to another bridge. Steeply climbing away from that bridge, the trail returns to level ground, where you will find mile marker 3. Soon it intersects a side trail to the right where a sign reads OVERNIGHT AREA.

A white-blazed trail leads across the

East Fork State Park trailhead

boat-ramp road, along an old fencerow, and into a woods to the camping area shared with the Perimeter Trail. Facilities there include toilets, picnic tables, and two low, floorless bunkhouses that will each accommodate two campers. There is no drinking water at the site. Tents are welcome.

Back at the intersection of the main trail and white-blazed side trail, the Backpack Trail soon emerges from the woods to cross the boat-ramp road and reenter the woods, continuing eastward. This is the last public road the trail crosses, although the next overnight area is within a short walk of one. Beyond this point the trail crosses a narrow, paved, abandoned road. The trail through here is sometimes difficult to follow. Keep checking for red blazes. Crossing ravines and washouts and moving up and down the slope, the trail passes mile marker 4. Eventually it swings south near mile marker 5 to follow the rim of the now impounded

valleys of Cloverlick and Poplar Creeks.

All along the trail the successional woods are full of alien "nuisance plants." Japanese honeysuckle, multiflora rose, bush honeysuckle, and *Euonymus fortunei* are ever-present. Add native brambles such as blackberries, and traveling along the edge of the abandoned fields can sometimes be difficult. But the trail is blazed well and can be followed if you watch carefully for marks. If the blazes do disappear, you have probably missed a turn. Just backtrack and you'll locate the proper route.

The trail crosses two more abandoned paved roads. Bantam Road—the northern extension of the still-open North Campbell Road—is crossed before the trail begins to swing southeast. From that crossing, the distance to the second campsite is just a little over 2 miles. About .5 mile farther down the trail, after it turns to the south, you cross Antibantam Road.

➤ The North Country National Scenic Trail in Ohio

Federal legislation authorized the establishment of the North Country National Scenic Trail (NCNST) in March 1980 as a component of the National Trails System. Planned primarily as a route for pleasure walking and hiking, when completed it will extend from the vicinity of Crown Point, New York, to Lake Sakakawea State Park on the Missouri River in North Dakota, where it joins the route of the Lewis and Clark National Historic Trail. It crosses seven states, including Ohio, and when done it will be the longest continuous hiking trail in the country. The best estimate is that the final length will be near 4,200 miles. The development and management of the trail is being accomplished in cooperation with many federal, state, and local agencies and private trail groups and individuals. It is being built and maintained primarily by volunteers, mostly members or associates of the North Country Trail Association. As sections of trail are finished, they are inspected by, and receive certification from, the National Park Service.

Thanks to the many years of trail building by the Buckeye Trail Association, the Ohio NCNST is the most completely usable part of the trail. Statewide, 24 segments totaling 287 miles have been certified. Much, but not all, of the NCNST utilizes the path of the Buckeye Trail. And like the BT, much of the marked trail is located on secondary roads. The trail is marked with vertical painted blue blazes, much the same as the BT. Blazes are on trees, or on posts in treeless areas. At intersections with roads and other trails, small blue and gold North Country Trail emblems are used.

From the east, the trail enters Ohio near Negley on the former Montour railroad right-of-way. The first state park land it encounters is Beaver Creek State Park. At last writing, the route was still not clearly defined in this part of the state, but the proposed general route parallels US 30 and SR 183 to Zoar. At that historic village it meets up with the Buckeye Trail, which it follows more or less for 600 miles around Ohio, heading first southwest through conservancy district, state park, and state and national forest and Ohio State Memorial lands toward the Ohio River. From there, it parallels the river for stretches out toward the Cincinnati area. Turning north toward Michigan, it uses a State Scenic Trail that parallels a National Scenic River and park district and municipal parklands and old canal towpaths to reach the Maumee River. In many places, by necessity and with the owners' permission, it uses private lands or occasionally resorts to lightly used roads. At Napoleon, the NTNST and the BT separate. From there to the Michigan line it utilizes the Cannonball Trail. It exits the state north of West Unity. Information about volunteering to help build and maintain the trail and the most recent information about its route is available at http://www.northcountry trail.org/explore/ex_oh/oh.htm.

If you are exploring the hikes in this book, you will encounter the NCNST at Atwood and Tappan Parks in the Muskingum Watershed Conservancy District and at Archers Fork in the Wayne National Forest, Fort Hill State Memorial, Shawnee State Forest, East Fork State Park, Lockington Reserve, and Oak Openings Metropark. Look for the symbols where it joins and leaves the trail you are on and dream about trekking east to Crown Point, New York, to the site of what was once a French, then English, fort, the setting for several of Kenneth Roberts's novels, including Northwest Passage and Rabble in Arms. Or the best of all dreams for a hiker, walk west to hit the Lewis and Clark Trail to the Pacific Ocean.

Next, the trail climbs slightly, passes an old fenceline, then drops steeply to the left to cross a wooden bridge. Beyond the bridge, the trail rises gently to a shrubby area in the direction of the lake and then reenters the woods. Just beyond here your outbound trail goes straight ahead while the return route comes in from the right. The 6-mile marker is approximately .5 mile beyond here.

There are many ravine crossings ahead, and the trail almost gets lost in tall grass a time or two. The blazes can be difficult to see where the trail passes through a peaceful pine planting, but the most difficult place to follow the trail is where it crosses under a high-tension power line. After coming into the right-of-way, go uphill, angling left. There are a couple of very small footbridges across the wash that are obviously part of the trail. Look uphill to the next tower, where there is a blaze. After passing the tower, follow the left edge of the woods to a blaze indicating that the trail is exiting the right-of-way. Mile marker 7 is about 400 yards ahead. The campsite and the end of the loop are only minutes from here. The power line actually lies farther south than shown on the USGS map, having been moved during construction of the lake.

The trail drops to near lake level and crosses a bridge. When it intersects an old dirt road that comes downhill to the lake's edge from the southwest, the campsite is just ahead. The site is under large oak trees

at the top of the hill beyond the road. White blazes lead to it. The two bunkhouses here are larger than at the other campsite and will house four people each on plywood bunks. There are also toilets and tables, but no water. Again, this area is shared with folks using the Perimeter Trail, so there may be horses and trail riders as well as long-distance hikers. In case of an emergency, North Campbell Road is less than .5 mile away; you can reach it by walking up the abandoned road below the campsite.

The entrance to the red-blazed return route isn't difficult to find if you know where to look. Return to the wooden bridge—sometimes washed out—that the trail came in on. A short distance after crossing a bridge, the trail goes left, not across the creek but following it upstream for about 50 feet before turning left up a steep diagonal climb. The hike now becomes easier than the outbound trail since the ravine crossings are farther from the lake. Even the power-line crossing is easier—go directly across the right-of-way. The trail passes through a nice grove of tall, well-spaced trees. There was a dump of old tires here when I walked the trail in 1989, and they were still here in 1996. Mile marker 8 is located nearby. After about 1 mile of walking, you will reach a familiar T. A left turn leads you back to the trailhead via the outbound trail. If you want to remain on the trail a third night, turn left at the white-blazed side trail 3 miles before reaching the trailhead.

38

Edge of Appalachia Preserve (Buzzardroost Rock Trail)

Total distance: 3 miles (4.8 km)

Maximum elevation: 992 feet

Vertical rise: 288 feet

Maps: USGS 7½' Lynx, map that accompanies CNC/TNC Edge of Appalachia Preserve System

On the back cover of *Walks and Rambles in Southwestern Ohio,* which I wrote in 1994, I am pictured standing on the platform atop Buzzardroost Rock. I was 65 when I last made that climb and took that picture. I never thought that I would again reach Buzzardroost Rock to marvel at the prairie plants that rim the platform and scan the beautiful valley of Ohio Brush Creek before me. But when I was considering what new trails to add to this edition of *50 Hikes in Ohio,* my mind kept returning to that special place and the trail that leads to it. So, at 10 A.M. on a hot day in mid-August 2006, with braces on both lower legs and 77 birthdays behind me, I hung a camera around my neck, put a hydration pack on my back, and, with two trekking poles, headed up the trail alone. Tucked in my pack were the necessities of the trail plus one of Manfrotto's Super Clamps to allow me to document the trip. At 11:47 A.M., I was standing on the platform, basking in the noonday sun, elated by my accomplishment. At 12:57 P.M., with photos of butterflies, flowers, scenery, and a self portrait taken, I started my return trip. By 2:47 P.M., I was back at my car, very tired, but very pleased with my hike.

I have made that climb probably 10 times since my trip in April 1997, no two by the same route. In recent years, the folks from The Nature Conservancy and the Cincinnati Museum Center, who manage the area, have established a good, stable foot trail to the promontory, albeit still a difficult climb. It's one that should be taken by every Ohioan who wants to stand on the western edge of the

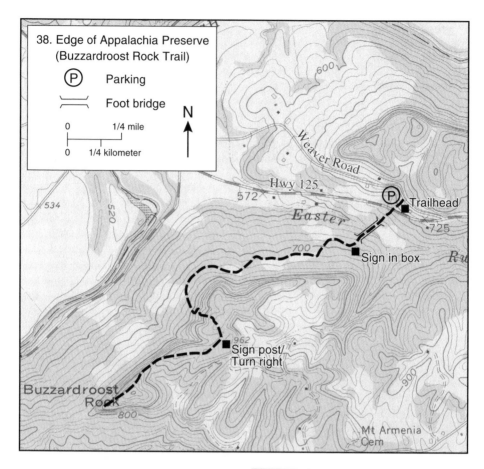

38. Edge of Appalachia Preserve (Buzzardroost Rock Trail)

P　　Parking

⌣⌣　　Foot bridge

N

0　　　　1/4 mile

0　　　1/4 kilometer

Weaver Road

Hwy 125

572

534

520

600

Easter

700

P　Trailhead

·725

Sign in box

R

962

Sign post/
Turn right

Buzzardroost
Rock

800

900

Mt Armenia
Cem

Allegheny Escarpment in the Outer Bluegrass Region of the state at the center of the 13,000-acre Edge of Appalachia Preserve, the "crown jewel of Ohio's natural areas." Open to the public since 1967, Buzzardroost Rock honors Christian and Emma Goetz. It is a National Natural Landmark.

How to Get There

From West Union—the intersection of OH 125 and OH 41 in the Adams County seat—travel on OH 125 east 5.8 miles to Weaver Road on the left (north). Follow Weaver Road 0.9 mile to the trailhead parking lot on the left. Stow your valuables out of sight and lock your car.

The Trail

Buzzardroost Rock Trail begins with four stone steps downhill from the rear right corner of the parking lot. Big bluestem, the dominant grass of the tallgrass prairie, grows here. This small patch of prairie is said to be the westernmost remnant of the prairie that at one time flourished around the town of Lynx. Look for the prairie forb hoary puccoon in this small prairie tract in May and for whorled rosinweed (recently reclassified as a subspecies of the southeastern species starry rosinweed) in July and August. Yellow-flowered leafcup (recently moved to the genus *Smallanthus*), a plant of the forest edge that I seldom see, was in bloom next to the trail when I made my hike in 2006.

Be careful as you cross the highway to then pass through an opening in the guardrail and continue downhill. Beyond the road, now traveling in young forest, the trail drops to Easter Run. The bedrock bottom of this stream is Brassfield limestone, the oldest of the Silurian rocks exposed at the Edge of Appalachia. More resistant to weathering than other strata, it forms small waterfalls on the lower slopes in Adams County. You can see one just downstream from the Easter Run bridge. Across the bridge, the trail turns right (downstream) alongside the creek for 50 feet before angling to the left to begin its slow climb. Please stop and sign in at the registration box.

The hardwood forest of the valley soon gives way as it reaches the Estill Shale Barren area of the slope. These areas were once covered with hardwoods such as sugar maple and tuliptree, but they were cleared in the late 1800s and early 1900s. This left the exposed slopes open to erosion, and once the thin topsoil was gone the mineral soil would support few plant species. In places, it takes bridges and boardwalks to carry the trail over the land made rough by years of erosion. Some of the forbs of dry prairies, such as little bluestem, orange coneflower, and shale barren aster, have taken hold here and red-cedar trees have invaded the area. I saw rose-pink, yellow partridge pea, ruellia, and orange coneflower in bloom as I passed through the barren area.

The trail continues to climb the hillside counterclockwise at a reasonable gradient. In the winter, you can look north across OH 125 and see a Peebles dolomite spire called the Devil's Teakettle. (Peebles is the massive layer of Silurian bedrock from which features such as Buzzardroost Rock and Red Rock are made, and you can see it exposed along OH 125.) In some places along the trail, Virginia pine, another pioneering species, shares that work with the red-cedars. The trail passes in and out of stands of hardwoods with spicebush in the shrub layer. Where water seeps from the hillside, there are large stands of pawpaw trees in the understory. Stop to examine a large dolomite slump block that tumbled down the slope a long time ago. Note the columbine and hydrangeas that grow in the pockets on the rock. Doubtless it is home to lots of creepy crawlers as well as ferns and mosses.

Beyond the rock is an area outside the preserve that was timbered not too many years ago. Hopefully it can be added to the preserve and allowed to revert to barrens and forest. The trail enters an area of more mature hardwoods with more slump block scattered here and there. This is an area rich in spring woodland wildflowers. The tighter contour lines on the map mean a steeper slope and soon the trail ascends on switchbacks and steeps. When the land begins to level out and the top of the climb is in sight, a sign indicates that the trail turns to the right. You are now almost 300 feet above the elevation at the Easter Run crossing. Between the sign and the Buzzardroost Rock promontory, the trail has been eroded by off-road vehicle tires. Riders enter the area unlawfully from the private property to the east.

It's about 2,200 feet to the platform on top of the rock, and the trail dips once along the way. The interesting thing is that the bedrock now beneath your feet is Ohio black shale and, consequently, the soil is acidic and the plant association is Appalachian oak woodland. Gone is the chinquapin oak of the limestone- and dolomite-derived soils of the hillside. In its place is the chestnut oak, so familiar on acid soils of the ridgetops of southeastern Ohio.

Buzzardroost Rock

Present too are several other species of oak, sassafras, hickories, and sour gum. When you cross the bridge to the Buzzardroost Rock platform, you will once again be on soils derived from alkaline bedrock. In the summer, such dry prairie plants as whorled milkweed, scaly blazing star, side-oats grama grass, and little bluestem hang on year after year. The master stream of the area, Ohio Brush Creek, lies 500 feet below, flowing south directly to the Ohio River. It was not always this way.

Prior to the Pleistocene epoch, which began about 500,000 years ago, Buzzardroost Rock was part of a ridge that extended across what is now the valley of Ohio Brush Creek. This ridge formed the southern divide for a northeast-flowing stream, possibly a tributary of the preglacial, north-flowing Teays River. Another river, probably one more tributary of the same system, flowed south from the ridge in the valley occupied by Ohio Brush Creek and the Ohio River, to the east of the present-day mouth of Ohio Brush Creek.

Ohio Brush Creek was formed, and Buzzardroost Rock exposed, when the north-flowing river system was blocked by the advance of an ice sheet. Upon melting, the glacier released a huge volume of water over an extended period of time, forming a lake between the ridge and the glacial front. Eventually the lake level rose high enough to reach a col, a low spot in the ridge. The water from the lake then cut though the ridge, eventually forming the south-flowing Ohio Brush Creek as a part of the newly created Ohio River system.

As you stand on the platform, look west, then to the south and north, to see if you can visualize that process in your mind. And don't forget to look skyward, because "buzzards," turkey vultures, do sometimes drop in and sit on the rails of the platform and/or nest in rock shelters of this escarpment on the edge of the Appalachian Plateau.

Return to the parking area the way you came, and do be careful as you descend the steps, steep trails, and switchbacks.

39

Fort Hill State Memorial (Fort and Gorge Trails)

Total distance: 1.4 and 3.1 miles (2.5 km and 5 km)

Hiking time: 4 hours

Maximum elevation: 1,290 feet

Vertical rise: 470 feet

Maps: USGS 7½' Sinking Spring; OHS Fort Hill State Memorial brochure

Fort Hill State Memorial, located off OH 41 in Highland County about a dozen miles south of Bainbridge, contains a prehistoric Native American hilltop enclosure that is one of the best preserved archaeological sites in Ohio. Equally important is the natural history of the area, with its rock outcrops and its great variety of plant and animal life. This tract of land is a piece of wilderness in the true sense of the word, an area not profoundly affected by human use. Over 10 miles of well-marked nature trails enable you to reach nearly all parts of the memorial. Deer Trail is the most rugged, taking you up and down the slopes, past most of the seven major plant communities identified there by the late E. Lucy Braun in her 1969 treatise, *An Ecological Survey of the Vegetation of Fort Hill State Memorial, Highland County, Ohio, and Annotated List of Vascular Plants.*

The presence of this ancient "fort" on this high hill in southwestern Ohio has been known by archaeologists for more than 150 years. John Locke wrote about it in 1838 in the *Second Annual Report on the Geological Survey of the State of Ohio.* The often-referenced *Ancient Monuments of the Mississippi Valley,* written by Squire and Davis in 1848, contained a detailed map of the 48-acre enclosure. No wonder, then, that when the opportunity arose in 1932 the state sought to protect it by purchasing a key 237-acre parcel. A plaque at the end of the parking lot provides some insight into how this site was acquired. It reads, "In memory of Morton Carlisle, 1869–1947, of

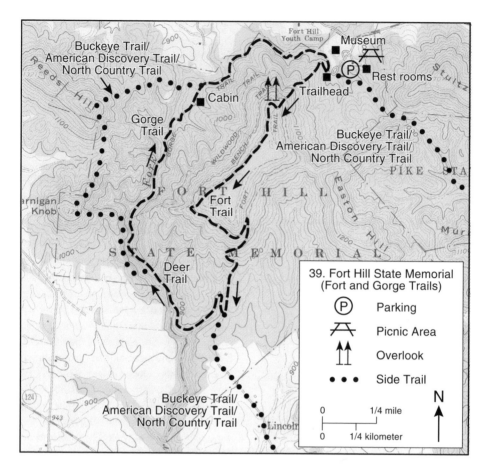

Buckeye Trail/
American Discovery Trail/
North Country Trail

Fort Hill
Youth Camp

Museum

Rest rooms

Trailhead

Cabin

Gorge
Trail

Buckeye Trail/
American Discovery Trail/
North Country Trail

PIKE STA

Fort
Trail

Deer
Trail

39. Fort Hill State Memorial
(Fort and Gorge Trails)

P Parking

Picnic Area

Overlook

Side Trail

Buckeye Trail/
American Discovery Trail/
North Country Trail

N

0   1/4 mile

0   1/4 kilometer

Cincinnati, Ohio, whose vision, zeal, and generosity were largely responsible for the establishment of Fort Hill State Memorial." Individuals do make a difference. Additional purchases have enlarged it to 1,200 acres.

The Depression-era Civilian Conservation Corps did much of the development work to open the area to the public. A monument near the museum reads, "In memory of the boys who served in Company 1505 Civilian Conservation Corps, Fort Hill, 1933–34." According to the records compiled by the Civilian Conservation Corps Alumni Association, this was an African-American company. They came by train to Peebles and were trucked to the worksite and camp

at Fort Hill. The small museum at the site was built in 1968 to provide interpretation of the natural and cultural history of the memorial.

Though the builders of the earthwork have not been clearly identified, it is presumed that the work was done by the Native Americans of the Hopewell culture that inhabited Ohio between 300 B.C. and A.D. 600. Interestingly, when Locke visited here in 1838, the hill was covered with virgin timber, including large trees on the "fort" wall and in the ditch. He estimated one large chestnut on the wall and a 7-foot-diameter tuliptree in the ditch to be 600 years old. Allowing some time for abandonment and reforestation, Squire and Davis suggested that, on the basis of Locke's observation, the fort was at least 1,000 years old. Carbon-14 datings put the Hopewell time in Ohio back about twice that far.

The unusual natural history of this tract of land has a number of causes. First, the geology here is uncommon: a hill of carboniferous shale with a sandstone cap and a dolomite base, which makes for acidic soils on the hillside and alkaline soils in the stream valley. Also, the area's proximity to the edge of the advancing glaciers seemingly left it rich in flora. Over 650 species of vascular plants have been found at Fort Hill. The size of the tract and the age of the trees apparently affect the number of bird species that use it for nesting—particularly the neotropical species that come north only to breed. Hiking at Fort Hill is like walking the pages of an ecology text.

This is not a hike for a hot and humid summer day, but rather a great one for spring or fall. The trails are open 8-8 daily, year-round. The museum was renovated in the mid-1990s as a part of the Ohio Historical Society's "Gateway Initiative." Picnic facilities, drinking water, and rest rooms are available during the warm months of the year.

How to Get There

From Columbus, travel south on US 23. At Chillicothe, take US 50 west (right) through Bainbridge, after which you make a left turn onto OH 41 south. Turn right onto Fort Hill Road and travel to the memorial entrance. The best route from Cincinnati is US 32 east to OH 41. Turn left (north) onto OH 41 and travel to Fort Hill Road on the left, which leads to the memorial entrance.

The Trail

This trail is for the hardy hiker. It has the greatest vertical rise of any hike in this book, 430 feet, and all of it occurs in the first half mile. This is a "semi-wilderness nature preserve." The hiker should carry a map and a good compass and know how to use both. There are places where the trail can be wet and very slippery, and some sections are quite primitive. A good hiking staff or a pair of trekking poles will serve you well. Extensive repair and upgrading was performed on the Gorge Trail during 2005–2006. Allow at least 45 minutes per mile of trail. There is adequate, but limited, signing and blazing. The Fort Trail has no paint blazes; the blazes on the Gorge Trail are yellow. The Buckeye Trail—marked with blue paint blazes—and the North Country Trail and American Discovery Trail—identified with distinctive symbols—pass through this area, using mostly the Deer Trail but overlapping the Gorge Trail in two places. To avoid becoming lost, stay on the trails and read all posted maps and signs carefully. Enjoy.

This hike begins on the Fort Trail, departing from a trailhead kiosk on the right side of the parking lot farthest from the entrance. You start with a turn to the right but quickly turn left to begin a 400-plus-foot ascent to the top of Fort Hill. Using switchbacks, the trail essentially goes directly up the hill. At one point it passes between the windthrown root balls of two large trees, exposing the shaley soil.

Fort Hill is very interesting geologically. The bedrock below the surface on the top of the hill is Berea sandstone of the Upper Devonian period. This is a gray compact rock composed of quartz grains firmly cemented by a small amount of clay. In most places in Ohio it is only 10 to 40 feet thick, but where it is still mined at South Amherst in Loraine County it's more than 200 feet thick. Because of its resistance to weathering, the slope of the hillside is steep at the level of the Berea rock. Directly below is the noncalcareous Bedford shale, also of the Devonian, and fairly resistant to weathering, especially when protected by the sandstone. The remainder of the hillside down to the parking lot is underlined by Ohio black shale, perhaps as much as 300 feet thick. There is a bench on the hillside at the top of this carboniferous shale.

This bare-ground trail up the hillside can be slippery when wet. The northeast-facing slope hosts a typical mixed mesophytic forest. You will know when you are close to the top, as the trail passes through the fort wall, conveniently pointed out by a sign. An old sign at the top reads, VIEWPOINT OVERLOOKING BAKER FORK AND THE BEECH FLATS AREA NORTHEAST OF FORT HILL. You will want to rest and take in the view of the countryside to the north. From here, the trail goes south-southwest on the nearly level hilltop, paralleling the fort wall. The forest here is dominated by several species of oak, hickories, sugar maple, and tuliptrees, with pawpaw prominent in the understory. The area has certainly been timbered at least once. The trees growing on the fort wall probably better reflect the pre-Columbian forest composition.

Somewhere on the top of the hill would be a good place to pause and contemplate what this area must have been like at the height of its use by Native Americans. Was it really a fort? Was there a village here? Was it only a place of worship or burial? Perhaps it was used for different purposes at different times of year or in different eras. Were there trees here then? How long did it take to construct the wall? Can you still hear the voices of the occupants here praying, mourning, gossiping, fighting, or just trying to keep warm on a cold winter's night? Let your imagination run wild.

After .5 mile, the Fort Trail turns left to travel around the hilltop and return to the parking lot via the incoming route. To continue this 4.5-mile hike, at the southwest corner of the hilltop go straight ahead down a rugged trail, passing through the fort wall. You will lose about 90 feet of elevation before reaching what looks like a service road where the trail makes a sharp left turn. Some old maps called this the Bench Trail and, in fact, it does run on a natural bench atop Ohio black shale. The rare wild pink grows in this area. This trail continues southeast on the bench for about 1,500 feet, then it makes a wide left turn toward the north and travels another 500 feet. Here a trail joins from the right rear. This is the yellow-blazed Gorge Trail, and a service road. A 6 x 6 post identifies the trails with abbreviations and provides the distances to destinations such as picnic areas. Make a hard right turn and follow the Gorge Trail downhill as it switches right, then left, before reaching another intersection. The Deer Trail goes straight ahead on the same roadbed as the Gorge Trail, and to the right to return to the parking lot. The latter is the last easy escape route if you want to cut short your hike. It's a slow, steady 1.25-mile drop from here to the parking area. In spring, the woodlands along this trail are full of Canada violets.

To enjoy the beauty that awaits you in Baker Fork Gorge choose the trail to the right, the combined Deer and Gorge Trails. The forest on this southwest-facing slope is chestnut oak. After a gentle downhill trek of less than .5 mile, there is another intersection. The trail straight ahead is the combined Buckeye, American Discovery, and North Country Trail heading out of the Fort Hill property. The trail to the right, the one you want to take, is the combined Gorge Trail, Deer Trail, BT, ADT, and NCT. A signpost indicates that you have 3 miles to go on the Gorge Trail before arriving back at the parking lot.

At this point, the trail has arrived at the

The Gorge Trail

bottom of the hillside underlain by Ohio black shale. Below you is the gorge of Baker Fork. It was created when the ponded waters of a former north-flowing stream, trapped by the advance from the north of the Illinoian ice sheet, found a new outlet to the sea by entrenching the massive Silurian-aged Peebles dolomite bedrock.

A hard right turn is the beginning of a new adventure. The trail enters the ravine of Spring Creek, which it crosses on a short bridge. Look to the right to see a small natural rock bridge. A large beech that lost its top to a wind storm is a source of food for the local pileated woodpeckers; near the base you'll find a rectangular hole made by one of these denizens of the deep forest seeking carpenter ants. Across the creek is the first of many water-shaped dolomite cliffs of the Baker Fork Gorge. In a very short time the trail reaches the main stem of Baker Fork. There it turns on itself to the right to climb a

set of wooden steps. Next is a short but difficult section that clings to the hillside near the mouth of Sulfur Creek. Walking fern nearly covers a dolomite slump block. There is fragrant sumac in the shrub layer, and on the cliff face above the stream grows *Sullivantia sullivantii,* the rare member of the saxifrage family named after the Ohio botanist William Starling Sullivant of Coumbus, who first collected it in the gorges of Highland County in 1839. Another set of stairs carries the hiker up a steep slope and away from the mouth of Sulfur Creek.

Where the trail drops to the floodplain, a post announces the Deer Trail's departure to the left, along with its traveling companions, the Buckeye Trail, the American Discovery Trail, and the North Country Trail. These combined trails cross the creek, gain about 25 feet in elevation, then turn right to cross over Keyhole Bridge. If you look carefully, you can see the natural arch from the Gorge

Trail just after you pass the junction. Beyond there, the trail works its way up the hillside to a set of steps where a post announces that you have come 2 miles and have 2 miles yet to go—in short, the middle of the Gorge Trail.

A 20-foot bridge carries the trail across the creek flowing from Beech Ravine. When I scouted the trail in August 2006, the hillside past there was full of mid-summer flowers, including both species of jewelweed blooming side by side. A wood frog crossing the trail in front of my feet made my day. The trail moves away from the stream and up the hillside, then returns to near the water's edge. A huge dolomite slump block lies along the creek and the trail slips between it and a rock wall. Just beyond where the trail crosses Shelter Creek on a short bridge, it hugs the side of a cliff before climbing 45 steps to a knob where you can take a dozen steps on a "wild" side trail to look directly down at Baker Fork. The floodplain widens out and sycamores, basswood, beech, and pawpaws reclaim the old streamside pasture.

A short way up the trail sits a wide-open cabin with benches inside where a hiker could retreat from a short rain shower or snack on an energy bar. Though the trail runs beside the cabin, it looks like most hikers actually include the cabin on the trail, going in one door and out the other. A 12-foot bridge carries the trail over Sunset Creek. Signs along the trail heading north from the cabin indicate that the Deer Trail, BT, ADT, and NCT are coming in from the left to again join the Gorge Trail. The distance to the picnic area and trailhead is shown as 1 mile. The combined trails turn right and then cross a 12-foot bridge, heading east. The trail still clings to the hillside, now in an area of open woods. In one place a section of boardwalk traverses a seepage area. A 30-foot bridge with a single rail carries the trail over a deep ravine. Now dropping to run along the stream, the trail includes a section of about 30 feet that has recently been rerouted to avoid a wet area. Ahead are three sets of four steps with some boardwalk between them. The trail leaves the tall trees and crosses some A-frame bridges and a mowed area. On a post near the edge of the parking lot there is a Buckeye Trail blue blaze and the emblems for the ADT and NCT, and in the distance the trailhead kiosk where the trail began.

➤ The Magnificent Chestnut

The American chestnut (Castanea dentata), *a large, rough-barked tree that sometimes grew to 100 feet with a trunk 10 feet in diameter, was once a dominant tree of the mixed oak forest of the dry, sandstone ridges and knobs of eastern Ohio, the Allegheny Plateau. This magnificent nut-bearing tree is virtually gone from its original North American range, the victim of a blight caused by an imported fungus,* Cryphonectria parasitica. *Introduced on Chinese chestnut, it was first reported in New York in 1904. It spread so fast among native trees that had no resistance to the fungus that by the middle of the 20th century, the American chestnut was virtually gone. Many of the shelter houses built in the state parks and forests in southeastern Ohio by the Civilian Conservation Corps during the 1930s were made of chestnut planks cut from salvaged victims of the blight. The search for a blight-resistant American chestnut or hybrid American/Chinese or Japanese chestnut continues to this day. Look for chestnut stumps on your walks; you may be lucky enough to find one with a few live sprouts.*

40

Germantown MetroPark

Total distance: 6.8 miles (10.9 km)

Hiking time: 4 hours

Maximum elevation: 900 feet

Vertical rise: 160 feet

Maps: USGS 7½' Farmersville;
FRMD Germantown MetroPark brochure;
FRMD Germantown MetroPark trail map
(not to scale)

Germantown MetroPark contains Montgomery County's largest tract of mature forest. Part of the park came into the public domain in 1918 when the Miami Conservancy District bought land along Twin Creek as a site for a flood-control dam. Dayton and the Miami valley had suffered a devastating flood in 1913, and leaders of the community were not about to let it happen again. Five flood-control dams were built on the major tributaries of the Great Miami River. Of a unique design, these dams do not hold permanent pools of water, nor do they have gates that can be closed at times of high water. Only when water collects behind the dam because it cannot pass through it fast enough does a temporary impoundment result. As of this writing, the last major flood was in January 2005. Fed by melting snow, the water level in Germantown Reservoir reached 58 feet. This was very close to a record level. Because these dams were not meant to produce power or to create large, permanent lakes, the land on the floodplains behind them has remained in a natural state, with forest and open fields. The valley behind Germantown Dam was mostly forested, and when the newly created Dayton and Montgomery County Park (now Five Rivers MetroPark) District began seeking park sites in 1967, it was able to lease 361 acres of this flood-control property from the conservancy district. The park district has subsequently added 1,173 acres, mostly upland.

The forests at Germantown MetroPark are exceptionally good for spring wildflowers, and the vast expanse of unbroken

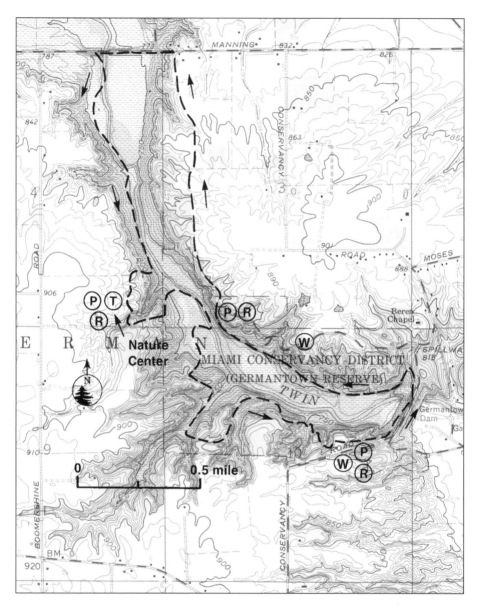

woodland is a spring breeding ground for many woodland birds. The nature center at Germantown is of an unusual design, being below ground. It features exhibits and displays about the natural history of the area with an emphasis on good land stewardship. They offer a series of public programs throughout the year. On a cool autumn afternoon a warm fire in the stove will take the chill off hikers while they watch birds through an observation window.

Native tallgrass prairie has been established on much of the unforested upland at Germantown, presenting a spectacular display of summer wildflowers and bringing grassland nesting birds back to the area. Look for the grassland along both sides of the road as you enter the park.

How to Get There

Germantown MetroPark is reached by traveling about 8 miles south of Dayton on I-75. Take Exit 44 right (west) onto OH 725. After passing through Miamisburg and Germantown, OH 725 climbs out of the valley of Twin Creek to pass Conservancy Road. Turn right on Boomershine Road, 12 miles from I-75. The park entrance is 1 mile north of OH 725 on the right. Take the first right turn inside the park to reach the nature center parking lot, 0.3 mile from the entrance. In addition to the nature center, the park's facilities include nearly 14 miles of foot trails and several picnic areas. Several short trails, and a long trail known as the Orange Trail, which circumnavigates the entire park, originate at a boardwalk overlook to the right of the nature center.

The Trail

The trails at Germantown are well marked with a color-coded system. Posts with colored disks mark the way, and posts with numbers identify trail intersections. (For anyone who's color-blind, the first letter of the color is located in the center of the disk; e.g., an O in the center of the orange disks.) The 6.8-mile Orange Trail described here passes three parking lots, so it is possible to start or end at Points 1, 15, and 16. The 0.5-mile White, 1-mile Blue, and 1.9-mile Yellow Trails all start south from Point 1. The 0.5-mile Red and 1.4-mile Green Trails both go north from Point 1. The 1-mile Silver Trail originates and returns to Point 16 at a parking lot off Conservancy Road 1.8 miles north of OH 725. The 1.2-mile Pink Trail begins and ends at Point 16. Thus, there are many ways to combine trails for hikes of various lengths. Be sure to follow the orange markers for this 6.8-mile hike, and remember to carry an adequate amount of drinking water with you.

Leaving the nature center to the west, the Orange Trail makes a short drop down wooden steps through a cedar thicket to Point 14. This is where the shorter Blue, Yellow, and White Trails loop back from the right. Along with the Orange, they leave Point 14 to the left. After fording a small creek, they follow an old roadway alongside a cedar-lined gorge cut through Ordovician limestone and shale. The combined trails curve to the right as they climb through oak/hickory/beech forest, soon to reach Point 10, where the blue and white routes turn up a ridge to the right.

After a slight rise, the Orange and Yellow Trails descend to the floodplain. During times of high water, this trail may be inundated. (You can bypass the floodplain by following the Blue Trail left from Point 10, past Point 11 to Point 12, where you take the Yellow Trail to the left to Point 9.) This streamside section of trail can be muddy and slippery if it has recently been underwater; exercise caution when hiking there. Watch for a huge cottonwood tree by the trail along the river's edge. After traveling downstream for .25 mile through a box elder/sycamore/cottonwood/ash floodplain forest, the trail swings back on itself and heads toward the hill, where it begins a moderately steep climb out of the valley. At the top of the hill the trail reaches Point 9, and the Yellow Trail exits right as it heads back to the trailhead.

The Orange Trail goes left but soon turns right to make a fairly steep descent into a ravine. It then curves right and heads up a valley. After crossing two side streams, the trail crosses the main stream and climbs a set of wooden steps back to the ridge, soon reaching Point 8. There it meets the Silver

Trail, which goes left and right. The Orange Trail joins it to the left.

Now following a ridgetop among tall red oaks, the trail drops into a low saddle, then makes an abrupt right turn to drop into another ravine. At the bottom, the path turns toward Twin Creek and curves to follow it, staying about halfway up the hillside. It then drops steeply into another ravine. In this area, the ravines expose sand deposited in preglacial valleys by a pre-Wisconsinan glacier. On the upland, the sands are covered by Wisconsinan-aged drift. Highly erodable, the gullies are so steep-sided that they have never been cleared for cultivation. The area supports a nice mature hardwood forest. The trail climbs very steeply out of the ravine, and then curves left to regain the high ground and reach Point 7, just downhill from Conservancy Road. The Silver Trail joins the Orange Trail to cross the head of a small ravine, going to Point 16 at a parking lot. Emerging from hardwood forest on the left side of the parking lot, the Orange Trail passes a bulletin board and latrines, then enters a young red-cedar and maple woodland.

Soon returning to mature oak/hickory/beech woods, the trail moves around the hillside to reach the upstream side of the earthen dam about 20 feet below the top. After crossing the dam at that level, the trail joins a gravel road just below a stand of Scotch pine. It crosses an old ridge road and drops to a T, where you make a right turn uphill to a natural material disposal area. Beyond a grass-covered fill area, the trail turns left down an old road as the service road turns right toward Conservancy Road.

The trail follows the old track to the left. Evidence of early park development in the form of disintegrated concrete picnic tables and stone posts can be seen in this area. After crossing a small creek, the trail nears a park driveway. To the left down the hill is an old borrow pit where gravel was obtained for construction of the dam. It once held water, but is now filled in and overgrown with tall weeds. Near the end of the park road loop, the trail climbs uphill to the right to Point 15. The Pink Loop Trail originates here. Turning left, away from the road, the Orange and Pink Trails pass to the right of a latrine and then head through some eroded upland with red-cedars. In a couple of hundred feet, the trail reaches Point 6. Continue straight ahead on the trail marked both orange and pink.

Following the border between old field and woods, the trail soon comes to Point 5, where the Pink Trail leaves to the right and the Orange Trail proceeds straight ahead. Shortly after this intersection, the trail breaks into the open under a power line. After following the right-of-way a short distance, the trail passes through a wooded fencerow and into more open fields. About 1,000 yards to the right is a platform where carcasses of road-killed animals are placed to feed vultures.

Now heading almost due north, for .3 mile the trail passes between older forest on the left and younger successional woodlands on the right to reach a corner of the property. After crossing the head of a ravine, the trail continues going north parallel to the boundary fence, entering more red-cedar thicket as it heads toward a junction with Manning Road.

At the road, the trail turns left and uses the left berm to reach a concrete bridge over Twin Creek. Two hundred feet beyond the bridge at the end of the guardrail, you exit the road to the right and go through a wooden gate. The trail makes a hard right to head downstream between more forest and an old field now succeeding to young forest. After another 1/8 mile, the trail cuts across the thicket to the left to reach a hill. Then it angles along the hill to the left to-

Germantown MetroPark

ward the rim, where it overlooks the river. Here, at a point where an unlabeled side trail enters from a grassy cedar glade to the right, there in an orange sign with arrows pointing upstream and downstream. The trail continues straight ahead.

The Orange Trail drops to the floodplain forest for a short stretch. Then, after crossing a side stream, it climbs to Point 4. In the summer, Indian pipe is often found growing near Point 4. The Green Trail comes in from the right and the combined trails then leave to the left. Again in mature hardwood forest, the combined trails travel midway along the hillside. This is an excellent area for spring wildflowers. Red-cedars are visible at the uphill edge of the woods. Side streams are again filled with flat pieces of limestone, indicating that the Ordovician-aged bedrock is not far below the surface. After following an old trace for about .3 mile, the trail climbs the hillside to the right on another old road. Near the top is Point 2; the Green Trail is joined by the Red Trail going to the left into a stand of red-cedars and the Orange Trail, also joined by the Red Trail, turns to the right into a beautiful stand of mature hardwood. Squaw-root blooms along here.

After about 100 yards, the trail passes a fire circle on the right and leaves the woodland as it arrives at Point 3. (The side of the green/red loops not traveled by the Orange Trail—between Points 1 and 2—is a good place to look for the terrestrial species of Ladies'-tresses in late summer.) The Green Trail then exits right and the combined Orange/Red/Green Trails head left through grassland toward a cedar glade. After crossing over the earthen dam of a small pond, the combined trails meet the other end of the Red/Green Trails coming in from the dense cedar glade that lies to the left. This is Point 1, and only a short connecting trail remains before you arrive at the nature center/boardwalk where the trail began.

41

Glen Helen Nature Preserve

Total distance: 3, 5, or 10 miles
(4.8, 8, or 16 km)

Hiking time: 2 hours

Maximum elevation: 1,003 feet

Vertical rise: 133 feet

Maps: USGS 7½' Clifton; USGS 7½
Yellow Springs; GHA Glen Helen trail
map

Antioch University's Glen Helen Nature Preserve has been described as one of Ohio's best-kept secrets. Its 26 miles of foot trails take the hiker past waterfalls, a national- and state-designated Scenic River, beautiful Silurian-aged limestone and dolomite cliffs, a National Natural Landmark woods, a 75-year-old pine forest, and the bountiful spring from which the nearby village of Yellow Springs got its name. Numbered posts on many of the glen's trails are keyed to *A Guide to the Historical Sites in Glen Helen,* generally available at the Glen Helen Building or at Trailside Museum. A map can be purchased at the museum, which also has the only rest rooms and drinking water in the glen.

Glen Helen was given to Antioch College in 1929 by Hugh Taylor Birch as a living memorial to his daughter, Helen Birch Bartlett. More land has since been added, bringing the total close to 1,000 acres. Beginning in 1969, local Boy Scout Troop 78 managed the Glen Helen Scout Hiking Trail in the preserve, one of the few such trails in the state located entirely off-road. Over the years, thousands of Scouts and their leaders walked the trail, earning an attractive commemorative patch and spending day in the woods, many for the first time ever. Though that opportunity may no longer be available, the trails of Glen Helen are open to anyone during daylight hours year-round.

Trailside Museum is where folks hiking the trails of the glen generally park and begin their trek. To help defray the cost of keeping the area open to the public, there

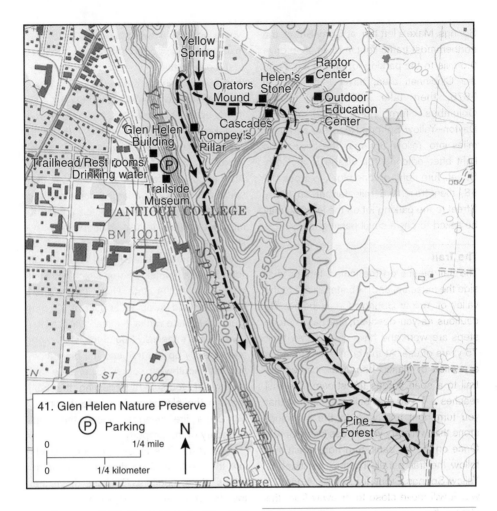

41. Glen Helen Nature Preserve

Ⓟ Parking   **N**

0 ———————————— 1/4 mile
0 ———————————— 1/4 kilometer

may be a small fee for parking. As the glen is not a park but a privately owned nature preserve, there are no facilities for camping or picnicking. Accommodations for both are available in John Bryan State Park, which adjoins the glen to the east.

Glen Helen is especially well known for its nearly continuous show of native wildflowers. Each season offers a new collage of nature. Hike and enjoy the trails of this natural treasure often. From 1973 to 1990, I was the director of Glen Helen and I never missed a chance to explore the natural world at my very doorstep. What a special privilege it was.

How to Get There

Begin hiking the trails at Glen Helen from Trailside Museum off the main Glen Helen parking lot on Corry Street in Yellow Springs. (The Glen Helen Building at 405 Corry Street and Trailside Museum at 505 Corry Street share the same parking area.) The sidewalk directly in front of you on the drive into the parking lot takes you to Trailside Museum.

To reach Glen Helen from central Ohio, travel I-70 west to US 68, the 52A exit. Turn left (south) and travel 8 miles to Yellow

Springs. Make a left turn at Corry Street, the northernmost traffic light in town, then drive 0.6 mile to the parking lot on the left. From the Cincinnati area, travel I-75 north to I-675, then take I-675 east toward Columbus. Turn right (east) at the Dayton–Yellow Springs Road exit and go 6 miles into Yellow Springs. The third traffic light after entering the village is at Corry Street. Turn right, go one block to cross US 68, then travel 0.6 mile farther on Corry Street to the parking lot on the left. You may be asked to pay a small parking fee.

The Trail

The trail begins on the Inman Terrace outside the museum, and 145 steps lead to the valley of Yellow Springs Creek below. Be cautious as you descend; the native stone steps are worn and have shifted over their 75 years of use. At the bottom of the steps a section of plastic boardwalk carries the trail to a span across the stream. The trail reaches a T 100 feet below. I suggest that you turn right and walk to the stepping-stone that will carry you across Birch Creek. Once on the far bank, turn right again and follow the trail paralleling the east bank of Yellow Springs Creek for .5 mile. Along the way it will move close to or away from the stream, but it always stays within hearing distance of the babbling water.

After about 1,000 feet you will see a trail leading toward the water and a set of stepping-stones crossing the creek. These lead to the south end of the Talus Trail. At the same point, a trail to the left goes away from the stream to Traveler's Spring. In April, detour up this trail to see marsh marigolds in bloom in that wet area. To continue the hike detailed here, keep on the trail headed south. Soon you will pass another trail leaving from the left that also goes to the spring. Ignore it and travel another 1,500 feet to

where you pass two steel posts that for many years supported a swinging bridge. Just beyond there, the trail turns left and then quickly right before splitting. The right fork continues downstream and the left fork heads uphill obliquely.

Take the heavily used left fork as it scrambles over rocks and gullies, then winds its way uphill at a gentle gradient. After about 200 feet, the trail arrives at the southwest corner of a large conifer plantation known as the Pine Forest. It's a bit of a misnomer, since it also includes Norway spruce trees. They were all planted in 1926 when this area of Glen Helen was part of John Bryan's Riverside Farm, which had just been given to the state. Hugh Taylor Birch worked a land swap to acquire it for the glen. It's a place with a magical quality all its own. This is especially true of the white pine area directly up the trail into the plantation from the southwest corner. Experience the feeling for yourself by following the trail through the plantation to where it comes out on a fire lane/road along the east boundary of the property.

Out of the Pine Forest, turn left and follow the fire lane along the east and north edges of the conifers. Continue down the trail that you came out on, except this time make a right turn after 60 feet. Follow this lane—actually a segment of the old Yellow Springs–Clifton stagecoach road—for almost a mile as it twists and turns toward the Glen Helen Outdoor Education Center (OEC). This was pastureland when the glen was acquired. Here and there in the forest to either side of the road you will see dead or dying red-cedar trees. These were the first trees to invade the old fields after grazing was halted, but they are now overtopped by the hardwoods. You will also see Osage orange trees that were originally planted as living fences. Students at the OEC have

Pompey's Pillar

adopted one as a climbing tree. Turn left after the fire lane passes a cable gate and an old stone bridge. This short trail leads to the bridge above the Cascades on Birch Creek. The view from below, looking upstream at the Cascades, is the most picturesque and best-known scene in Glen Helen. A photograph of the Cascades graced the cover of the second edition of this book.

The OEC lies to the right of the fire lane, opposite the entrance to the trail to the Cascades. It is the location of the glen's year-round school camp program and in summer hosts Ecocamp, a natural history-oriented camp for youngsters of all ages. At the Glen Helen Raptor Center, located at the OEC, ill, orphaned, and injured birds of prey are treated in an effort to return them to the Ohio sky. To visit the Raptor Center, go straight ahead on the fire lane instead of turning toward the Cascades bridge.

Birch Creek marks the eastern edge of the 250-acre National Natural Landmark section of the glen. At the west end of the Cascades bridge, enter the woods on the middle trail directly ahead. Soon you will pass Helen's Stone, which bears a poem written by the glen's namesake. Directly south of here, but not visible, is the site of an 1826 Owenite settlement. In quick succession, the trail passes a Hopewell Indian mound; a kiosk telling the story of a white oak that fell nearby; the site of the late-18th-century Neff House resort hotel; the spot where in 1803 pioneer Lewis Davis built the first cabin in the area; and, lastly, the famous spring from which the village gets its name. Flowing year-round at 52 degrees and 70 gallons per minute, the spring is not really yellow but rust-colored from iron impurities in the bedrock through which the water travels before reaching the surface. Neither this nor any other spring in Glen Helen is approved as a source of public drinking water.

Beyond the human-landscaped spring is Bone Cave, a small cavern that can hold a dozen or more schoolchildren all scrunched together. The trail arcs downhill to the left. On the right are the ruins of a dam that at one time impounded Yellow Springs Creek. There was a dance hall overlooking the lake's upper end. Can you picture people traveling to Neff Park by interurban to fish, boat, ice-skate, promenade alongside the lake, or just dance the night away? Just beyond on the left is the Grotto, where the water from the springs falls into a man-made pool before running to the creek. The water deposits some dissolved limestone as it tumbles over the falls, causing the lip of the falls to build out like a tongue rather than be eroded back as most falls are. Next is an area where you can see some of the 10,000 years of tufa deposits that have created the travertine mound on the slope below the spring.

A walk through the forest is a walk among giants, specifically the three or four giant bur oak trees that have been growing on this floodplain since Native Americans were the only people here. Pileated woodpeckers have nested in this area for many years. The spring flora in this rich river bottom is as good as it gets. Spicebush forms a solid shrub layer and such trees as wafer ash, blue ash, pawpaw, redbud, and bladdernut occupy the understory. On the hillside to the left a tall tower-like slump block called Pompey's Pillar has been creeping downhill away from the cliffs for centuries. At the intersection where you began your hike, turn right toward the span over Yellow Springs Creek and the boardwalk beyond. Under towering chinquapin oak trees, climb the 145 steps to Inman Terrace. Stop to smell a crushed leaf of the fragrant sumacs outside of Trailside, and make sure your hiking shoes are clean before heading home.

42

Hueston Woods State Park and Nature Preserve

Total distance: 2 miles (3 km)

Hiking time: 1.5 hours

Maximum elevation: 960 feet

Vertical rise: 140 feet

Maps: USGS 7½' College Corner; USGS 7½' Oxford; ODNR Hueston Woods State Nature Preserve brochure; ODNR Hueston Woods State Park map

In 1797, Matthew Hueston returned to the fertile ground in southwestern Ohio that he had seen as a soldier marching with General "Mad" Anthony Wayne to the Battle of Fallen Timbers. Eventually, the pioneer farmer owned several thousand acres in Butler and Preble Counties. Though most of Hueston's land was soon cleared for farming, a 200-acre tract of beech/maple forest along Four Mile Creek missed the ring of the ax. Perhaps it was too steep to farm, or maybe, since cane sugar was not available on the frontier, Hueston considered the sap of the sugar maples too valuable to lose. For whatever reasons, the hilly tract of timber remained untouched by successive generations of the family. When the last Hueston family member died in 1935, local banker Morris Taylor recognized the educational and scientific value of the virgin woods. He purchased it and protected it until 1941, when the state bought it as a forest park. Additional land around the "big woods" was acquired, and eventually Hueston Woods State Park was developed. In 1969, the original tract of virgin forest was declared a National Natural Landmark, and in 1973 it was dedicated as a state nature preserve.

Hueston Woods is especially lovely in the autumn. The Main Loop Road affords good vistas on the reds and golds of the beech/maple forest. Deer are often seen in the meadows and at the edge of the woods along the road.

Hueston Woods State Park, in which Hueston Woods State Nature Preserve is lo-

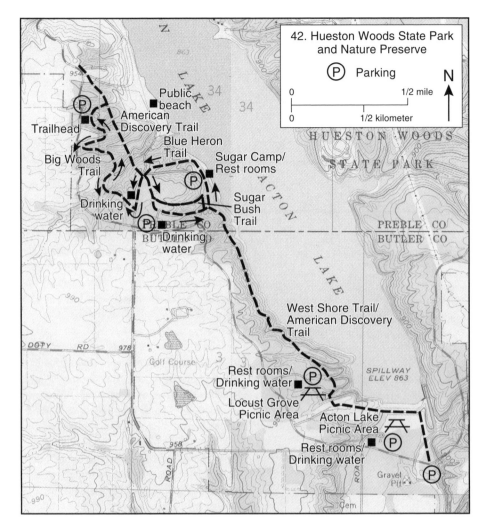

Public beach

American
Discovery Trail

Trailhead

Blue Heron
Trail

Big Woods
Trail

Sugar Camp/
Rest rooms

Drinking
water

Sugar
Bush
Trail

Drinking
water

PREBLE CO
BUTLER CO

West Shore Trail/
American Discovery
Trail

DOTY RD

Golf Course

Rest rooms/
Drinking water

Locust Grove
Picnic Area

SPILLWAY
ELEV 863

Acton Lake
Picnic Area

Rest rooms/
Drinking water

Gravel
Pit

HUESTON WOODS
STATE PARK

cated, is a full resort park with cabins, a lodge, campground, beach, marina, pioneer museum, nature center, hawk and owl rehabilitation center, and golf course. Information about the park facilities can be obtained from the Division of Travel and Tourism or the Department of Natural Resources.

How to Get There

Hueston Woods is located on the Butler/Preble county line about 5 miles north of the college town of Oxford. From all of Ohio except Cincinnati, it is most readily reached by traveling west on I-70 to US 127, 10 miles from the Ohio/Indiana line. Travel south 6 miles on US 127 to Eaton, then south 15 miles on OH 732 to the park entrance. From Cincinnati, follow US 27 north 38 miles to Oxford. Then take OH 732 north 5 miles to the park entrance.

The nature preserve trailhead is located at a cul-de-sac off the Main Loop Road, approximately 5 miles from the park entrance. At the split in the road about 0.6 mile past the park entrance, take the left fork. This road leads clockwise around 625-acre Acton Lake, passing the spillway and then following the boundary between the state park golf course and the nature preserve. A little over 0.5 mile after crossing Brown Road, a cul-de-sac appears on the right side of the road. Here is the trailhead for the Big Woods Trail.

The Trail

The trailhead is on the right side of the parking lot. After passing through an opening in a rail fence, the trail immediately plunges into tall timber. About 44 percent of the canopy of Hueston Woods is made up of gray-barked beech trees, 28 percent is sugar maple, and 19 percent is white ash. A variety of other hardwoods, including red and white oaks, make up the remaining 9 percent. In these mature and reasonably undisturbed woods, a distinctive layered effect is visible. Under the canopy is an understory of saplings such as the shade-tolerant sugar maple. Beneath that is a layer of shrubs such as spicebush. Close to the ground is a layer of herbaceous plants. There is a similar stratification in the animal populations, with birds such as the Cooper's hawk nesting in the canopy and smaller birds like the red-eyed vireo in the understory. Many visitors to the woods are treated to the noisy call of the pileated woodpecker, a species once thought in danger of extinction but now common in large tracts of Ohio woodland. Also, because it is protected from grazing, the forest hosts a wide variety of wildflowers, and it is known to have a good population of terrestrial amphibians. The deer herd here must be culled by hunting at times to protect the herb and shrub layers—and the recruitment of young canopy tree species—from severe overbrowsing.

Once in the woods, the trail goes in and out of three ravines, crossing streams on bridges or flat rocks. Steps have been installed on steep slopes to help prevent erosion. Just before the trail climbs to Brown Road, note the large burl on a white oak tree. Where the trail reaches the road, .6 mile from the trailhead, there is a water fountain. Before the construction of Acton Lake in 1956, Brown Road crossed the valley of Four Mile Creek. It has now been rerouted and goes only to a demonstration sugaring operation on the edge of the woods near the lakeshore. Shoreline anglers also use this road and the Sugar Bush parking lot.

Where the trail reaches Brown Road it is necessary to turn left and follow the paving for just over 0.1 mile. Just before the road curves to the right, there is a bulletin board and an entrance to the American Discovery Trail (ADT) coming from the north. The ADT utilizes the road to connect with the Sugar Bush Trail (SBT), just as this hike does. The entrance to the combined SBT/ADT is located on the right side of the road, about 150 feet beyond the curve. Turning right onto this 0.8-mile loop trail leads you into the largest timber in the preserve. After walking 150 feet, take the Blue Heron Trail, which exits to the right. (The ADT continues on the SBT until it meets the West Shore Trail, where it turns right toward the Lake Acton dam area and then leaves the park.) All of this 200-acre tract slopes steeply to the valley of Four Mile Creek, now flooded to form Acton Lake. The Blue Heron Trail soon passes through the area with the highest elevation in the preserve. It next goes to another cul-de-sac parking lot, which it skirts.

Shortly after the trail leaves this second lot, you cross a stream on stepping-stones and climb to a ridge, which you then follow

A marker for the Blue Heron Trail

downhill to the lake. After crossing another stream on stepping-stones, the route for this hike turns left onto the West Shore Trail. There is also a trail straight ahead that leads to a fisherman's trail along the lakeshore. Don't take it. Following the West Shore/Blue Heron Trails brings you to the south end of the open grass around the Sugar House. During maple syrup season, usually in March, the woods are strung with sap-collecting lines, and the sweet smell of steaming hot sap hangs heavy in the air. Park naturalists and volunteer work to re-create the age-old method of making sugar by boiling down the sweet maple sap. Rest rooms are available at the sugar camp.

It is possible to complete the loop back to the Big Woods Trail either by following the blacktopped road up the hill or by taking the combined West Shore/Sugar Bush Trail from the north end of the parking lot. After a couple of hundred feet, the latter moves gently upslope to reach a knob, where the West Shore Trail goes straight to return to the lakeshore and the Sugar Bush Trail goes left up the ridge to eventually reach the road. Continue on the Sugar Bush Trail to the road, where you turn right to take it back to the head of the Big Woods Trail. Follow the .6-mile trail back to the trailhead.

43

Shawnee Prairie Preserve

Total distance: 2 miles (3.2 km)

Hiking time: 1.5 hours

Maximum elevation: 1,025 feet

Vertical rise: 21 feet

Maps: USGS 7½' Greenville West, DCPD Shawnee Prairie Preserve Pathfinder

One of the younger park districts in Ohio, the Darke County Park District was created in 1972, named for Revolutionary War general William Darke. The county is probably best remembered as the site of the signing of the Treaty of GreeneVille [sic] entered into on August 3, 1795 by General Anthony Wayne and the chiefs of 12 allied Indian tribes. It brought peace to the area and opened up the Northwest Territory for settlement. History says Fort GreeneVille was the largest log structure ever built in North America. It stood for only six years.

The famous travel writer Lowell Thomas called Darke County his home, as did the equally famous lady marksman, Annie Oakley. At 118 acres, Shawnee Prairie Preserve is the largest park in the county system. There is a fine nature center here and 2.25 miles of trail with benches and observation towers. It comes by its name legitimately. According to Robert B. Gordon's 1966 map, *The Natural Vegetation of Ohio at the Time of Original Land Surveys,* there was prairie along both sides of Mud Creek, where the park lies. And according to archeological evidence, at least a portion of Shawnee Prairie Preserve was the site of Prophetstown, the village founded by Tecumseh's brother—called the Prophet—to rally 15 woodland Indian nations to gather and demonstrate their living and hunting rights under the treaty mentioned above. Thus, Shawnee Prairie Preserve is a good fit.

Geologically, the site is on a late Wisconsinan outwash plain, deposited by meltwater in front of glacial ice. The prop-

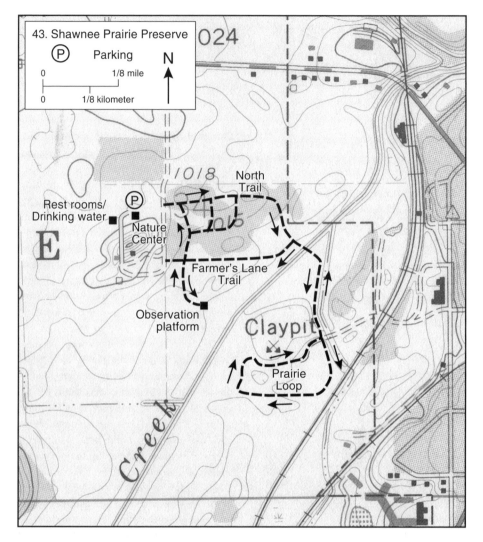

43. Shawnee Prairie Preserve

P Parking

N

0   1/8 mile

0   1/8 kilometer

024

1018

North Trail

Rest rooms/
Drinking water

P

Nature
Center

E

Farmer's Lane
Trail

Observation
platform

Claypit

Prairie
Loop

Creek

erty is dissected by slow-flowing Mud Creek and Appenzeller Ditch. Ponds occupy areas of earlier mineral removal. Most of area is wetland—both seasonal and permanent—grassland, and woodland. Bring insect repellent and carry binoculars for observing birds, especially waterfowl, and insects. This would be a good hike on which to tuck the Stokes *Beginner's Guide to Dragonflies* and *Beginner's Guide to Butterflies* in your day pack or pocket.

How to Get There

To reach the county-seat town of Greenville (though named after Nathanael Greene, a Revolutionary War general, Greenville dropped the third "e" in its name many years ago), travel west on I-70 to OH 49. Turn northwest on OH 49 and continue to the center of downtown Greenville. There, turn left (southwest onto OH 502 (West Main Street) and follow it as it turns right

Beaver dam–flooded swamp forest

onto Vine Street and west onto Winchester Avenue. Pass the Tecumseh Boulder Historic Site on the right. The entrance to Shawnee Prairie Preserve is about .25 mile beyond on the left. Except for a small wetland area, the park does not front the highway. Instead, you reach it by a long driveway. Watch carefully, as the sign is easy to miss. Park at the nature center, where you'll find the only drinking water and rest rooms. You can also pick up a map of the preserve here.

The Trail

Begin walking on the plastic boardwalk of the North Trail as it heads east past a large white oak just across the driveway from the bulletin board. The trail turns to gravel just beyond a sign that reminds you about the problem of alien plants. Boardwalk is used throughout the preserve, but only where experience has proven it necessary. This is mixed oak forest, not the typical beech/maple woods seen in most of western Ohio. There are some nice oaks here that somehow missed the axe and saw. Continue east on the North Trail, ignoring three possible right turns. Soon you will be traveling on grass over a dam that was built to create a wetland between the trail and OH 502; but it hasn't really done so, no matter what the map indicates. Along here to the left you can see one of the major alien plant problems in many of Ohio's woodlands, bush honeysuckle. After passing the wetland on the left, the trail makes a right turn into what is now swamp forest. Just before the trail makes a half turn to the left to cross Mud Creek, there is a juncture on the right with the Farmer's Lane Trail. To continue hiking, cross the bridge. Now on Trail 6, the Prairie Loop, there are hackberry trees to the left and Appenzeller Ditch lies just beyond. When I explored the trail, a family of mallards was in the ditch and farther on a beaver had built a dam.

On the right is an area of old field being transformed to wet prairie. Follow the trail as it passes an area to the right that was once a clay pit mined by The Greenville Tile Company, still in business just across the railroad tracks to the east. It is now a swamp where nesting boxes have been set out for wood ducks. The ditch remains along the left side of the trail. Before the trail begins to encircle an old field, there is a sign that quotes from a May 5, 1795, journal entry of James Elliot, calling the area, "A Terrestrial Paradise." Elliot was at Fort GreeneVille in 1795–96, a soldier in the army of Mad Anthony Wayne and probably a witness to the signing of the Treaty of GreeneVille.

To continue hiking, return to the bridge over Mud Creek and cross it. Then turn left onto Farmer's Lane and skirt the south edge of the big woods. After it makes a half turn to the right, a cluster of farm building are visible on a rise to the west. These are being restored for program use. To the left, across wet grassland, an observation platform is accessible via a wooden boardwalk. A sign along the trail speaks about "an ocean of grass" encountered by pioneers. At the trail intersection where the boardwalk goes west to the platform, turn right and head east into the forest. This is the Savannah Trail, and after passing an entrance to the Oak Trail on the right the plastic boardwalk carries you back to the North Trail. A left turn here leads to the parking lot and nature center.

Be sure to check out the prairie garden beside the nature center and the window on wildlife and fine exhibits inside. The careful observer visiting this park and trail system will be well rewarded with the sounds and sights of a wet terrestrial environment that stands apart from most others in this book.

44

Stillwater Prairie Preserve

Total distance: 1.5 miles (2.4 km)

Hiking time: 1.25 hours

Maximum elevation: 975 feet

Vertical rise: 64 feet

Maps: USGS 7½' Versailles; MCPD Stillwater Prairie Preserve brochure

Western Ohio's Stillwater River meanders east from near the Ohio-Indiana boundary, passing over progressively older Silurian-age bedrock before making an abrupt turn south to join the Great Miami River in Dayton. In most places, it is not possible to see the rock beneath the river. Where Stillwater Prairie Preserve straddles the river in Miami County, the bedrock is obvious. The river carved its way through layers of ancient rock, and a bare limestone ledge lines the north shore.

Here, prairie plants thrive on the thin soil that overlies the limestone and dolomite bedrock, as they have done for millennia. Nodding onion, partridge pea, and that delicate beauty, harebell, hang on in pockets of soil in the exposed rock on the north bank. On the south side of the river, where the calcareous bedrock is covered with glacial outwash, prairie dock, purple coneflower, tall coreopsis, bergamot, big bluestem, and dozens of other prairie grasses, forbs flourish. Like grasslands elsewhere in Ohio, they are thought to be remnants of the prairie that extended farther east during a post-glacial period when the climate was warmer and drier. They probably remained after cool weather returned due to soil and hydrologic conditions.

The Miami County Park District acquired the original 217-acre tract of this park in 1977 to protect the unusual vegetation. Since that time, the property has grown to 380 acres. In addition to the prairie along the river, the park includes a mature oak/hickory forest on the morainal upland.

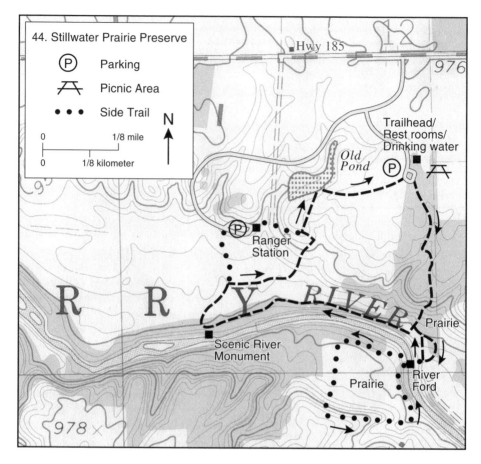

A well-designed and well-maintained trail system enables the visitor to know and enjoy the varied habitats of this special reserve. Seeing the best of the original prairie habitat may even include a wade across the river.

Seventy-five miles of the Stillwater River and its principal tributary, Greenville Creek, have been designated by the Ohio Department of Natural Resources as State Scenic River. And the river's run through this reserve is certainly one of the most scenic. The river also has a wide reputation among anglers as one of the finest small-mouth bass streams in the state. The Miami County Park District also has a small park at

the falls of Greenville Creek, not very far south of Stillwater Prairie about 1.5 miles west of Covington on Gettysburg Road. It's a place of beauty well worth a visit while you're in the area.

How to Get There

Travel north from I-70 through Covington on OH 48 to OH 185. Turn left (west) and travel 1.7 miles to the entrance on the left (south) side of the road. The park is open year-round from 8:00 A.M. until a half hour after sunset. After entering, make a left turn past the flagpole and park at the main picnic area. The only rest room and a source of drinking water are located here.

Wildflowers line the boardwalk in the Stillwater Prairie Preserve

The Trail

To begin hiking, cross through the wooded open picnic area to the bulletin board and head into the forest on the wide gravel trail. The strip of woodland is narrow, but it contains some nice-sized oak, hickory, beech, and maple. Bush honeysuckle has found its way into the shrub layer and garlic mustard has begun to appear, but the spring flora is still quite abundant. About 200 yards beyond the trailhead a bridge crosses a small wash. Just beyond there is a split in the trail. Take the left fork and continue walking toward the river. After another 200 yards, the trail begins to drop toward the water.

A sign at a trail intersection introduces you to the Stillwater River Prairie, and to the left a plastic boardwalk carries you through the big bluestem and prairie forbs to the river's edge. This is a special place, where plant life clings tenuously to soil-filled pocks in the limestone bedrock. Here, when the sun comes out after a shower, look for butterflies such as the giant swallowtail sipping from puddles on the stone. Prickly ash, the larval food plant for these biggest-of-all-Ohio butterflies, grows nearby and I have photographed the species here. (Because they're so big, they seldom stop flapping their wings when taking nectar on plants, but they do stop when sipping water on the rock.) Watch, too, for damselflies and dragonflies patrolling the area in search of flying prey.

There is a much larger prairie across the river. If the water isn't too high and cold, you can wade the river to reach the plastic boardwalk that allows you to explore the prairie with minimum disturbance to the plants. If you are wearing sneakers that you don't mind getting wet, keep them on. I usually wear leather hiking boots, though, so I remove them, stuff my socks inside, and throw them over a shoulder with the laces tied together. I then sidestep across the river with my toes pointed upstream, using my hiking staff to carefully test the depth of the next step and to keep my balance. If you want to visit the south-bank prairie but don't want to wade the river, drive east and then turn south at the first road crossing after you leave the park's front entrance. On the other side of the river, you'll find a parking area on the right. A hiking trail takes you from there to the prairie. The round trip is about a mile.

After you have had enough of the prairie, return via the plastic boardwalk to the trail intersection and head upriver on the wide trail of the north bank. Along the way you'll find a place to sit, rest, and watch the river. Just beyond a boulder with a plaque marking the designation of the Stillwater as a Scenic River, the trail turns right on an elevated boardwalk. To the left an earthen dike built in 1993 collects runoff from the slope to the north to create an artificial wetland.

Up the hill is a small pond open to public fishing. No license is needed. There are a few picnic tables at the forest edge just beyond the pond and a short boardwalk nature trail in the woods.

Cross the open field at an angle to the right. You will see an old farmstead, springhouse, and barn off to the left. This is a service area, and the trail stays between the building and the river. The trail crosses a small stream, then eventually winds its way up the hill to a T with another trail. Take a left, then a right to pass to the south of another pond where fishing is permitted. Continue east on the mowed trail. After the trail passes through a hole in the fencerow, you should be within sight of your car.

Stillwater Prairie Preserve offers a lot for the nature lover to see in any season.

45

Goll Woods State Nature Preserve

Total distance: 3 miles (4.8 km)

Hiking time: 2 hours

Maximum elevation: 715 feet

Vertical rise: 10 feet

Maps: USGS 7½' Archbold; ODNR Goll Woods State Nature Preserve booklet

The first European to explore the northwest corner of Ohio was, in all probability, the French fur trader Robert Cavelier La Salle. He visited the valley of the Maumee River in 1679, finding it inhabited by Chippewas, Ottawas, Wyandottes, Delawares, and Pottowatamies. More than 150 years later, German pioneer families became the first whites to settle in what is now German Township in Fulton County. By 1834, the Native American tribes that La Salle encountered had been pushed out of Ohio, the Shawnee who replaced them had long since been defeated, and only a handful of Wyandottes remained on a reservation near Upper Sandusky.

In June 1836, Peter F. Goll, his wife, Catherine, and their young son, Peter Jr., immigrated to America from Dobs, France. The next summer, Goll made his way to the federal land office in Lima, where he purchased 80 acres of what we now know as Goll Woods for $1.25 an acre. Goll's farm prospered and he continued to buy land, eventually owning 600 acres.

The timber at that time was described as "dense throughout the whole area: it was tall and the whole of an extremely vigorous growth. The varieties included Elm in abundance, Basswood, Oak of several varieties, Hickory, Black Walnut, Whitewood [tuliptree], Butternut, Sugar Maple, and a sprinkling of beech in some parts, and in the lowest lands Black Ash, and White Ash prevails throughout the township." Timber wolves howled in the forest close to settlements and cougars roamed at will, as did

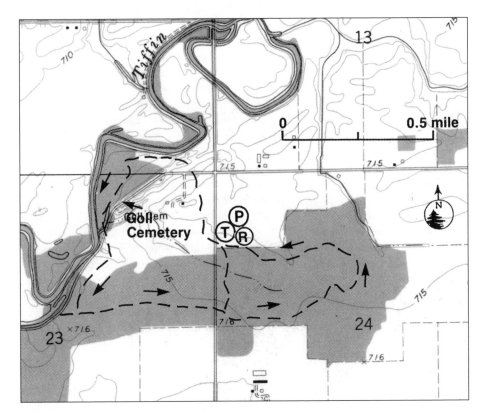

bison, elk, black bear, Canada lynx, and many other mammals that have long since vanished.

The area was the wet forest of Ohio's Great Black Swamp, land that was under the western extension of Lake Erie after the exodus of the Wisconsinan ice sheet from the Ohio. The land was flat, with soils that did not drain well. They were black from the decay of vegetation that flourished in the shallow postglacial lake basin and rich enough to grow big timber.

Settlers needed that timber when they first arrived—to build houses, barns, and wagons. But they needed more than trees to survive and raise families. They needed tillable land, and every farmer knew that any land that could raise such trees as these of the Black Swamp could surely raise great

corn and wheat. In 1859, therefore, a law providing for extensive ditching was passed by the county commissioners, and in a few decades the swamp that once covered two-thirds of the county was almost gone.

Almost, that is, except for this 80-acre tract we call Goll Woods. The Goll family stayed on the land for four generations. The land was passed on from Peter F. Goll Sr., to Peter Goll Jr., to George F. Goll, and then to his son and to his daughter, Mrs. Charles Louys. Although Goll and his descendants were farmers, they loved the big trees, and they carefully guarded the Big Woods from the timber operators. At the urging of citizens and conservation groups from north-western Ohio, the Ohio Department of Natural Resources (ODNR) purchased 321 acres of land, including Goll's 80-acre Big

Woods, from Mrs. Louys in 1966. It was dedicated to the people of Ohio as Goll Woods in 1969 and in 1975 became Goll Woods State Nature Preserve.

The closest thing to a stand of old-growth woods in northwestern Ohio, Goll Woods holds visitors in awe. Many of its magnificent trees were large when the Pilgrims landed at Plymouth Rock. Trees commonly found in three different types of forest—elm/ash/maple swamp forest, mixed mesophytic, and beech/maple—are found here. Swamp forest is found in the wet area, beech/maple grows on the moist but well-drained sites, and mixed mesophytic, a blend of many species, frequents the transition areas between.

Goll Woods is a place of beauty during all seasons. Many special creatures such as tree frogs, barred owls, red-headed woodpeckers, red foxes, and several species of salamanders make their homes here. So, too, do many kinds of ferns and wildflowers, including the delicate purple, white, and yellow Canada violet and the three-bird orchid. Unfortunately, it is but a small remnant of the once vast forest of this part of Ohio.

We can only hope that some of the countries of the world just now undergoing "development" will do better than we did protecting larger tracts of these original forests.

How to Get There

Travel I-80/I-90 (the Ohio Turnpike) west from Toledo to Exit 3. Turn left (south) on OH 108 and go 1.5 miles to Alternate US 20. Turn right (west) and travel 8.3 miles to OH 66 in Burlington. Here, turn left (south) and go 1 mile to Township Road F. Turn right (west) and travel 3 miles to Township Road 26, where you turn left (south) to the preserve entrance.

The Trail

A walk through Goll Woods is a walk through a precious remnant of the primeval forest characteristic of northwestern Ohio's Great Black Swamp. Start exploring by heading into the eastern 160-acre tract. Take the right fork at Post 1 on the Goll Woods self-guided nature trail. A guidebook is available at the kiosk at the parking lot or by mail from the ODNR's Division of Natural Areas and Preserves office in Columbus. The area near Post 2 was probably swamp forest at one time, but with the water table dropping in recent years, it is undergoing a transition. The red maple and ash are still there, but so, too, are trees that don't tolerate being in standing water all year, such as tuliptree, basswood, bur oak, chinquapin oak, sugar maple, and shagbark hickory. This is the transitional mixed mesophytic area.

Goll Woods' vernal flora is special. On a May trip, I was struck by the light color of the wild blue phlox compared to what I've seen in central Ohio, where I grew up. The trail guidebook provides a checklist of the more common flowers of the preserve. Remember, "Let them live in your eye...not die in your hand." Between Post 3 and the next stop on the trail, a side trail enters from the right. This will be your inbound trail at the end of our hike.

At Post 4, let the statistics speak for themselves. Bur oak (*Quercus macrocarpa*) diameter at breast height (DBH): 56"; height: 112'; estimated board feet: 4,270. A bur oak that stood at Post 5 was struck by lightning in 1970 and has now fallen. The lightning scar is still visible along the full length of the trunk. The trail now turns east to explore more of the Big Woods. Every Ohioan should know the tree at Post 6. This is the buckeye from the Native American

An old-growth Bun oak tree stands out in the fall woods

word *hetuck*—"the eye of a buck deer"—and it is the official state tree.

Perhaps by this point you will have discovered one of the nuisances that plagued early settlers in the Black Swamp region—mosquitoes. A good warm-weather walker is always prepared with a head net or repellent close at hand. In early Ohio, mosquitoes were more than a nuisance; they were a hazard because they carried malaria. The papaws at Post 7 are Temperate Zone members of the largely tropical custard-apple family. Dark maroon flowers in May change to yellowish-green, banana-like fruits in the fall—food for opossums and raccoons. Before reaching the next stop, you'll pass a trail to the left that takes a short route back to the trailhead. Continuing on this hike, however, you will come to Post 8, where the "Elder of the Woods," a 122-foot-tall bur oak, has occupied the site for close to 500 years. It died in 1984, but when I last visited the woods it was still standing. What stories it could tell! No hiker needs to be told about the poison ivy pointed out by Post 9: "Leaves three, let it be."

Nature is the grand recycler. Post 10 reminds the visitor that letting dead trees rot and return to the soil allows their nutrients to be used again. That philosophy is central to the management of nature preserves. White ash like the one at Post 11 provide the wood for such products as baseball bats, tool handles, and furniture. This giant is 104 feet tall with a 32-inch DBH. Four of North America's 18 species of ash grow in Goll Woods.

The cross-section of the bur oak that fell during the winter of 1968 at Post 12 is nature's time capsule. From the growth rings, you can read of dry years and wet ones, lightning strikes, fires, and the disease and death of the old oak.

All along, the elevation of the trail has

➤ Lichens: Complex Organisms

Lichens are the pioneers of the plant world. They grow on rocks, soil, and wood in the harshest weather conditions; and they are found in forests, fields, backyards, and urban parks. They are sensitive to acid rain and air pollution, a characteristic that allows them to be used as monitors of air quality.

Found in unique shapes and colors, they are not really a single organism but two, comprising a photosynthetic organism and a fungus that have formed a symbiotic mutualism. Each organism gains some advantage from this cooperative living arrangement. In most lichens, the photosynthetic partner (or photobiont) is a green alga and/or a cyanobacterium (what we used to call blue-green algae). The other partner is a fungus and is referred to as the mycobiont.

There are estimated to be 13,500 species of lichens. They grow in four general forms: crustose, growing closely attached to the substrate; squamulose, which are scale-shaped with a free edge; foliose, which are flattened from top to bottom or leaflike; and fruticose, which are bushy and most often attached at the base. The familiar reindeer moss is an example of the last.

To photograph lichens, you need a good macro lens. I prefer to use a 90 to 105 mm focal length, so as not to make a shadow with my camera. Their study requires a hand lens and a reference book or two. How to Know the Lichens, *by Mason E. Hale (Wm. C. Brown Co.), has good keys, and* Michigan Lichens, *by Julie Jones Medlin (Cranbrook Institute of Science), has topnotch color illustrations. How many different lichens can you find on your next wilderness walk?*

been changing subtly. At Post 13 the forest has become true swamp forest, with black ash, red maples, and silver maples dominating. Swamp white oak also occurs, but the American elm has been gone for nearly 40 years. The trail rises now, only a few feet, to a well-drained sandy knoll, and once again the composition of the forest changes. At Post 14 American beech and sugar maple dominate. In time, as the area becomes better drained, this combination will probably dominate Goll Woods.

People who live downwind from a cottonwood like the one at Post 15 have probably wondered aloud about the worth of these trees. The "cotton" can be a real nuisance! The red squirrels that live in this one, however, could easily sing the cottonwood's praises, as could the other mammals and many birds that are cavity dwellers. The much larger fox squirrel also abounds in this woods. By examining the tooth marks on the opened acorns, you should be able to distinguish which of the two squirrel species found in Goll Woods made them: the smaller or the larger species?

Now heading west, the trail reaches Post 16. This is the location of a tall tuliptree, a living fossil. Geologists have found evidence that this genus has existed for as long as 100 million years. Because it grows tall and self-prunes its lower branches, it was often used by pioneers for log structures in this part of Ohio. A relative of the magnolia, its green and orange tulip-like blossoms grow on the top of the tree, usually out of sight. Small ponds such as the one at Post 17 support life of all sorts, including frogs, salamanders, dragonflies, and mosquitoes, which only spend one phase of their life there. Others, like fairy shrimp, are tied to the pond throughout their lives. Bigger creatures like raccoons and skunks feed off the turtles and frogs in ponds.

Ferns similar to those at Post 18 have been around for 400 million years. They need moist environments like this to survive. Lichens, like the greenish white Parmelia lichen on the trunk of the tree at Post 19, are examples of two different life-forms that coexist to their mutual benefit. The plant is composed of both a fungus and green alga cells, living harmoniously as one structure. Hummingbirds and eastern wood-pewees use bits of this species of lichen for lining the insides and outsides of their nests.

The shortcut side trail enters from the left as you approach Post 20. The giant white oak at this stop would provide enough wood to construct half of a small frame house. This tree is 44" in DBH. At the time of settlement, thousands of trees like this one were felled and burned in huge piles to clear the land for agriculture. Forests like that at Post 21 were often burned by Native Americans to keep the brush from growing up and hindering hunting. When pioneers found these burned areas, they called them oak openings.

As this interpretive trail ends, continue exploring the other environments of Goll Woods by taking the trail across the road from the other end of the parking lot. While passing through the pine planting east of the manager's residence, try to figure out what year it was planted. The planting will probably be crowded out by hardwoods eventually. Here the trail crosses the road toward the Tiffin River. There is an especially large patch of toadshade, the maroon sessile trillium, here in April and May. The trail goes through a stand of beech/maple and tuliptree between the river and the Goll Cemetery. Take time to read the tombstones in the graveyard and to reconstruct the lives of those buried here from the facts gleaned from the stones.

The trail reenters the woods on the east side of the road 200 feet to the right (south) of where it emerged. From there it swings south through more pines and secondary-succession scrubland. It passes a parking lot before turning left (east) past more large trees. After .5 mile, the trail reaches the road that bisects the preserve. Angle across the road to the right to enter the trail and connect with the east woods loop. Upon reaching the T intersection with the nature trail, turn left to return to the parking lot.

46

Kelleys Island

Total distance: 7.5 miles (12 km)

Hiking time: 6 hours

Maximum elevation: 615 feet

Vertical rise: 40 feet

Maps: USGS 7½' Kelleys Island;
ODNR Lake Erie Islands State Parks map;
KICC Kelleys Island map

Early maps call it Cunningham Island, but for more than a century the 2,800-acre solid limestone island that lies in Lake Erie, 11 miles north of the mainland city of Sandusky, has been known as Kelleys Island. Between 1833 and 1841 the Kelley brothers of Cleveland, Datus and Irad, purchased the entire island for $1.50 per acre. The name Cunningham—that of a squatter who had built a house on the island in 1808—was lost to geographers forever. With the establishment of the Kelleys Island Stone Company, quarrying—the industry that was to bring people and fame to the island—was under way in earnest.

By 1842, grape cuttings had been set out on the island, marking the beginning of the second industry that was to carry the name far and wide. Fermented from grapes grown on the sweet soils of the island, the products of the Kelleys Island Wine Company were known for their quality. The 1990 census listed 200 residents for Kelleys Island, where there were once several thousand people working in jobs related to the fishing, quarrying, and winemaking industries. Though now supplemented by air service, the principal way to reach Kelleys Island remains, as it was in the 1830s, by boat. The ferries do haul cars and trucks to and from the island year-round (weather permitting), but the number of vehicles on the island remains small. It is thus a wonderful place to explore on foot.

In addition to the artifacts from the early industries, the island has other points of interest. Inscription Rock, on the south shore,

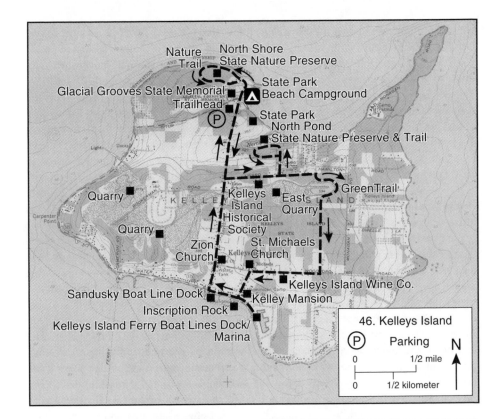

Nature Trail
North Shore State Nature Preserve
Glacial Grooves State Memorial
Trailhead
State Park Beach Campground
State Park North Pond State Nature Preserve & Trail
Quarry
Kelleys Island Historical Society
East Quarry
Green Trail
Quarry
Zion Church
St. Michaels Church
Sandusky Boat Line Dock
Kelleys Island Wine Co.
Kelley Mansion
Inscription Rock
Kelleys Island Ferry Boat Lines Dock/ Marina

46. Kelleys Island

Ⓟ Parking   N

0   1/2 mile
0   1/2 kilometer

is covered with Native American drawings. The glacial grooves scratched in the limestone bedrock that are visible at Glacial Grooves State Memorial are world famous. There are also homes and churches left from the island's heyday to be admired. The Ohio Department of Natural Resources (ODNR) operates a 661-acre state park with a beach, boat-launching ramp, and campground on the island. Local merchants and restaurateurs ply their goods to tourists during the vacation season. The Kelleys Island Chamber of Commerce will gladly send you a packet of material with a map and information about local businesses, including accommodations. Its phone number is 419-746-2360; web site is kelleysisland-chamber.com; and e-mail address is kelleyschamber@aol.com.

How to Get There

At least two ferry operators serve Kelleys Island. The Kelleys Island Ferry Boat Line (419-798-9763) runs from a dock at Marblehead year-round, with an expanded schedule from early May until late September. It will transport vehicles and their passengers as well as pedestrians. Between Memorial Day weekend and mid-September, Jet Express operates catamaran passenger ferries out of downtown Sandusky (1-800-245-1538).

Sandusky is 54 miles east of Toledo via I-80/I-90 and US 6; 105 miles north of Columbus via US 23 and OH 4; and 64 miles west of Cleveland via I-80/I-90 and US 250. To get to Marblehead, which is only 3.5 miles from the island, take OH 2 west from Sandusky across the Sandusky Bay Bridge. Turn right (north) on OH 269, then right (east) on OH 163. Free parking is available at both terminals. Each of the ferries will bring you to the south shore of Kelleys Island and Water Street. When you get off the ferry, be sure to note the time of the last returning boat. If you plan to take the last one, get to the dock early, as it is often crowded.

If you are carrying camping gear, you should proceed to Kelleys Island State Park at the north end of Division Street to obtain a campsite and to stow gear. The Kelleys Island Ferry comes into the Seaway Marina, less than .5 mile east of Division Street, the center of town. The park campground entrance is not quite 1.5 miles north on Division Street on the right side. Use the sidewalk and take time to study the homes and other structures along the route. You may want to stop at the Kelleys Island Historical Society's stone church museum on the right side of the road just north of the business district. Be sure to walk through the cemetery, studying the names and inscriptions. And don't miss the Butterfly Box, where you can walk amid live butterflies in a plastic hoop house and shop for butterfly- and beetle-related gifts. Islanders have had a long love affair with butterflies, especially the monarch, as the island is an overnight resting place for that long-distance flier in the fall. The chamber of commerce can provide details about the butterfly festival held each September.

The Trail

After setting up camp (or leaving your luggage at some other accommodation), I suggest that you walk north from the campground entrance to the Glacial Grooves. There is excellent interpretive signage along the grooves, or you can stop at

the park office and purchase an inexpensive booklet entitled *A Glacial Grooves Fossil Walk on Kelleys Island*. The grooves are nothing short of awesome—400 feet long, 30 feet wide, and 15 feet deep. They are scars that were scratched along the surface of the limestone bedrock by the mile-deep glacial ice as it advanced to the south many millennia ago. The glacial groove site is a state memorial owned by the Ohio Historical Society but operated by the Division of Parks and Recreation.

The 1-mile North Shore Loop nature trail originates just north of the grooves. It goes into the quarry only briefly, and then swings to the right to travel through woods to the rocky shoreline. As you would suspect on an island that is solid limestone, the woods are composed of trees that do well on sweet soils: hackberry, redbud, blue ash, water ash, basswood, chinquapin oak, and, early in succession, red-cedar. Where the trail continues west, paralleling the shoreline, the sparse vegetation on the rock surfaces between the trail and the lake is an unusual natural community known as a stone alvar. At a point just after the trail turns west, back from the shoreline, a path leads over to the shore and a low-to-the-ground display case with interpretive material about the alvar plant community. This is a dedicated state nature preserve. I recommend that you not try to descend to the bare rock for a better look. I did, and I tripped and fell against the rocks and into the poison ivy, bloodying myself badly. (One of the best examples of this kind of habitat is found at Lakeside Daisy State Nature Preserve just south of the village of Marblehead on the mainland. It is open to the public during May, when its namesake plant is in full bloom.) Back on the North Shore Loop Trail, turn right and continue going west. The trail eventually swings

The famous glacial grooves along the trail on Kelleys Island

south and east to return to the parking lot. One summer I walked it in the evening and saw many deer in the scrubby area along the way.

Return to Division Street via the driveway and walk south on the sidewalk on the east side of the road. The next area to explore is the North Pond Trail. To reach this, continue walking south along Division Street to Ward Street. Turn left (east) and follow the sidewalk 0.4 mile until you reach the entrance to the 20-acre North Pond State Nature Preserve, managed jointly by the Division of Natural Areas and Preserves and the Division of Parks and Recreation. Turn left to enter the trail system. A sign along the trail speaks of the designation of the site as an important birding area by Ohio Audubon. The trail leads north down a considerable slope toward the lake. A pile of granite boulders (glacial erratics) to the right indicates that at one time the area was

cleared for agricultural use. Soon it reaches a fork where a sign describes the mission of DNAP. Continue north toward the lake. After 150 feet the trail changes to boardwalk, where signs provide information about the trail's construction and the plastic lumber used. Just beyond is a five-paneled kiosk where the natural history of the area is illustrated with pictures and text.

From there one trail goes north to the beach. There are interpretive signs and a bench along the way. After looking at the beach community, return to the kiosk and take the other trail. At another fork in the trail there is a raised observation area, allowing a view of North Pond from overhead. The winding trail continues through the heavily vegetated sand dune community. The pond does not always contain water; it's dependent upon rainfall and the very fickle nature of the level of Lake Erie. When I visited in July 2006, it was essentially dry and completely overgrown with emergent vegetation. From the tower I could see neither waterfowl nor wading birds. The trail circles counterclockwise, the boardwalk ends, and the environment becomes more "old field" in nature. When the loop trail meets the access trail, turn right (south) to exit the preserve where you entered.

Now, back at Ward Road, turn left (east), walk on the sidewalk, and look for the entrance to the East Quarry Trail area of the state park on the right (south) side of the road. It's a distance of about .25 mile. Stop and look at the map of the area on the trailhead sign to fix the lay of the land firmly in your mind. There are so many exits that it's unlikely you'll get lost. On the other hand, it is easy to end up somewhere other than where you intended. If it's a sunny day, it's a good idea to check the position of the sun before you enter the area. That should enable you to reorient yourself any time you wonder what direction you are moving. The object is to go in from Ward Road on the north, circle around the east end of Horseshoe Lake, and then exit to the south onto Woodford Road. Go around whatever is blocking the road and walk toward the lake. If you can find them, follow the green blazes around the east end of the lake between red-cedars, planted pines, and brush.

After you have rounded the lake and are more or less heading west, turn left at the second exit headed south. If you take the first, or the third or the fourth, you will still get there. And if you choose to go straight west you will eventually come out on Division Street Road, knowing exactly where you are. A self-guided trail brochure with a map of East Quarry Trail is available free at the park office. The trail is about a mile from north to south, and it shouldn't take more than 40 minutes unless you loiter too long basking on rocks overlooking the lake. Be careful with your scrambling if you decide to explore the lakeshore.

Once on Woodford Road, continue your Kelleys Island hike by turning right (west). If you need nourishment, the new Kelleys Island Wine Company is on the left. At Addison Road, St. Michael's Church stands on the right. Turn left toward the lake. The Kelley Mansion, built in 1863, sits on the left corner of Addison and Water Streets. About a dozen years ago, 78 archaeological sites and 316 buildings, including this mansion, associated with the settlement and history of the largest American island in Lake Erie, were added to the National Register of Historic Places as the Kelleys Island Historic District. And the work of sorting out the interesting history of the island goes on, carried out in no small part by the active Kelleys Island Historical Association. (If you have time, visit their museum on Division Street about a third of the way up the road to the state park.) Prehistoric sites on the island show evidence of human occupation from Paleo-Indian times through the Late Woodland period, or from 12,000 B.C. to A.D. 1,300. Among those sites is Inscription Rock, which sits under a protective shelter to the right across Water Street from the mansion.

Many more places to explore and things to see await on Kelleys Island. There are excellent eating establishments on the island, and fishing trips can be arranged on the waters of Lake Erie. The route that I have suggested is about 7.5 miles long, but you can easily pick a route to suit your interests. Bicycles and electric golf carts can be rented on the island. For a day, a weekend, or a week of walking, leave your automobile on the mainland and visit this enchanting island.

47

Lockington Reserve

*Total distance: 3.5 to 6.5 miles
(5.7 to 10.7 km)*

Hiking time: 2 to 3.5 hours

Maximum elevation: 960 feet

Vertical rise: 70 feet

Maps: USGS 7½' Piqua East and Piqua West; SCPD Lockington Reserve map; BTA Buckeye Trail map; St. Marys section map

The 1913 flood devastated the Great Miami River valley. Nothing on the floodplain was spared, and farmers and city folk alike suffered. Downtown Dayton was awash with water like no one had ever seen. City fathers decided that such a flood should never recur. The Miami Conservancy District was thus created, and five flood-control dams were built on the great Miami and four of its principal tributaries. These dams are unique because they impound no permanent pools and have no gates to close, even in times of flood. Only when the rainfall upstream exceeds the amount of water that can pass through the dam does water pool behind it. As the rain lets up and the water drains out, the water level drops. When no floodwater is being retained, which is most of the time, the hundreds of acres behind the dams are available for recreation. The genius behind this design was Arthur Morgan, later to become the president of Antioch College at Yellow Springs.

In Montgomery County, those lands form the heart of four park district reserves. Lockington Dam on Loramie Creek, in southern Shelby County, is the fifth of the conservancy's flood-control reservoirs. The Shelby County Park District now manages 200 acres around the reservoir as Lockington Reserve. Because it is a flood-control area, at times of heavy rainfall the trails may be inundated. If in doubt, call the park district office at 937-773-4818.

Loramie Creek, the West Branch of the Great Miami, originates on the flatland of

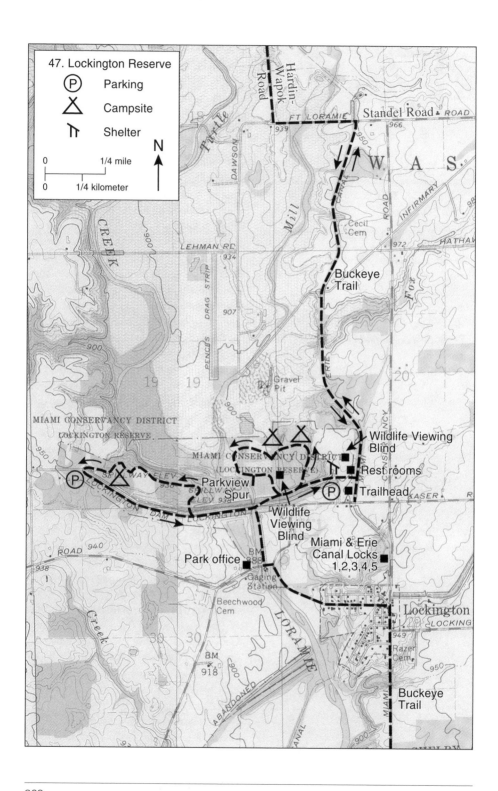

47. Lockington Reserve

P Parking

△ Campsite

⋔ Shelter

N

0   1/4 mile
0   1/4 kilometer

Hardin-Wapok Road

Tuttle

FT LORAMIE   Standel Road ⋆ ROAD

W   A   S

939

966

DAWSON

950

CANAL

ROAD

INFIRMARY

Cecil Cem

LEHMAN RD

934

972

HATHAW

Mill

CREEK

900

907

FOX

DRAG STRIP

PENCE'S

Buckeye Trail

ERIE

Gravel Pit

900

20

MIAMI CONSERVANCY DISTRICT
LOCKINGTON RESERVE

Wildlife Viewing Blind

950

MIAMI CONSERVANCY DISTRICT
(LOCKINGTON RESERVE)

Restrooms

P

SPILLWAY   LEV

950

Parkview Spur

P

Trailhead   KASER ⋆   R

LOCKINGTON DAM   SPILLWAY   LEV

Wildlife Viewing Blind

ROAD   940

938

BM
888

Park office ■

Miami & Erie Canal Locks
1,2,3,4,5 ■

Creek

Gaging Station

Beechwood Cem

30

LORAMIE

Lockington

S LOCKING

949

BM
918

Razer Cem

950

ABANDONED   CANAL

900

MIAMI

Buckeye Trail

SHELBY

Shelby County between the Lake Erie and Ohio River watersheds. It gets its name from Pierre Loramie, a Frenchman who operated an Indian trading post, Loramie's Station, at the present site of Fort Loramie from 1769 until 1782. In the early 1840s, the headwaters of Loramie Creek were dammed to make Loramie Reservoir, which fed the Miami & Erie Canal. The summit at Loramie was 512 feet above the level of the Ohio River at Cincinnati, so a series of locks was needed to allow boats to make the 99-mile trip. The first of these, Locks 1-5, were at the village of Lockington, 18 miles from the feeder that brought water from Loramie Reservoir to the canal. During the late 1800s, Lockington thrived, and in its heyday it boasted 19 industries. The 1880 census reported a population of 219, and those are only the ones who got counted. But by 1913, when floods sounded the death knell for the canal system statewide, water traffic had already ceased in Lockington. The locks, located in the middle of the village, are preserved by the Ohio Historical Society in cooperation with the Shelby County Park District. The canal towpath, north of the town, is the route of the Buckeye Trail (BT).

When the flood-control reservoir was built on Loramie Creek, it was named for the closest town on the 15' USGS quadrangle, Lockington (those were the days before every reservoir was named for a politician). The area includes trails for hiking and cross-country skiing, several bird blinds, a camping area available for a fee by reservation, and two picnic shelters. The park district offers an already assembled "Rent-a-camp" if you do not have, or do not want to bring, your own gear. The Buckeye Trail passes along the eastern edge of the preserve, and there is a connecting trail to the BT from the shelter and rest room area. Due to the vagaries of public wells, carrying water from home is advisable.

How to Get There

Lockington Reserve is reached by taking US 36 west from I-75 into Piqua. Turn right (north) on OH 66 and follow it 4 miles to Hardin Road, where you turn right. At a T with Fessler-Buxton Road, turn right. After crossing Loramie Creek, turn left onto Kaser Road, which leads to the park entrance at Lockington Dam Road.

The Trail

The Buckeye Trail and the trails of the reserve start at the parking lot at the east end of the dam. To walk the section of the BT north of here along the Miami & Erie Canal towpath, go east from the parking lot 200 yards, following the blue blazes. Turn left at the towpath. For the next 1.5 miles, the BT follows the path once trod by horses and mules as they towed canal boats between Cincinnati and Toledo. At Dawson–Fort Loramie Road, the BT leaves the towpath for pavement. Turn around there and return to the picnic area at the reserve. A relatively new trail leaves the picnic area going north along the edge of the old field, hugging the forest on the left. It is headed for high ground where there is an observation deck from which you can see the pond in the valley below. It's a dead-ender. Return to the parking lot to begin your exploration of the main area of the preserve.

To continue the hike for another 3 miles, head downhill on the service road at the base of the dam. Turn right and go down a set of steps. After crossing a bridge that spans a stream between a small pond on the right and a large borrow pit pond on the left, the trail crosses a smaller bridge. As it reaches a pine growth, it splits. Follow the right fork as it goes uphill and curves left

A bird blind assists in viewing wildlife

through the pines. It soon reaches a point where a trail to the right leads to the group camping area. Make a half-right turn. There will be an area of successional forest (an old farm field now reverting to forest by the process of natural succession) to the left and woodland on the right. Watch for a wildlife-viewing area; you may want to spend some time there.

Soon, a quarry pond becomes visible on private property to the right. After 100 feet, the trail reaches a spot where you can see another meadow being overgrown with shrubs and young trees a short distance ahead through the woods. Follow its left edge. Shortly, the trail splits. The right fork is a spur that leads through the woods to Loramie Creek for a good view of the dam. After studying the unusual open dam, return on the same spur trail and turn right to continue on the main trail. After 100 feet, the trail turns into the woods and approaches

two bird blinds, where you can view birds at feeders.

Departing the bird blinds, continue toward the dam on the paved trail. Where the trail reaches an old road, turn right. The borrow pit pond will be on the left. When this trail reaches the base of the dam, turn left (east). There you have a choice. To bring your hike to an end, continue east up the old road to the parking lot where you began. If you want some more hiking, travel up the road to where you can climb to the abandoned road on top of the dam. Travel this path west for 1 mile, across the dam and over the spillway to the west parking lot. There, turn right where you see the trail entering the brush and forest to the north. A colored marker there indicates the trail but sometimes it's difficult to see. The trail crosses a boardwalk between two ponds, then passes another pine planting as it heads to the 90-foot-high bluff overlooking the creek. Upon reaching the edge of the bluff, the trail turns right to loop back to the trail along the foot of the dam. This west loop trail is not heavily used and may be a little difficult to follow; however, the dam is always in view, so there is no chance of becoming lost even if you end up bushwhacking around a deadfall or a place where the trail has grown over. Return to the trailhead parking lot via the old road atop the dam.

A visit to the Lockington Reserve area would not be complete without spending some time in the village viewing the locks and the 150-year-old homes that remain from the canal days.

48

Maumee Bay State Park

Total distance: 2.25 miles (3.6 km)

Hiking time: 2 hours (if you are looking at things along the way)

Maximum elevation: 575 feet

Vertical rise: 5 feet

Maps: USGS 7½' Reno Beach and Oregon; ODNR Maumee State Park brochure; Maumee Bay Boardwalk map

Note: *This trail and its ancillary facilities meet the standards of the federal Americans with Disabilities Act (ADA).*

Ohio is said to be second only to California in its loss of natural wetland habitat. Since settlement, millions of acres of fens, bogs, swamps, wet prairies, and marshlands have been drained for agriculture or to make managed "duck marshes." At Maumee Bay State Park, a small expanse of Lake Erie marsh has been preserved and a boardwalk constructed to allow visitors to have a closer look at this rare habitat. The Milton B. Trautman Nature Center, with exhibits that interpret the natural and cultural history of the Lake Erie marshes, is located at the entrance to the boardwalk. No matter how many times you walk this trail, you will always have a unique experience. Visit it in different seasons when different land birds and waterbirds are using the area. Experience the many moods of the various weather Mother Nature throws at the boardwalk. See how many different species of dragonflies, damselflies, and butterflies you can see on a summer walk. Come when the male frogs are singing their "aren't I pretty, come mate with me" call over the months of spring. Learn the blossoms of the plants of the wetlands by visiting often during the growing season, with short-focusing binoculars, a 100 mm macro lens on your camera, and a wildflower book in your pack. And remember, it's a wetland, so be prepared for the six-legged hummers. These female mosquitoes need a blood meal to ensure that there will be a next generation to help feed the birds and other insects.

How to Get There

To reach Maumee Bay State Park, with its lodge, cabins, campground, Milton B. Trautman Nature Center, and Maumee Bay Boardwalk, take OH 2 east from I-280 on the east side of Toledo. At North Curtice Road turn left (north) toward Lake Erie. This road will lead you into the park, where signs will direct you to the nature center.

The Trail

This hike begins with a visit to the Milton B. Trautman Nature Center, reached by sidewalk and a bridge over a small pond. Note the cutout steel artwork in the pond to the right. The center is dedicated in memory of Drs. Milton B. and Mary A. Troutman. Milton was author of the monumental treatise *Fishes of Ohio,* and Mary was his steadfast helpmate during the writing of this book and the completion of many other projects. They were dear friends of mine and of the community of naturalists in Ohio and beyond. How fortunate we are that they passed our way. There is an exhibit related to their lives in the nature center. During the spring and summer, the nature center's hours are 10–5 Monday through Friday and 1–6 Saturday and Sunday. In the off season, the hours are 1–5 Wednesday through Friday and 10–5 on Saturday. I attended the nature center's dedication ceremony on May 21, 1993.

The 2-mile boardwalk system that reaches out into the coastal marsh from the nature center was built in 1992 by the proud young people of the Ohio Civilian Conservation Corps, a division of the Ohio Department of Natural Resources. In addition to serving park visitors, the center offers special programs for visiting school groups and people of all ages from the surrounding communities. To the left of the center is a wooden screen house, named the Doris N. Stifel Monarch Gazebo in honor of The Monarch Lady of Toledo, who ran monarch rearing and tagging programs here each summer. Beyond the gazebo is a handicapped-accessible butterfly garden maintained by staff and volunteers. It is an official Monarch Way Station in the program run by MonarchWatch, based at the University of Kansas.

On the opposite side of the nature center there is a small pond and a bird-feeding area that can be viewed from a window in the center. Rest rooms available from the outside are open even when the center is closed. The elevated trail through the marsh begins from the right rear corner of the center and is accessible by stairs or ramp. The 5-foot-wide trail was built of treated wood to the standards of the Americans with Disabilities Act. There is a .25-mile loop close to the center that can be reached from the center and the park lodge, and a 1-mile loop available via a single connecting trail from the smaller loop, a connecting trail to the cabin area, a spur trail to a two-level observation deck, and a spur trail to an observation blind. There are large interpretive signs with color photos and text at nine places along the trail. Most, but not all, are at trail entrances or intersections. At the bottom of each you'll find a map routed in wood with a red dot showing the location and station number, not necessarily in sequence. The numbers are useful in giving hikers the approximate location of plants or animals being seen by others. I have not provided the information on the signs here as they are better understood when you read them onsite. In addition, at least eight smaller interpretive signs on tall posts scattered along the trail provide information about such topics as reptiles, poison ivy, dead trees, bat boxes, woods ducks, swamp forest, and decaying logs. On the

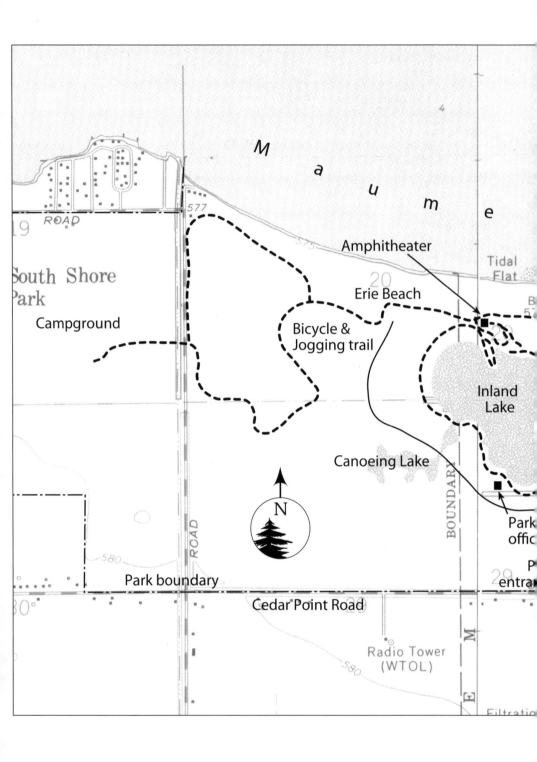

South Shore Park

Campground

Amphitheater

Erie Beach

Bicycle &
Jogging trail

Tidal Flat

Inland Lake

Canoeing Lake

BOUNDARY

Park office

N

Park boundary

Cedar Point Road

Radio Tower
(WTOL)

Park entrance

577

575

580

580

20

29

19

M a u m e e

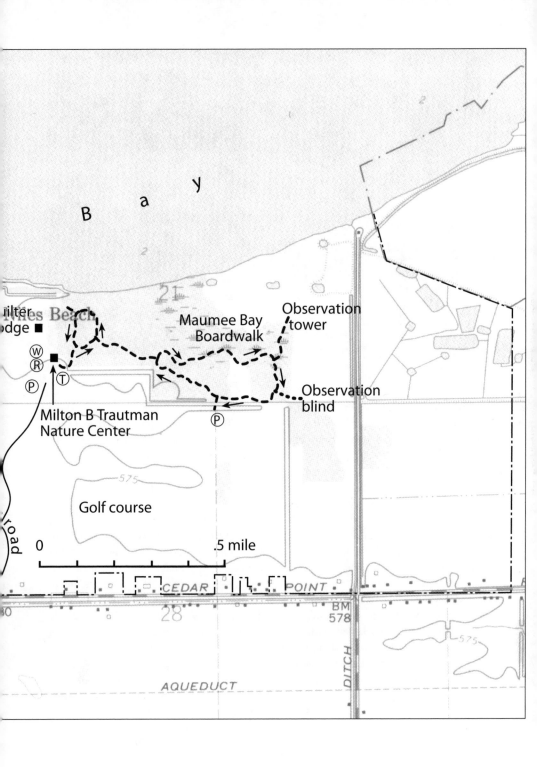

B a y

B a y

uilter
dge ■

Observation
tower

Maumee Bay
Boardwalk

W
R

T
P

Observation
blind

Milton B Trautman
Nature Center

P

Golf course

0   .5 mile

575

CEDAR   POINT

28

BM
578

575

DITCH

AQUEDUCT

Phragmites *along the park's boardwalk trail*

short loop, small red signs with white letters (also in Braille) are located on the top of a handrail and are keyed to an interpretive guide for the disabled, including those with a visual handicap. Ask for the accompanying material at the nature center. There are places to sit and rest at each of the nine stations, plus at a few other good places for wildlife watching along the way.

A lake and shoreline marsh represent a dynamic environment, changing over time spans both short and long. I have walked this trail perhaps a dozen times since its construction and it has never been the same. In the 1990s, the lake level was high and there was standing water along much of the trail. As I write this, Lake Erie is near a historic low level, thus the marsh and adjoining swamp forest have been devoid of water. Most woody plants such as the swamp forest trees and the stands of buttonbush survive those changes, but some

do not, and you will see standing dead trees. These become feeding and nest sites for many creatures. Herbaceous plant populations tend to respond more quickly to changing water levels. Needless to say, so too do the populations of reptiles and amphibians.

On the left side of the boardwalk, just beyond Station 1, the welcome sign, there is a concrete slab on the forest floor that identifies the imprint of eight mammals that might be seen along the trail. This is one of several Scout projects along the trail. Study it closely so you can recognize any tracks you come across. Rabbits have sometimes been fairly abundant along the trail, but the presence of the canine carnivores such as red fox and coyote make that a balancing act that tilts back and forth between predator and prey. White-tailed deer are nearly always seen in the swamp forest. I counted nine on a recent early November day. Some

50 Hikes in Ohio

folks I talked with on one fall walk reported seeing 28.

The boardwalk starts out through swamp forest with only an occasional open area. At Station 2, turn right and continue through the woods along the outer part of the handrailed short loop. Soon you reach Station 3. The short loop continues straight ahead toward the lake. Take the trail to the right to access the long loop, the observation tower, and the blinds. This is a good area in which to spot deer. Soon you emerge from the woods and experience the first large stand of *Phragmites* along the trail. This very tall grass with its plume-like inflorescence is often called reed grass. It competes with cattails for dominance in the marsh. In the early spring, red-winged blackbirds can be seen swaying back and forth near the tops of last year's reed grass, advertising their availability with a squeaky *kiong-ka-ree* song.

At the next station, No. 6, turn left toward the lake. From here on the swamp forest will give away to stands of herbaceous reed grass or cattails or the woody buttonbush. On a June walk along here, I saw several viceroy butterflies, and photographed one that was basking. This is typical habitat for that monarch-look-alike species. There are cottonwoods and willows here too, both species that are known to be host plants for viceroy larvae. After nearly .5 mile of walking, you will really feel that you are out of the woods and wholly into a Lake Erie marsh. Notice that both the common cattail and narrow-leaved cattail are present here—and probably the hybrid between the two.

At Station 7, take the spur to the right to a two-level observation tower. On the upper level there is a map that will help you identify the man-made objects you can see across this broad sweep of Lake Erie's western basin. Note the Little Cedar Point

➤ Dutch Elm Disease

The American or white elm was once an important part of Ohio's forests. A component of the elm/ash/maple forests of poorly drained bottomlands, it was also part of the mesic woodlands in the northern part of the state. Forest-grown American elms had tall columnar trunks. For many years, the largest known white elm grew at Marietta. It was 26 feet, 6.5 inches in circumference at breast height. American elms, with their wineglass shape, once lined the streets of most Ohio cities and villages. The Dutch elm disease is a fungus, Ceratocystis ulmi, carried by the European bark beetle. It was first discovered to be affecting elms in Cleveland in 1930. By 1933 it was being seen at the port of New York, but by then no amount of quarantining could prevent its spread across eastern North America.

At the same time, a second disease was attacking the elms in Ohio. Originally called phloem necrosis, but now referred to as elm yellows, this phytoplasm-caused disease was first seen in Ironton, Ohio, in 1918. It was likely as devastating to Ohio's elms as Dutch elm disease. In any case, by the late 1940s, Ohio towns had lost nearly all of their lawn and street shade trees, and the elm was gone from the swamp forests.

Today, an occasional young elm tree can be seen in places like Cedar Bog (where giant elms once stood), but they hardly ever make it past the 6-inch-diameter size. A few municipalities in the East still use the American elm as a street tree, but they have to use an aggressive spraying program to halt the spread of the two diseases that all but wiped out the species in the Ohio woods.

National Wildlife Refuge jutting into the water along the shore to the right. As a naturalist, it grieves me to see that the shore-vine visible from here is armored with rip-rap, but this is probably necessary to protect the area against further shoreline erosion. A great egret was fishing in the marsh beyond the tower on one early summer day when I walked this way. The nearest egret rookery is on West Sister Island, over 16 miles northeast from Maumee Bay in Lake Erie, so these wading birds make a long flight back and forth daily to feed in these shallow protected waters.

Backtrack on the spur to the main trail. Note that enough people get confused about where they are that directions have been painted on the decking at most intersections. A hard left turn will carry you past more marsh, but soon you will reenter the swamp forest. If the alien emerald ash borer that is spreading across Ohio reaches this area, as it is quite likely to do, another important element of the wetland communities, the ash trees, will surely disappear, as did the American elm nearly a century ago.

Now headed back toward the trailhead, you will soon pass a small pond off to the left and arrive at Station 8 and the spur trail to the observation blind. This trail-level structure, with slots through which to peer, offers a chance to observe all sorts of wildlife close up. Returning to the main trail, turn left to continue through the swamp forest. Shortly, there is a seating area in the middle of a stand of *Phragmites.* At Station 9, you'll find a repeat of the station welcome sign as this is an entrance for the cabins-area vacationers. There are at least two large nesting boxes high in trees along the trail here, probably meant for barred owls or squirrels. Two additional rest areas provide for a respite as you continue toward the trailhead. As I passed this way one mid-summer day, a wood-pewee was calling. It's one of the species that continues to sing long after the nuptial season.

Upon returning to Station 6, make the right turn to connect with the short loop. There, once again at Station 3, I suggest you turn right toward the lake. As the trail curves left to parallel the shoreline, it rises ever so slightly because it is on a beach ridge. Station 4, the only one not at an intersection, is the place to stop and contemplate what role wetlands play in the ecosystem. From here, it's only a short way to Station 5, and another repeat of the welcome station. Take the right if you want to go to the lodge. The left fork will allow you to complete the short loop, and at Station 2 you can catch the connector back to the nature center.

Now that you have had an introduction to the Lake Erie wetland, return often to see what a new hour or season will hold for you in this wondrous shoreline environment.

49

Oak Openings Preserve Metropark

Total distance: 16.6 miles (25.9 km)

Hiking time: 12 hours or 2 days

Maximum elevation: 690 feet

Vertical rise: 50 feet

Maps: USGS 7½' Swanton; USGS 7½' Whitehouse; MPDTA Oak Openings Preserve Metropark map

The Oak Openings is a sandy tract of land, about 130 square miles in area, in western Lucas County and extending into adjoining Fulton and Henry Counties. Though the area is mostly flat, there are sand dunes as high as 25 feet scattered throughout. Underlain by an impenetrable Wisconsinan-aged clayey till, the land is covered with loose, permeable sand deposited on or near the shoreline of glacial Lake Warren, a precursor of present-day Lake Erie. The underlying glacial till is alkaline, but the sand is acidic. Rainwater that collects in low places and soaks into the soil becomes alkaline when it contacts the underlying limy till. The sand dunes and dry hills, however, remain acidic. In addition, the local accumulation of organic material in ancient swamps has led to locally acidic sites. Many native tree species that require rich soils or a neutral soil are thus absent from the area. On the other hand, small areas of wet prairie similar to those that occurred in presettlement days do remain, and the region is home to many rare and endangered species of plants and animals.

The incredible diversity of habitat and the presence of many species of plants and animals not commonly found elsewhere in the state make this trail especially attractive to naturalists. From mid-February, when the skunk cabbage comes into bloom, until late October, when heavy frost knocks down the last of the gentians, there is always an unusual flower in bloom somewhere in the Oak Openings. Among that number are at least a dozen species of native orchids. In

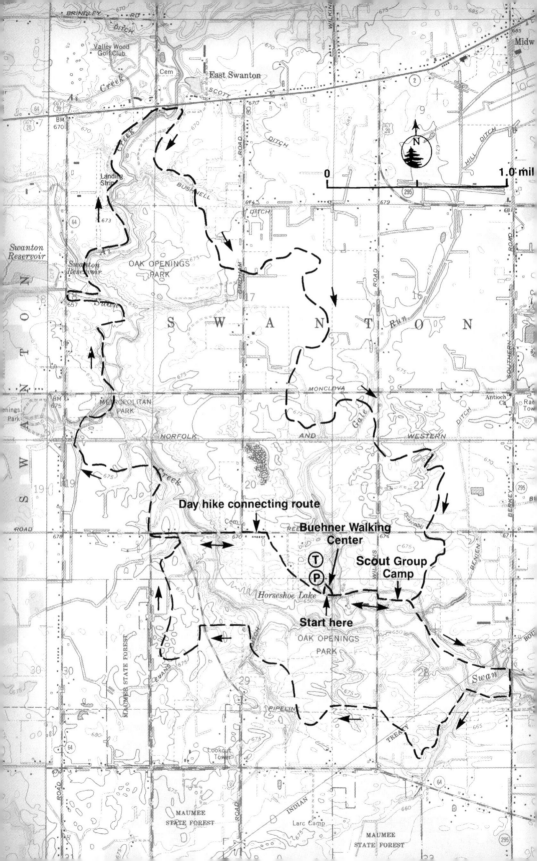

the open areas where prairie and old field species occur, butterflies are common, and many species of mammals and birds reside in this vast park year-round. Reptiles with habitat requirements as different as those of the spotted turtle and the hog-nosed snake reside here. The rare lark sparrow is known to nest in the park. It's a place to come often with your senses tuned to the wonderful world of nature that abounds here.

In 1939, when the Metropolitan Park District of the Toledo Area was formed, plans were made to "revitalize" the sandy area west of Toledo. An initial 67 acres was acquired, and thousands of pines and other evergreens were planted in an attempt to stabilize the soil. One major sand dune area was conserved within the park so that future generations of visitors could see this type of Ohio habitat. The original development, known as Springbrook Park, is now only a small part of the 3,744-acre Oak Openings Preserve Metropark. The complex includes a reservable lodge, picnic areas, and many miles of bicycle, horse, and foot trails, including a 16.2-mile loop trail (described below) that goes around the perimeter of the park.

The Oak Openings Hiking Trail was originally developed as a Boy Scout hiking trail and is still used for that purpose. Its 50th year of operation was celebrated in 2005. It is said to have been developed by Max Shepherst, then commissioner of the Metroparks, and Ben Long. They and the Scouts of Explorer Post 55 at Burroughs School did the original walking and blazing of what was then a 17-mile trail. It was a two-day hike with an overnight at the Springbrook Scout Camping Area. In the many years since it first opened, thousands of Scouts from throughout the region have walked its earthen path. Scout units wishing to walk the trail should contact the Trails

Committee, Erie Shores Council, BSA, 1 Stranahan Square, Suite 226 Toledo, OH 43604, phone number 419-241-7293, for information on reservations, awards, and camping. The trail can be hiked as a single 16.2-mile loop or, by adding a 2.5-mile connector that utilizes public roads and the parkway, you can do it as two segments of close to 10 miles each. There are no campsites available to the general public, and camping is not permitted along the trail. There are, however, two privately operated campgrounds within a mile or two of the trailhead. There is a group camping area at the trailhead available to youth groups only, on a reservation basis.

Dogs are not allowed on the trails. This is a wet area, and during some seasons of the year insects will be bad. A prudent hiker will be prepared. Be especially careful about matches and cigarettes because of the flammability of the prairie grasses and pine needles. Water is available at pumps located at picnic areas along the trail. There are no concessions serving food anywhere within the park.

How to Get There

To reach the entrance to Oak Openings, take OH 2 west from I-475/US 23 at Exit 8 on the west side of Toledo. Travel 8.5 miles to Wilkins Road. Turn left (south) and travel 2.75 miles to the park entrance on the right side of the road. Park in the Mallard Lake Picnic Area lot on the right side of Oak Openings Parkway, 1.25 miles beyond the entrance.

The Trail

There is a trailhead kiosk near the Buehner Center for Oak Openings at the parking lot on the west side of Mallard Lake. This serves all of the trails in the park. The Oak Openings Hiking Trail is well signed and marked with yellow blazes. To begin the hike, walk east to the lake edge, then turn right to follow the trail around the southern end of the lake. Follow the trail along the left side of the parkway to its intersection with the orange-blazed Evergreen Trail. Turn right and cross the parkway to a kiosk in front of the lodge. There, turn left (east) and begin following the yellow-blazed trail.

After 200 feet, the trail crosses the road and enters a deciduous forest. Here it passes the area designated for group camping. It is used by Scout groups that arrive on a Friday so they can camp near the trailhead and get on the trail early the next morning. After you have walked about .25 mile, the trail divides into inbound and outbound forks. I suggest hiking the southern loop first, but the choice is yours.

Turning right, for .75 mile the trail travels between Swan Creek and the parkway, soon reaching OH 295. After another right turn, walk the berm of the road across Swan Creek toward the entrance to the Evergreen Lake Picnic Area. About two-thirds of the way between the creek and park entrance, the trail turns right on a path through the woods. It soon joins the paved All-Purpose Trail just a few feet from the trailhead signs alongside the parkway. Turn right on the All-Purpose Trail and follow it across Evergreen Lake Dam. Don't miss the turn at the far end of the dam. The All-Purpose Trail goes straight, the hiking trail left.

Now tracing the shoreline, the trail passes a stand of hemlock where a horse trail comes in from the right and follows it along the lakeshore. Where the two trails enter a pine grove, a shelter house, horse stalls, and rest rooms serve those using the bridle trail. Having almost reached the southern boundary of the park, the trail crosses the bridle trail to the left, and then makes a tight clockwise turn as it begins

heading northwest. As it passes through a narrow pine plantation, it crosses an east-west-running fire lane. After leaving the pines and entering a woody wet area, it crosses a second fire lane. A quarter mile later, the hiking trail turns west, crosses the All-Purpose/Wabash Cannonball Trail Connector, and then travels along the edge of a deciduous forest for another .25 mile. Next it crosses a horse trail and angles left, beginning a sweeping semicircular arc through pine and regenerating fields. A fire lane going straight ahead can be easily mistaken for the footpath. This is the Pine Ridge Area, where prairie forbs such as Carolina puccoon can be found in the grassy openings. A quarter mile later, the path crosses the fire lane as it begins heading north through a nice deciduous woods.

Winding its way to the northwest, the trail stays among the hardwoods on high ground for about .5 mile before passing through more pines and crossing two horse trails in quick succession. Now turning toward the north, the trail crosses another horse trail, then Evans Ditch, which drains into Swan Creek. This ditch is part of a large network of ditches in Oak Openings, built many decades ago in an attempt to make the land suitable for agriculture. After crossing the ditch, the hiking trail turns north, then west to cross another horse trail.

Regenerating fields are now on the right and older woods on the left. After .25 mile, the trail reaches and crosses Jeffers Road near a picnic area. Beyond Jeffers Road is a good place to look for badgers, or at least for sign of badger. Seventy-five yards past the road the trail turns south, crosses a small bridge, and makes a large loop through a wet woods, crossing two horse trails as it does so. It next heads north on slightly higher land, paralleling the west

The Oak Openings Hiking Trail

boundary of the park. A fire lane enters from the right after .5 mile, and several hundred feet beyond that the trail makes an abrupt right turn to follow another ditch toward Jeffers Road. After crossing another horse trail and turning left across the ditch, the trail travels the road's edge as it goes west to reach Reed Road near its intersection with Manore Road.

Your hike has now covered about 5 miles. This is a good place to return to the trailhead if you wish to reduce your mileage. To do so, turn right (east) on Reed Road and walk .75 mile to Oak Openings Parkway. Turn right and follow the drive .5 mile to the Mallard Lake parking lot, for a total walk of 7.5 miles.

Return to the trail another day by reversing the 1.25-mile cutoff described above. To continue walking the 16.2-mile trail, angle left across Reed Road and across a horse trail to where the yellow-marked trail leaves

the road, headed north between a white pine plantation and regenerating old field. As pines blend to hardwoods, the trail angles slightly right for a couple of hundred feet, turns north on the highest land in the park, then west, continuing through oak forest. At the edge of the older forest, you cross a north-south horse trail just as the hiking trail turns north northeast to cross the All-Purpose/Wabash Cannonball Trail on the former Norfolk & Western (N&W) Railroad right-of-way. The Springbrook Picnic Area and the Springbrook Lake Trail (formerly a part of the hiking trail) are located about .25 mile west of this crossing beyond OH 64. They can be accessed via the All-Purpose Trail. There is also a rest room there.

Many years ago the park district began experimenting with pines to stabilize the sand blowouts of Oak Openings.

Beyond the railroad right-of-way crossing, the hiking trail follows the yellow markings on a path to the north. It crosses an old service road that is now a horse trail leading to a horse resting area (at one time a group camping area that was used as a midpoint campsite for the hiking trail). This is the site of the original dedication monument for the Oak Openings Scout Trail. On relatively high land above a creek, the woods has one of the largest red maples I have seen in Ohio. Beyond the horse trail, the hiking trail drops to the creek valley, traveling north. Just before the trail reaches Monclova Road, it turns left across a small stream before crossing the road at the west end of the Swan Creek bridge.

For the next 3.25 miles, the Oak Openings Hiking Trail follows the west bank of Swan Creek. Except for one place where it moves nearly .25 mile away to cross the stream coming in from Swanton Reservoir, the path stays alongside the stream. Crossing side ravines on small bridges, it passes through riverine forest and more white pine plantations. When the trail comes within sight of OH 2, it stays off the highway berm as it uses the right-of-way to get over Swan Creek. At the east end of the bridge, watch the utility poles and the end of the guardrail for blazes and arrows.

The return route from this point, the northernmost on the trail, provides a diversity of habitat. The trail passes through prairie openings, old fields, mixed black and white oak forest, pin oak swamp, sand dunes, and pine forest. The soil varies from alkaline in the wet prairie to very acidic in the pin oak swamp forest.

At the east end of the OH 2 Swan Creek crossing, the trail turns south into regenerating old fields and old mixed oak forest. After crossing almost flat land, the trail begins to swing left as it drops toward Bushnell Ditch. Turning left at the ditch, the trail travels upstream (east) through more evergreen forest for .25 mile. Near a property line corner it turns south again, traveling through deciduous woods, brush, and meadow. Where it reaches an east-west-running horse trail, the footpath turns left (east) to share the equestrian path for a couple of hundred yards. Turning south once more, the trail next travels through dry, sandy terrain with prairie grasses and forbs between small stands of oaks. Here and there the mounds of harvester ants can be seen.

After traveling .3 mile through mostly open land, the trail enters a large stand of red pine, where it turns left (east) and soon reaches Girdham Road. Many of the pines are dying and being removed. After crossing the road, the trail skirts another evergreen planting and then continues east through swamp forest. The hiking trail crosses a fire lane and then makes a left turn and crosses a horse trail, turning right shortly thereafter. After another .125 mile traveling east, the trail swings south in a reverse S-curve. This is the flattest area of the preserve. The trail meets and then leaves the horse trail once more as it turns left to follow the edge of the woods.

South of Monclova Road, the trail crosses the All-Purpose/Wabash Cannonball Horse Trail connector then turns left (east) on a fire lane along deciduous woods for .25 mile. The trail next turns north until Monclova Road is visible through the trees; then it turns right (east), parallel to the road and connector trail. As it approaches Wilkins Road, it crosses the connector one last time and turns right (south). Traveling along the road and the connector trail, it crosses a small bridge, then passes a lovely stand of cinnamon fern before reaching the Wabash Cannonball Trail.

The hiking trail crosses the Wabash Cannonball Trail and Wilkins Road together, then shares an old track with a horse trail and the connector trail as together they head uphill to the southeast. Moving through oak woods, the trails split as they reach high land. The hiking trail takes the left fork through a wet area, and the connector trail continues east for a short way and then makes a half turn to the north parallel to the hiking trail. The horse trail swings to the right (south) toward a large evergreen forest. The hiking trail next swings south and crosses the bridle trail just prior to where it joins the Wabash Cannonball Trail to exit the park. Traveling through rough, very wet pin oak woodland, the hiking trail utilizes corduroy road and boardwalk to keep hikers dry. About a mile after the Wabash Cannonball crossing, the Oak Openings Hiking Trail emerges from the swamp onto Reed Road amid a stand of black oaks.

After a direct road crossing, the trail goes a short distance into a spruce forest, and then turns left (east), then south to continue among the evergreens. When it reaches a fire lane coming in from the left, the trail turns right and soon leaves the spruce stand, headed south through more mixed oak forest. After two jogs to the right, it crosses a horse trail before curving right to cross Oak Openings Parkway. In the forest just beyond the road, the trail meets the outbound 16.2-mile trail, thus closing the loop. A turn toward the west takes the trail past the main Group Camp and the Oak Openings Lodge. Turn right onto the orange-blazed Evergreen Trail, follow it across the road, and turn left to follow the path around the lakeshore to the trailhead and the Mallard Lake parking lot.

➤ Flowers of the Air

Adult butterflies are considered to be creatures of the summer by most Ohioans, but I have encountered them in forest and field in every month of the year. As cold-blooded creatures, they need heat from an external source to allow them to move about. In nearly every case, that means an ambient air temperature above 60 degrees Fahrenheit and unfiltered sunlight in which to bask. Though the vast majority of the 144 species that are found in Ohio overwinter as pupae or eggs, a few make it through the winter as adults in a condition called reproductive diapause. Instead of breeding shortly after emerging from pupae in late summer or fall, they wait until warm weather the following spring. During one of those rare warm spells in January or February, one of these insects may take to the air. I once saw a Milbert's tortoiseshell along the boardwalk at Cedar Bog State Memorial in January, and I have seen mourning cloaks along the trails at Glen Helen in many February warm spells.

At least two species found in the summer in Ohio, the monarch and the painted lady, do not overwinter here. While some species, notably the cabbage white and the clouded and orange sulphurs, seem to breed continually, with overlapping broods from April through November, most species have only one, two, or three broods. When there is more than one brood, there is usually an overlap. If you are out and about much you will soon come to recognize the peak period of each hatch. To learn more about Ohio butterflies, look for Butterflies and Skippers of Ohio, *by Iftner, Shuey, and Calhoun (Ohio Biological Survey, OSU, Columbus).*

50

Ottawa National Wildlife Refuge

Total distance: 4.5 miles (7.25 km)

Hiking time: 3 hours

Maximum elevation: 575 feet

Vertical rise: Virtually none

Maps: USGS 7½' Metzger Marsh; USFWS Ottawa National Wildlife Refuge Wildlife Foot Trails map

Established in 1961 to preserve diminishing Lake Erie marshes, Ottawa National Wildlife Refuge (NWR) is a very special place. A remnant of the once vast swamp forest and marshland that stretched from Sandusky to Detroit prior to settlement, the area has been set aside as a haven for wildlife, especially waterfowl, wading birds, and shorebirds. More than 265 species of birds have been recorded using the area. The refuge is also used by bald eagles as both a nesting and a feeding area. America's national bird was once a common nester along the entire Lake Erie shoreline. Unfortunately, the places where eagles like to nest are also choice sites for lakeshore homes. Today, Ottawa is one place in Ohio where you can almost always see this majestic raptor.

Ottawa NWR is also a very special place to the thousands of people who visit it each year. You can walk along the more than 5.2 miles of dikes and see thousands of geese and ducks, including mallards, blacks, blue-winged teals, wood ducks, American wigeons, and canvasbacks. In late winter, tundra swans pass through the area on their way from their wintering area in Chesapeake Bay to their nesting grounds near the Arctic Circle. During the summer, many beautiful flowers grow along the edges of the dikes; plants like swamp rose-mallow and swamp milkweed, many of which are not only attractive to the human eye, but attractive to butterflies seeking nectar. During the bald eagle nesting season, you can spend hours watching

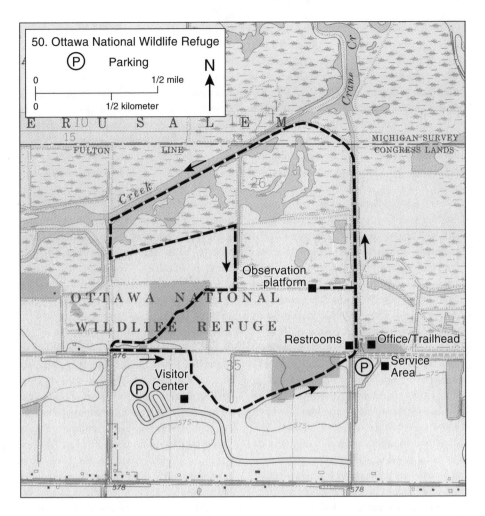

50. Ottawa National Wildlife Refuge

(P) Parking

N

0 — 1/2 mile

0 — 1/2 kilometer

Observation platform

Restrooms

Office/Trailhead

Service Area

Visitor Center

courtship flights and the feeding and fledging activities from the comfort of a bench along the dike roads.

Seasoned hikers know that any area with standing water suitable for waterfowl and shorebirds is also likely to have a good insect population during the warm months. Such is the case at Ottawa. An ample supply of repellent, a head net, and loose-fitting clothes covering exposed skin are necessary during the summer. A cap with a visor, sunglasses, and sunscreen are also essentials. Hikers need to wear good footwear and carry drinking water on the trail. Binoculars, a bird guide, and perhaps a spotting scope enhance the wildlife watching.

Though the refuge is operated primarily for wildlife, there are now fine new facilities for the human visitors. A new entry road going west from the original entrance leads to a visitor center that includes many new exhibits, a gift/book store, and a third floor observation deck. Eventually, there will be new connecting trails to the dikes originating at a plaza/gathering space on the north

---

Ottawa National Wildlife Refuge

side of the visitor center. There is adequate parking space for cars and buses. Future plans call for an outdoor rest room, a trailside environmental education shelter, a boardwalk through a wetland, and an additional pedestrian bridge. When you arrive at the refuge entrance, look for a sign directing you to the trails. For the foreseeable future, trails will remain accessible from the trailhead at the north end of the entrance road.

The trails are well labeled and have a good surface. Don't be fooled by the map. distances are farther than they appear. For example, a walk by the shortest route to the best place to watch the eagles is more than a mile one way. The ponds between the dikes will be empty of water at some periods during the year. They are drawn down to allow the growth of plants, and then flooded before the arrival of waterfowl. Because the refuge is first and foremost managed for wildlife, trails are subject to closure. You can check the refuge web site to find out about marsh conditions and to learn what is being seen at the moment. The refuge has an active "friends" organization and is always seeking good volunteers. Information about this and the many public programs offered at the refuge can be obtained at the visitors center. Trails are open from sunrise to sunset throughout the year.

How to Get There

Ottawa NWR is located about halfway between Port Clinton and Toledo off OH 2; a prominent sign along OH 2 identifies the single entrance to the area of the refuge open to the public.

The Trail

The refuge trails begin at a parking lot off to the left (west) at the end of the road. There you will find educational exhibits, brochures and maps, and the only public rest rooms along the trail system. With binoculars, a bird book, and an area bird checklist in hand, head straight north along the dike. The area across the ditch to the right is known as Goosehaven, a good place to see nesting Canada geese at the right time of the year. After walking less than .25 mile, you will reach an intersection where the Blue Heron Trail goes to the left and a sign points to an observation platform. If you are interested in seeing waterfowl or wading birds, turn left and walk the .25 mile to the observation platform. This fine facility was built in 1995 with financial support from the Ohio Audubon Council (OAC). Return to the dike you were following to continue north. Muskrats are frequently seen in this and other waterways of the refuge.

After going 1 mile due north, the trail swings northwest, then west-southwest. Along this 1-mile stretch, you might see eagles in the distance to the right. During nesting season, one of the adult birds may be hunting in this area. At the west end of the trail, which has been following Crane Creek, turn left (south) for .25 mile, then left again (east) for .5 mile. The trail turns right (south) for .25 mile before turning right again (west, then southwest) into a swamp forest. Here you can expect to see wood warblers during the spring and fall migration. Some species, such as the yellow warbler and common yellowthroat, nest in the area, and even the beautiful prothonotary warbler has been seen here during some summers.

After emerging from the woods, the trail turns left (east) along the edge of the woods and then goes right (southeast) through a brushy thicket. It travels through more swamp forest before returning to the parking lot. There are rest rooms here, but no facilities for picnicking or camping. The

A wildlife-viewing area

latter are available at Maumee Bay State Park near Toledo and East Harbor State Park east of Port Clinton. The refuge office is located just east of the information kiosk. Construction of the bridge to the office was also supported by the OAC.

Index

Index